Healing, Rebirth, and the Work of Michael Eigen

This important book features collected essays on the distinguished psychoanalyst Dr Michael Eigen, who is an influential innovator within and beyond psychoanalysis.

Drawing on the ideas of Bion, Winnicott, Kabbalah, and artists, Eigen's work is noted for fusing spirituality with psychoanalysis and his extraordinary creativity. The book begins with Dr Eigen's new essay "Rebirth: It's been around a long time." The other essay's feature a rich array of subjects and reflections, with many clinical examples and applications to domains beyond psychotherapy and include such titles as "Healing longing in the midst of damage: Eigen psychoanalytic vision" and "Breakdown and recovery: Going *Berserk* and other rhythmic concerns."

Dr Eigen is one of the most influential psychoanalysts of the current era and this collection of essays provides insightful discussion on his ideas. This celebration of Michael Eigen will fascinate any psychoanalyst interested in his work.

Ken Fuchsman (EdD) was President of the International Psychohistorical Association from 2016 to 2020. He is Emeritus faculty from the University of Connecticut, where he taught American history, interdisciplinary studies, the nature of being human, and the family in interdisciplinary perspective, and was Executive Programme Director of the Bachelor of General Studies Programme. Along with Michael Maccoby, Dr Fuchsman co-edited *Psychoanalytic and Historical Perspectives on the Leadership of Donald Trump*, published by Routledge.

Keri S. Cohen is a Licensed Clinical Social Worker and a Board-Certified Diplomate in clinical social work. She is a psychoanalytic psychotherapist in private practice in Lancaster, PA. Her work is with adults, adolescents and children. She is a graduate of the University of Pennsylvania's School of Social Policy and Practice and holds a certificate from the William Alanson White Institute's Online Intensive Psychoanalytic Psychotherapy Programme. She is a published writer, has presented papers at national and international conferences, and is a co-moderator of the international online Studying Eigen group. She teaches and has attended Michael Eigen's Bion seminars for nearly 15 years.

Healing, Rebirth, and the Work of Michael Eigen

Collected Essays on a
Pioneer in Psychoanalysis

Edited by
Ken Fuchsman and
Keri S. Cohen

Routledge
Taylor & Francis Group

LONDON AND NEW YORK

First published 2021
by Routledge
2 Park Square, Milton Park, Abingdon, Oxon OX14 4RN

and by Routledge
52 Vanderbilt Avenue, New York, NY 10017

Routledge is an imprint of the Taylor & Francis Group, an informa business

© 2021 selection and editorial matter, Ken Fuchsman and
Keri S. Cohen; individual chapters, the contributors

British Library Cataloguing-in-Publication Data
A catalogue record for this book is available from the British Library

Library of Congress Cataloging-in-Publication Data
A catalog record has been requested for this book

ISBN: 9780367484286 (hbk)
ISBN: 9780367484231 (pbk)
ISBN: 9781003039761 (ebk)

Typeset in Bembo
by codeMantra

To Michael Eigen,
a timeless presence, embodying the light.

Keri

To Tom, Bill, and Jim.
Extraordinary individuals, wonderful sons.

Ken

Contents

Notes on contributors

Robin Bagai (PsyD) is a licensed psychologist in Portland Oregon, practicing for over 30 years. Previously, he performed comprehensive psychological evaluations with children and adults in a variety of treatment settings. His current practice is limited to psychoanalytic psychotherapy with adults. Since 2015 he has been leading seminars on the work of Michael Eigen (PhD).

Rachel Berghash (CSW) was born in Jerusalem. She has been a teacher of Interior Life Seminar, combining religion and philosophy and has published a memoir, *Half the House, My Life In and Out of Jerusalem* (Sunstone Press). Her poetry and poetry translations have appeared in numerous magazines and anthologies. Berghash was a producer of "A World Elsewhere," a poetry program that featured interviews with prominent poets and writers, including Czeslaw Milosz and Seamus Heaney, broadcast on WBAI, NYC. Her book, *Psyche, Soul, and Spirit: Interdisciplinary Essays*, with co-author Katherine Jillson, has been published by WIPF & STOCK, Publishers.

Keri Cohen is a Licensed Clinical Social Worker and a Board Certified Diplomate in clinical social work. She is a psychoanalytic psychotherapist in private practice in Lancaster, PA. Her work is with adults, adolescents and children. She is a graduate of the University of Pennsylvania's School of Social Policy and Practice and holds a certificate from the William Alanson White Institute's Online Intensive Psychoanalytic Psychotherapy Program. She is a published writer, has presented papers at national and international conferences and is a co-moderator of the international online Studying Eigen group. She has attended Michael Eigen's Bion seminars for nearly 15 years.

Howard Covitz (PhD, ABPP) is a psychoanalyst in the Philadelphia area. He was a training analyst at the Institute for Psychoanalytic Studies of Philadelphia, and the Institute for Psychoanalytic Psychotherapies. He was Director of the latter from 1986 to 1998. His book, *Oedipal Paradigms in*

Collision, was nominated for the Gradiva Book of the Year Award. He is a contributor to the best seller *The Dangerous Case of Donald Trump*.

Loray Daws is a registered Clinical Psychologist in both South Africa and British Columbia, Canada. Loray is currently in private practice and serves as senior faculty member at the International Masterson Institute for Psychoanalytic Psychotherapy in New York. He has published and works in the areas of daseinsanalysis, psychoanalytic psychotherapy, disorders of the self, psychosomatic difficulties, and mental health ethics. Loray serves as assistant editor for the *Global Journal of Health Sciences* in Canada, evaluator and international advisory board member for the *International Journal of Psychotherapy*, assistant editor for EPIS (Existential Psychoanalytic Institute and Society), and both teaches and supervises in South Africa, Australia, and Turkey in the psychoanalytic approach to disorders of the self. He is also the editor of four books.

Michael Eigen is a psychologist and psychoanalyst. He is Associate Clinical Professor of Psychology in the Postdoctoral Program in Psychotherapy and Psychoanalysis at New York University (adjunct), and a senior member of the National Psychological Association for Psychoanalysis. He is the author of books including, *The Challenge of Being Human*, *Dialogues with Michael Eigen: Psyche Singing*, *Toxic Nourishment*, *The Psychoanalytic Mystic*, *Feeling Matters* and *Flames from the Unconscious*. Eigen has led a weekly seminar on the works of Bion, Winnicott and Lacan for over 40 years.

Ken Fuchsman (EdD) was President of the International Psychohistorical Association from 2016 to 2020. He is Emeritus faculty from the University of Connecticut, where he taught American history, interdisciplinary studies, the nature of being human, and the family in interdisciplinary perspective, and was Executive Program Director of the Bachelor of General Studies Program. Along with Michael Maccoby, Dr. Fuchsman co-edited *Psychoanalytic and Historical Perspectives on the Leadership of Donald Trump*, published by Routledge. He is also the author of the forthcoming *Movies, Rock & Roll, Freud: Essays on Film and Music*.

Ziva Bracha-Gidron is the founder and manager of The Jerusalem Psychodrama Institute: "Hakol Koreh", associated with the "David Yellin Academic College of Education". She is a psychodramatist and psychotherapist who counsels individuals, couples and groups. She works as a senior lecturer in the "Crisis, Stress and Suicide Treatment Unit" of the Israeli Ministry of Education. She is also a senior lecturer in Professor Mordechai Rotenberg's institute. Writer and director of monodrama experimental theater performance. The title of her doctoral dissertation in Psychology (PsyD) is "Hope in Psychodrama Group Psychotherapy Based on the Jewish Hassidic Spiritual Approach".

Ruth Golan is a clinical psychologist, a psychoanalyst, and poet. Living and working in Tel-Aviv, Israel, she is researching psychoanalysis according to the teachings of Lacan and his interpretation of Freud. Golan is also a supervisor in Bar-Ilan University and heading The Freudian Place in Jaffa. In the last few years she has been practicing and researching the evolution of consciousness as a student and partner to the path of the teacher and philosopher Andrew Cohen. She is the director of EnlightenNext Israel. She published many articles. Her acclaimed book in English is *Loving Psychoanalysis* (Karnac, 2006). She has also published five poetry books. In 2013 her book *The Consciousness Bearers: When Psychoanalysis Encounters the Evolution of Spirit* was published by Contento.

Sean Harrell (PsyD) is a clinical psychologist and psychoanalytic psycho-therapist. While completing his doctoral studies in clinical psychology he also earned a Masters in Theology and completed a one-year fellow-ship at the Chicago Center for Psychoanalysis, and his doctoral research culminated in a theoretical integration of psychoanalytic self psychology, relational psychoanalysis and the theology of Jürgen Moltmann. He has formed and continues to co-lead a psychoanalytic study group in Grand Rapids, Michigan where he lives and practices.

Katherine Jillson, early in her career, taught students in elementary schools in New York State and in U.S. Army schools in France. Based on this experience, she wrote many educational materials. After studying in inter-disciplinary Interior Life seminars with the psychiatrist and psychoanalyst Dr. Preston G. McLean, she taught similar seminars. She co-authored, with Dr. McLean, two Survey Reports for American Management Associations. With Rachel Berghash, Katherine wrote the book *Psyche, Soul, and Spirit: Interdisciplinary Essays*, which has been published by WIPF & STOCK. Katherine lives in New York City, where she continues to write interdisciplinary essays with Rachel Berghash.

Alitta Kullman (PhD, PsyD, LMFT) is a psychoanalyst and psychoanalytic psychotherapist in private practice in Newport Beach, CA. She is the au-thor of "The Perseverant Personality: A Pre-attachment Perspective on the Etiology and Evolution of Binge/Purge Eating Disorders" (*Psychoanalytic Dialogues*, 2007), and *Hunger for Connection: Finding Meaning in Eating Disor-ders* (Routledge, 2018), and a longtime member of the MEigenWorkshop.

Shalini Masih (PhD) is a psychoanalytic psychotherapist in private practice in New Delhi, India. She has supervised and taught psychoanalytic psycho-therapists training in the MPhil Psychoanalytic Psychotherapy program of the School of Human Studies, Ambedkar University Delhi. Her doctoral thesis was a Psychoanalytic Study on Beauty in Ugliness in Spirit Posses-sion and Exorcism. She has presented papers at national and international psychoanalytic conferences and contributed her writing in edited volumes like *Psychoanalysis from the Indian Terroir: Emerging Themes in Culture, Family, and Childhood, Counterdreamers: Analysts Reading Themselves* and *Rethinking the Relation between Women and Psychoanalysis: Loss, Mourning and the Feminine.* Her paper titled "Devil Sing me the Blues – A Life Struggling to be Born" received the Critics Award for Best Psychoanalytic Writing in the Fifth International Psychoanalytic Conference held in New Delhi, India in 2018. She has also received the Scholar Award from the Society for Psychoanalysis and Psychoanalytic Psychology, Div 39, APA for the year 2020.

Merle Molofsky is a New York State-licensed psychoanalyst in private practice in New York City. She is committed to furthering psychoanalytic education, and to writing and editing in the service of psychoanalytic education. She is on the Editorial Board of *The Psychoanalytic Review*, and the Editorial Board of *The Journal of Psychohistory*. A member of the Training Institute of NPAP, she serves on the NPAP faculty, is a member of the NPAP Clinical Experience and Supervision Committee, and is former Dean of Training. She serves on the Advisory Committee of Harlem Family Institute (HFI) and on the HFI faculty. She is former Director of Education, the Institute for Expressive Analysis (IEA). Merle has served as Editor of *Other/Wise*, an IFPE journal of psychoanalytic writings, literature, and creative arts, from Spring 2010 to Winter 2012. Merle is a published poet, fiction writer, and produced playwright. Her novel, *Streets 1970*, was published by International Psychoanalytical Books in January 2015.

Willow Pearson (PsyD, LMFT, MT-BC) is Assistant Professor and Director of Clinical Training, Clinical Psychology Department, Notre Dame de Namur University, Belmont, California. A licensed Clinical Psychologist, licensed Marriage and Family Therapist, and nationally board-certified Music Therapist, Dr. Pearson has a private practice in Oakland, California, where she sees individual adults and couples. Dr. Pearson is also a singer and composer. She has four albums of original music and a fifth album of Tibetan Buddhist songs of realization. Dr. Pearson is co-editor and contributing author of *The Spiritual Psyche: Mysticism, Intersubjectivity and Psychoanalysis in Clinical Practice.*

Louis Rothschild (PhD) is a clinical psychologist in Lutherville, Maryland. Specializing in psychoanalytic psychotherapy, he also provides supervision, writes, and occasionally reviews manuscripts. His publications have ranged from quantitative to qualitative, social-cognitive to psychoanalysis, and clinical to philosophical. Presently, his scholarly focus is centered on rapprochement between fathers and sons. Most recently, he served as a member of the steering committee for the 38th annual spring meeting of Division 39. He is a past-president of the Rhode Island local chapter of the Division of Psychoanalysis (39) of the American Psychological Association.

Ashis Roy (PhD) is a psychoanalytic therapist and faculty at Centre of Psychotherapy and Clinical Research, Ambedkar University, Delhi. He works with both young adults and adults, and is interested in mental states of fragmentation and negation. He is interested in clinical and cultural psychoanalysis. His doctoral work has been on the translation of otherness in intimacy in Hindu–Muslim couples. His publications include "Imagining Undreamt Selves" in *Counterdreamers: Analysts Reading Themselves* (2016).

Neetu Sarin is an Assistant Professor and psychoanalytic psychotherapist at the School of Human Studies, Ambedkar University Delhi. She is a training candidate at the Indian Psychoanalytic Society (International Psychoanalytic Association). Her doctoral work is an inquiry into dissociative states arising out of trauma in the second and third generation survivors of the India-Pakistan Partition. Clinically, she works with states of autism, dissociation and psychosis. Her most recent publication is titled 'Sexual abuse, sexuality and desire of daughters: A reflection on changing familial relationships' (*International Journal of Social Sciences Review*, 2019).

Burton Norman Seitler (PhD) is a psychoanalyst/clinical psychologist, with offices in Ridgewood and Oakland, NJ. He is the Editor-in-Chief of the *Journal for the Advancement of Scientific Psychoanalytic Empirical Research* (*JASPER*), which just won the Gradiva Award from the National Association for the Advancement of Psychoanalysis (NAAP). He is the Director of the Training Board of the New Jersey Institute for Training in Psychoanalysis (NJI). He has contributed over 100 articles, book chapters, book reviews, videos, and scholarly presentations on topics including: randomized controlled trials, autism research, ADHD, psychosis, neurological impairment, trauma, separation-individuation, castration anxiety, soma-psyche, myopia, dreams and sleep apnea.

Adam Shechter is a psychoanalytic psychotherapist in private practice in New York City. He began his career working at community-based clinics throughout Manhattan. Mr. Shechter's writing explores the intersection of interpersonal states and textual reality in terms of psychoanalytic theory and practice. His work has appeared in numerous print and online journals, and has been presented at academic conferences and cultural events. His chapbook, *Paul Celan and the Messiah's Broken Levered Tongue: An Exponential Dyad* was co-authored with Daniel Y. Harris and published by Cervena Barva Press. He is also the book review editor for the psychoanalytic journal, *Vestigia*.

Stefanie Teitelbaum (MSW, BMusic) is a supervisor, training analyst, and on the faculties of the National Psychological Association for Psychoanalysis (NPAP), The Object Relations Institute (ORI), and the Institute for Expressive Analysis (IEA). She was formerly an IEA Education Director and Dean of Students. Her papers have been published in the *American*

Journal of Psycho-Analysis, *Other/Wise* (the On-Line Journal of IFPE), *Psychoanalytic Inquiry* and *The Psychoanalytic Review*. She is a member of Psychoanalytic Review Editorial Staff. She is a former staff psychotherapist at the Lower East Side Service Center Drug-Free Out-Patient Program. Stefanie maintains a private psychoanalytic practice in New York City. She was formerly a classical music singer.

Acknowledgements

Many thanks to Ken Fuchsman for conceptualizing this book which contains many of the Eigen papers presented at the 42nd International Psychohistorical Association Conference held in New York in the spring of 2019. It has been an honour to work on this project with Ken, who has steadfastly brought this book to fruition.

Thank you to Routledge for the opportunity to publish a diverse group of papers, which will add creative resources to the psychoanalytic field.

Michael Eigen has been both a background and foreground presence in my life for over 20 years. Sometime around 2008 or 2009, he began for about five years, subtly and directly encouraging me to write. When I finally took the plunge, it bore fruit. His gift of making introductions to parts of yourself opens worlds. I am forever grateful for his encouragement and ability to teach me how to mine the depths, an ongoing journey, along with so much more.

Thank you for contributing your paper on Rebirth to this project.

To the authors, contributors. It is with joy, awe, intrigue, laughter, and touching intimacy that your papers bring additional light to Eigen's work and spirit. Your individual lenses allow new ways to see and advance his work in the field. There is so much light and beauty in your papers.

Jeff Eaton, Brent Potter, and Loray Daws gave generous support and help with my paper. Loray generously agreed to read it through multiple times, giving feedback, while Jeff and Brent graciously helped me articulate certain concepts better.

Ofra Eshel helped me flesh out the Radical Group of psychoanalysts for the Preface.

Finally, I wish to thank my family. My husband gave support, time, and counsel for which I am entirely grateful. His love and dedication supporting me with this project was ever present. My children provided much comedic relief when I needed a break. The presence of children, no matter what age, helps one put things in perspective. My family is as much a part of this book as I am.

Keri S. Cohen

****

Michael Eigen has been gracious and generous from the time I invited him to speak at the 2019 International Psychohistory Association Conference until the present. This book would never have materialized without his connecting me to his friends and colleagues. He also listens carefully, as one would expect, and has given me sage advice on how to proceed. As Mike is in much demand, he could have published his Rebirth essay in other places, but kindly contributed it here. For this I am very grateful.

I also owe a great deal to my co-editor Keri Cohen. Her emails early in planning for the Psychohistory Conference educated me about Eigen's work and about who else might be interested. She was so helpful I asked if we could talk on the phone, which we did. As she kept being so encouraging and informative, I asked her to be co-editor of this book. She has continued to be a guide.

Alitta Kullman has been a wealth of ideas and enthusiasm from her first contact with me to the present. She is another generous soul, and her essay in this collection is outstanding. Thank you, Alitta.

Loray Daws continued his devotion to Eigen in the ways he encouraged and assisted me and others in the planning of the conference and since then.

Emeritus History Professor and psychoanalyst Dr Jacques Szaluta reads and makes essential critiques of everything I write. He also listens to my thoughts and helps me sort things through and has done so with this project.

NYU Professor Theresa Aiello has a wealth of knowledge and wisdom that she generously shares each time I call her. I have been educated by her in many ways, including with this book.

Talented poet and memoirist Carol Bonci reviews my writing, and gives honest, insightful, and thought-provoking feedback. She does the same not only with what I write, but has done so with each step of editing this book, which I deeply appreciate.

Last is social worker Lisa Kleckner. For the last decade, no one has encouraged me more than Lisa, has listened more attentively to my interminable expounding of my notions, and has made so many inspiring suggestions, including throughout my work on this tribute to Michael Eigen. There is no way to sufficiently thank her.

Ken Fuchsman

Preface

Michael Eigen's work has been on the cutting edge of psychoanalysis for over 50 years, forging a path for psychoanalytic freedoms of expression and experiential possibilities. His work pushes sentient life to new dimensions and depths, opening new radical ways to be present with patients. Eigen seems ahead of his time by 50 years or more, given how strongly he presses into expanding the frame. He is a visionary leading the way to radical openness.

Ofra Eshel has included Michael Eigen in what she calls the Radical Group of psychoanalysts (Eshel, 2019). This group, which has its foundations in Winnicott, Milner, late Bion, and late Lacan, focuses on a more radical dimension of being and becoming in the experience rather than an epistemological exploration of conventional psychoanalytic work. It is a more soulful way to work with patients. Use of the full self is paramount. Eigen's radical openness uses everything in his being, bringing patients to a deeper, compassionate place in their inner lives.

Michael Eigen's work is influenced by the Tao, mysticism, mythology, Kabbalah, Lacan, Winnicott, Milner, Bion, Elkin, Jung, Freud, Shakespeare, poets, musicians, and many others. His creativity serves as a springboard for others to feel the freedom to express themselves, unabated. There is nowhere his mind will not wander which gives his readers, patients and others the courage to accept their madness and sanity, all mixed into one.

This book grew out of the 42nd International Psychohistorical Association Conference held at New York University in May 2019. Papers on the work of Michael Eigen were a subset of presentations, many of which are included in this book.

These papers illuminate and expand upon Eigen's brilliant playfulness as an analyst, his compassionate wisdom, how he uses time, music, Kabbalah, dream work, case studies, Bion's grid, F in O, Psychospiritual approaches and more. Authors weave everything from comic books to dissociative patients into their papers, giving the reader a psychic taste of what it is like to enliven the field of practice, bringing play, love and compassion to our patients.

I suppose these papers remind us that nothing is too small or insignificant and that every little bit counts, something Eigen professes over and over again. His psychoanalytic faith along with his faith in the elements of the universe shine through in these papers. Turning into a barnacle becomes a jumping off point for deep reverie. Every morsel of every phrase has something to offer the psyche. Eigen believes in moments. These papers bring moments to life, with tears, laughter, heart and soul, emanating from the soul of what it means to be human, a soul Eigen shares openly with love.

Keri S. Cohen

Reference

Eshel, O. (2019). *The emergence of analytic oneness: Into the heart of psychoanalysis.* Routledge.

Introduction

Ken Fuchsman

The distinctiveness of Michael Eigen

In the pantheon of psychoanalytic thinkers, Keri Cohen and I believe that Michael Eigen has carved out a unique place. Building on predecessors, he has expanded vistas and explored territory that have regularly been either alien to or at the fringes of the field. Permeating Eigen's work is an exploration of psychic reality from emotional deadness to mysticism to ecstasy. What has garnered him much attention is the vitality with which he explores a full range of the peaks and valleys of our inner being.

While Freud famously labelled psychoanalysis the science of the unconscious, Eigen can be called a humanist of experience. William James, for instance, describes experience as a "stream, a succession of states, or waves, or fields … of knowledge, of feelings, of desires, of deliberations, etc., that constantly pass and repass, and that constitute our inner life" (James, 1914/1899, p. 15). Similarly, Eigen puts the full scope of human feeling, thoughts, and ideas front and centre; he derives much of his psychoanalytic perspectives from the depths and heights of our thoughts and feelings. The titles of many of his works reflect his interest in the spectrum of emotional and spiritual experience. This includes *Psychic Deadness, Emotional Storm, Ecstasy, Damaged Bonds, The Psychoanalytic Mystic, Toxic Nourishment, Kabbalah and Psychoanalysis, Lust, Contact with the Depths, The Sensitive Self,* and, of course, *The Challenge of Being Human.*

His humanism is connected to a revelatory experience that happened to him as a young man. He writes that in his 20s he was in "emotional agony" that somehow led to "radiant light." While his "pain did not vanish" neither did "the light." He concludes that "suffering and ecstasy nest in one another" (Eigen, 1998, pp. 41, 167). For Eigen the experience of radiance is connected to that "Divine sparks work in us." Psychoanalysis needs to "touch the infinite unknown … All kinds of unknown emotional transmissions" (Eigen, 2012, pp. 62, 26). We see here that an inner journey leads him to bring both transcendence and agony into the psychoanalytic realm in ways that has opened up less explored vistas within this specialty.

Eigen is, as I said, a humanist. What is meant by this term? There are at least four meanings of humanism: (1) those who do not recognize a Supreme Being and focus on human reality, (2) people concerned with what it means to be human, (3) practicers and believers in the humanities, and (4) humanistic psychologists. I see Eigen as concerned with the challenge of being human and an adherent to the humanities. It should not be forgotten that he was an undergraduate English major. He wonders what psychoanalysis would look like "if literature had not been a core part of its background. In one way a science, but even more a form of literature" This adherence to literature and other humanistic disciplines is evident to anyone listening closely during his legendary Tuesday seminars; for he regularly drops allusions to fiction, poetry, spirituality, and philosophy into his remarks. Michael Eigen can be called a humanist, in the sense of being focused on the fullness of being human.

His extraordinary spiritual and intellectual journey has captured the attention of some prominent psychoanalysts. Adam Phillips wrote of Eigen's "new kind of moral seriousness" and added, "No-one in contemporary psychoanalysis writes with this cunning, wholehearted openness" (1999). In a similar vein, British psychoanalyst Christopher Bollas said of Eigen: "No one else thinks like this, writes like this, or puts psychoanalysis into a separate realm ... this is literature for the ages" (2009). Philosopher and analyst Jon Mills wrote that "Michael Eigen is one of the greatest psychoanalysts of our time" (2018). Psychoanalytic chronicler of Wilfred Bion, James Grotstein, nominated Michael Eigen "as an (inter)-national treasure" (Grotstein, 2018, p. xxiii).

Jessica Benjamin said how Eigen is "a person of rare wisdom, courage and heart" who has "the mind of a brilliantly creative thinker" (2007) and uses "language in a way that opens and deepens psychic reality." Relational psychoanalyst Lewis Aron talked of how Eigen "dazzles" with "gems of wisdom" and "love" that help people "survive the inevitable catastrophic condition of life" (2012). Another relational analyst, Adrienne Harris, said that in reading Eigen one learns "about the creative power of disruption and turbulence" and the need for analysts to do as Eigen does and go "deeply into the awesome terrain that lies within oneself" (2018).

Unlike some others, Dr Eigen has garnered this recognition without establishing a new school of thought, a la Freud with psychoanalysis, or Kohut's self-psychology, or Stephen A. Mitchell with relational psychoanalysis, among others. In the history of psychoanalysis, many who have become influential, such as Melanie Klein and Heinz Kohut, have often claimed new ground for their endeavours. Acknowledging their predecessors may be part of their writing, and yet they focus on their own innovations. Eigen stresses much less his originality than his debts to others. This regularly includes his former analyst Henry Elkin, his enormous personal and intellectual gratitude to Wilfred Bion, what he has gained from D.W. Winnicott, Marion Milner, or

Jacques Lacan. At a workshop, he said, "In a way, I am a Winnicottian-Bion analyst" (Fetting, 2015, p. 178).

Of the psychoanalysts listed as influencing him, only one, Elkin, is American. The rest are European. Yet this long-time New Yorker's interests go beyond Western culture. They are close to global. Not only has Michael Eigen written three books on the Jewish mystical tradition of Kabbalah, he incorporates religious and humanistic traditions from across the planet. Eigen is receptive to experience in many of its forms no matter where it appears. A humanist of experience should embrace humanity not only in the worlds where he or she grew up and received training, but most anywhere. And this Michael Eigen does. He goes beyond the mainstreams of psychoanalysis by incorporating perspectives from all over the intellectual, experiential, and spiritual map into his writings.

What is also striking about Dr Eigen is the enormous power his writings have for many. Here are a few examples. Clinical psychologist Robin Bagai describes his first experience reading a Michael Eigen book,

> I was surprised to discover that my face had become wet with tears. I found myself unexpectedly weeping ... I was taken aback, and wasn't quite sure *why* I was crying, just knew I was being deeply touched. The second thing I noticed: I found myself in a very quiet contemplative state, similar to what happens, if lucky, while meditating.

Robin then wonders, "Who is this guy Michael Eigen and how does he manage to speak to my insides, affecting me like this?"

Similarly, clinician Dr Margaret Fetting says that Eigen's "insides talked to my insides" Being immersed in Eigen's writings for her "began an opening, a blossoming of self that deepened my capacity for experience, radically expanded my view of living, took my clinical work and teaching to new depths, and emboldened my writing. I felt I was in a different world" (Fetting, 2015, *Living Moments*, pp. 176–7). Psychoanalytic psychotherapist Sean Harrell writes in this book, "I was looking for a creedal formulation and found a mystic; looking for a ship safely above the *waves* and found someone signalling me to dip into the waters ... I needed to find Eigen's work to find something of my own voice." Eigen's writings have helped these individuals get more in touch with their own insides, and flourish as a result.

A good number of persons so impacted by Dr Eigen's writings and person gathered together at the May 2019 International Psychohistorical Association Conference at New York University. Dr Eigen was a plenary speaker and about 30 others delivered papers on his contributions. When, as then President of the Psychohistory Association, I invited Eigen to be a speaker at our conference, and I mentioned including a panel on his work, inviting others to present, and hopefully a book, Mike not only said yes but gave me names to contact. Before I knew it Loray Daws phoned me from Canada, soon Keri

Cohen had written me a lengthy email suggesting what to cover and whom to contact. Many submitted proposals and presented at the conference. All the chapters in this book were delivered at the 2019 Psychohistory Conference. After the conference, each of the presenters were invited to send in a contribution for the book. Our contributors come from various sections of the United States, Canada, India, and Israel. Keri Cohen and I as co-editors collected the papers, and proceeded on the project of transforming publicly presented papers into a book to be published.

Eigen on rebirth

This collection begins with Dr Eigen's plenary talk on rebirth, then presents chapters by the three plenary panellists: Robin Bagai, Keri Cohen, and Loray Daws. There are then a series of chapters on psychic reality in Eigen's work followed by discussions of spirituality and faith. The book ends with chapters that are reflections on psychoanalysis and various ways of knowing the ins and outs of psychoanalytic frameworks.

Rebirth, Eigen writes, has been associated with circuitous change and on the other hand with nourishing new senses of being and possibility, of re-animation, rejuvenation. Part of this process of rebirth is encountering the dialectic between being born and dying. The Hebrew God's Biblical creation is first good and soon Cain kills his brother. How do we make sense of this? Eigen writes, "There are ways life feeds on death as well as the reverse." He wonders, "Could good exist without evil? Is evil a moral growth of pain?" Hercules is a central figure is this chapter, as he suffered "boundless agonies" and went from "madness to divinity." But he is a figure who embraced his trials and confronted his challenges, and as wanton a murderer as he was as Eigen presents him Hercules has a bit of a heroic in him. Humans have demons and need to make our demons better meet the challenge of being human, To Eigen, we are all beginners still learning, and still beginning. Beginning like rebirth is without end.

Eigen in time

This part consists of chapters by the three members of the plenary panel on Eigen's work given at the Psychohistory Conference. "Encountering Michael Eigen: A personal retrospective" is the title of psychologist Robin Bagai's plenary panel delivered at the Psychohistory Conference. Dr Bagai is a clinical psychologist who leads a weekly seminar on Eigen's work. His approaches combine his interest in thought from the East and the West. This seminar covered ten of Dr Eigen's books. His chapter talks about the immense impact reading Eigen's work has had on him, and also how leading the discussion groups on Eigen's work has deepened his therapy practice and enabled him to be more resilient and spontaneous in sessions. This is quite a tribute from one professional to another. Dr Bagai also says that the complexity of Eigen's work has yet to be fully appreciated and assimilated. A central motif in Eigen's writing is the unknown, the ineffable. Another element for Eigen is faith as a living reality and also as Bagai says "a capacity waiting our encounter." To Bagai, what makes Eigen so important is the way "he circles unflinchingly around areas humanity needs most help grappling with: Sufferings of madness, trauma, destructiveness, and murder." In this day and age, what Bagai thinks we need is to further develop our capacities rather than become embroiled in unproductive conflicts.

Co-editor Keri Cohen is a clinical social worker who co-leads the international Studying Eigen Listserve. Her chapter "On the importance of time as a background object" is the second of the three plenary panel chapters. She sees Eigen as someone who artistically uses Time as a background support, as a third in the room. He uses Time creatively as a good object, one that nurtures rather than persecutes. Cohen describes how Eigen's use of time becomes part of the analysis, ultimately serving as a welcoming object, thus becoming a healing salve. For in Eigen's "graceful practice," Cohen writes, he makes "time feel effortless," and this grows out of his "lifetime of meditation" and "contact with the depths." He has the capability of "nursing damaged souls" in ways that helps them transform trauma into "new psychic experience." Eigen can do this by "playing for time" and being "not in a hurry." His sense of "therapeutic time becomes an incubator for the psyche." It allows the "damaged Self" to be become transformed and to gently take shape. Among other things, his use of time becomes a healing salve.

Loray Daws' chapter is entitled "Healing longing in the midst of damage: Eigen's psychoanalytic vision." He is a clinical psychologist and a senior faculty member with the International Masterson Institute, and has edited two books on Eigen. The most recent is *Dialogues with Michael Eigen: Psyche Singing* (2020), and earlier with Stephen Bloch, he co-edited *Living Moments: On the Work of Michael Eigen* (2015). Dr Daws has gone through Eigen's total publications and selected out essential quotes to portray the dimensions and scope of Eigen's contributions. He focuses in on archetypical rhythms in Eigen's writings, including birth–growth–damage–rebirth rhythms, trauma–nourishment rhythms, nourishment as trauma rhythms, breakdown–recovery rhythm, and a unique rhythm of faith. This includes a trust that the Other can come through the trauma-recovery sequence and develop his or her own inherent generative capacity. Daws sees Michael Eigen as being sober, realistic and "sensitively hopeful."

Tasting the psyche through Eigen's writings

In this part of the book, we have a variety of perspectives on the ways Eigen portrays psychic reality. "Breakdown and recovery: Going *Berserk* and other rhythmic concerns" is the title of the first chapter in this part. It is by clinical psychologist and psychoanalytic psychotherapist, Louis Rothschild. He has published in professional journals and books on topics ranging from essentialism and prejudice to chronic depression and personality. In his chapter here, Dr Rothschild adeptly integrates into his presentation such diverse authors as Canadian philosopher Charles Taylor, Nobel prize winner Bob Dylan, and classicist Edith Hamilton, among others. Rothschild finds that for Eigen a breakdown and recovery rhythm is basic to being human. Being faithful to this rhythm, Rothschild says, entails "an uncertain journey … a willingness to take another breath and see." This involves faith in the unfolding process. Because the way things unfold involves accepting being shattered and that one is never whole. Rothschild finds that in going through this never-ending journey that "Eigen's master surfing is helpful," to say the least.

Dr Shalini Masih is a psychoanalytic psychotherapist in New Dehli, India. She was given the Scholar Award in 2020 by Division 39 of the American Psychological Association. "Reading the work of Michael Eigen: Artitst of the Invisible" is her chapter title for this book. This is a wide ranging chapter. Dr Masih faces a dilemma in relation to a certain client, and turns to Eigen's writings for assistance in how to confront her internal struggle. She also has a number of sessions with Dr Eigen in his Manhattan office. As Masih relates one of them, we witness what makes Eigen such an extraordinary therapist and human being. This example helps us understand a good deal of why Michael Eigen is treasured and revered by so many. Dr Masih writes about how important for the therapist it is to cultivate psychic sensing, and the illustration from her session with Eigen is illustrative of his sensing capacities. This is part of her section on shame, where she also relays two of Eigen's experiences and then discusses her own reflections on shame. There are also other encounters between Eigen and Masih connected to important issues for her.

Sean Harrell's chapter is entitled "Chasing the uncatchable: Mystery and metaphor in the work of Michael Eigen." Harrell has both a doctorate in clinical psychology and a master's degree in theology, and seeks to integrate self-psychology, relational psychoanalysis, and theology. He focuses on the connection between Eigen and Winnicott and Bion in relationship to mystery and metaphor. He does this by recounting an interview of Eigen with a patient who had been much hospitalized until encountering Eigen as a therapist. While this client's statements and associations may be hard to comprehend, Eigen stays with him. The client feels listened to. Harrel quotes Eigen that psychoanalysis is more about hypothesis than answering; it is open-ended exploring. Again, he quotes Eigen writing about therapy being about rebirth rituals that involve destruction and rebuilding. Harrell also finds selections from Eigen's writings that connects the therapeutic and the religious.

Robin Bagai delivered a second paper on Eigen's contributions at the 2019 Psychohistory Conference, and it is included in this volume. The chapter title is "Michael Eigen and evolution of psyche." Eigen, Bagai says, captures many of the forms of doubleness and paradox within us. One of these paradoxes is that the aggressiveness and destructiveness within us can be thrilling and enlivening. Throughout his work Eigen increases awareness of the complexity of our emotional life. He also shows us that the emotional life is more than we can grasp, sustain, and experience fully. Still, Bagai says Eigen "emphasizes the value inherent in partnering the flow between any two polarities, tendencies or capacities." He quotes Eigen that in our lives as we go through "shock and grief" we "we come closer to being artists of the pain of existence." Bagai affirms that becoming such inner artists is a worthy goal.

"On not knowing Michael Eigen" is the intriguing title of Alitta Kullman's chapter. She is a psychoanalyst and psychodynamic psychotherapist and author of *Hunger for Connection: Finding Meaning in Eating Disorders*, and "The perseverant personality: A pre-attachment perspective on the aetiology and evolution of binge/purge eating disorders." To Dr Kullman, Michael Eigen's "boundless openness and curiosity" stems from his "willingness not to know." He is able to mine the "inner and outermost element of human experience" without a need to find answers or to pretend to know. Her essay is designed to illustrate Eigen's gems of insight and wisdom. As Dr Kullman does not believe she can capture the nuances and the spiritual and emotional connections in Eigen's writings, she does so by sequencing extraordinary quotes from Eigen's many books and articles. She has picked out many highlights for the reader to take in and absorb.

Ashis Roy is a psychoanalytic psychotherapist and a member of the faculty at Ambedkar University in Delhi, India. He has done research on the Self and the Other in Intimate Hindu–Muslim relationships. His chapter is entitled "Canvassing *Faith* and *Illusion* in fragmentation: An Indian perspective." It is primarily a case study of a client of his he names Sarah. Dr Roy derives his approach from *Eigen in Seoul: Madness and Murder*, Winnicott's work on illusion, and Emmanuel Ghent. The latter was a psychoanalytic psychiatrist, who according to Lewis Aron "was in many ways the leader of the relational group at NYU" (Aron, 2009, p. 14). Roy's chapter engages with reveries, co-fragmentation, infantile states, shame, a sense of annihilation, and how out of this whirlwind selfhood and psychic growth can emerge.

"More than a word: Reverberations between Eigen's notions of deadness/aliveness and Bion's grid" is the title of Adam Schechter's chapter. He is a psychoanalytic psychotherapist, book review editor of *Vestigia*, a psychoanalytic journal, and co-author of *Paul Celan and the Messiah's Broken Levered Tongue: An Exponential Dyad*. This chapter explores how in Eigen's published writings his use of language anchors the intricacies and intimacies of psychoanalytic experience. Eigen takes from Bion, yet in his own way uses language to be clinically alive in psychoanalytic sessions and on the printed page throughout his writings.

Dr Neetu Sarin is a psychoanalytic psychotherapist and Assistant Professor in the School of Human Studies, Ambedkar University, Delhi. Her research centres in the area of the role of body as a unit of thinking and finding agency in the human psyche. Her chapter, "Psychoanalysis a prayer: The construction and breakdown of faith in dissociative states" is an extension of her work on trauma and dissociative states among survivors of the second and third India–Pakistan partition. In this instance, it is a case study of a young significantly unintegrated young woman. Dr Sarin sees her work with this client as an application of Eigen's ideas about touching madness in manageable doses, how muteness arises out of the strain of everyday living, and primary and non-cognized support in therapy. Her client at first is remote, relatively mute, and dissociates. In the course of therapy, the young woman comes into psychic birth.

Spirituality and becoming

A central component of Eigen's focus on psychic reality is connected to religious and spiritual traditions across the planet. This portion of the book has chapters on Eigen's work in these areas. The first article in this section is co-authored by Rachel Berghash and Katherine Jillson, and is entitled "Difficulties of faith." Berghash is a clinical social worker, a teacher of Interior Life seminars which combine religion and philosophy. She is also an accomplished poet, and a published memoirist. Jillson has been a student and then teacher of Interior Life seminars, has co-authored reports for the American Management Association. These two writers in 2016 co-authored, *Psyche, Soul, and Spirit: Interdisciplinary Essays*. Faith needs to be distinguished from belief, Berghash and Jillson contend. Belief is a system that organizes experience, while faith is concerned with the unknown and unseen. A difficulty of faith is surrendering to the unknown parts of reality. To be within faith requires an openness to exploration, a capacity to wait, and courage to accept doubt and despair, and that catastrophes may occur. To illustrate their concerns, they cite the work of Michael Eigen extensively, but also poets such as Rilke, Wordsworth, Rumi, and TS Eliot, and philosophers such as Alfred North Whitehead and Paul Tillich.

Dr Ziva Bracha Gidron is a senior lecturer in a unit of the Israeli Ministry of Education and founder and manager of the Jerusalem Psychodrama Institute. Her chapter has the title, "Unity of opposites": Hope in psychodrama group psychotherapy based on the Jewish Hassidic spiritual approach and Michael Eigen's psychospiritual relational approach." She discusses how hope can emerge in a special way from the Jewish mystical tradition that sees a dialectic between opposites that reveals a unity between them. The Jewish traditions to which Dr Gidron is referring are Kabbalah and Hasidim. What she also discusses is how Michael Eigen's focusing on emotional growth has a parallel in Kabballah. Both Eigen and certain Jewish mystical traditions focus on this dialogue between opposites, and how it is this dialectic that can be a source of hope where it might have seemed that these opposites were a barrier to such optimism.

Our second Israeli writing about Jewish mysticism is Ruth Golan. She is a clinical psychologist, a psychoanalyst, an author of five poetry books, a volume in Hebrew on Kabbalah, and in English, *Loving Psychoanalysis: Looking at Culture with Freud and Lacan*. Her chapter is "The influence of Kabbalah's conception of Eros on the psychoanalytic Eros, according to Michael Eigen." As an author of a book on Kabbalah, Golan begins by describing some important elements of Kabbalah. She then shows how Eigen has been influenced by this Jewish mystical tradition, while his writings are poetic and erotic. His aim is to "create a more holistic understanding of the psyche." Golan shows the roots of Eigen's efforts in this regard in both Freud and Kabbalah. Eigen believes that God is everywhere, and he somehow "unites sex with God." In Plato's dialogue about the realms of the erotic, *The symposium*, the category of philia, Golan declares, is "the love of wisdom or erotic knowledge." Evolving Eros expands the limits of the self, and in Eigen's hands "contains a wellspring of knowledge and experience."

"'My kingdom for a widdler': Michael Eigen: A beta-watcher's midwife" is by psychoanalyst Stefanie Teitelbaum. As well as being in private practice, she is on the faculties of the National Psychological Association for Psychoanalysis, the Object Relations Institute, and the Institute for Expressive Analysis. She has studied under Michael Eigen. For this chapter, among other things, she shows how Eigen uses Wilfred Bion's Beta concept in his own work, especially in *The Birth of Experience*. She also applies Eigen's notion of the distinction–union structure to one of her long-term clients, discusses Freud's Little Hans case and the boy's references to widdlers, hence the title of this paper. She writes about Eigen's use of literature in his work, and also makes reference to a variety of art forms herself in this chapter.

Expanding the psychoanalytic frame

Burt Seitler is a psychoanalyst, and founding editor of the journal *J.A.S.P.E.R.*, which stands for *Journal for the Advancement of Scientific Psychoanalytic Empirical Research*. His ambitious paper here is entitled "A tribute to Michael Eigen's brave opposition to a legacy of dogma and manufactured truth." Dr Seitler holds up Eigen as a counter-example to a reductionist tradition that diminishes the human psychic reality. He begins his indictment of reductionism with Descartes and his many intellectual descendants, then shows how the tradition of psychological behaviourism also lessens the complexity of the human being. Seitler details how the *DSM*'S, with their focus on diagnosis from DSM-III in 1980, overly categorize humans in ways that fits them into boxes rather than shows their full being. Seitler then returns to how Eigen brings out the entire psychic reality, and declares that is what we need in this fragmented time.

"Missed opportunities in the history of psychoanalysis" is Howard Covitz's contribution to this book. Dr Covitz is a psychologist-psychoanalyst, a contributor to Bandy Lee's *The Dangerous Case of Donald Trump*, author of *Oedipal Paradigms in Collision*, and was Director and on the Training Faculty of the Psychoanalytic Studies Institute in Philadelphia. His chapter is a wide ranging, wide reaching account of the chequered history of psychoanalysis in the United States and elsewhere. He finds that there are both Good-Enough Analysts and Analysts Acting Badly. He singles out Michael Eigen as one of the select analysts who are actually more than good enough. Covitz also discusses the long-standing division in American psychoanalysis between the exclusivity of psychiatrists and non-medical analysts. He finds this division to be artificial.

Dr Willow Pearson wears a variety of hats. She is licensed both as a clinical psychologist and a marriage and family therapist and is a board-certified music therapist. In addition, she is Assistant Professor at Notre Dame de Namur University in Belmont, California. Her chapter is entitled "From madness to mysticism: Celebrating the work of Michael Eigen." It focuses on Dr Pearson's connection with Eigen's work. In particular she believes the distinction–union perspective is helpful in understanding the dialectic between madness and mysticism. Eigen's reverie "Be a light unto the world" is a conduit for herself and others to make soul to soul contact with the depths of Eigen's teachings.

This book closes with Merle Molofsky's tribute to Michael Eigen, "Permission and gratitude: Michael Eigen's gateway to possibility and freedom." Dr Molofsky is a woman for all seasons. As well as being a licensed psychoanalyst, she is also a novelist, a poet, playwright, and is on the Editorial Boards of *The Psychoanalytic Review* and the *Journal of Psychohistory* and has been the Director of Education for the Institute for Expressive Analysis, among other positions. To her, Eigen has both expanded psychoanalysis in theory and therapy, but has enabled her to become her true self. Eigen respects the boundaries of others as persons, and in ideas and concepts he "bypasses boundaries and borders." Despite our limits, Eigen helps us to see the extensiveness of our capabilities, of envisioning a future, of consciously and unconsciously shaping the world. Many of us are wounded and fragmented yet can survive and go beyond these difficulties. Eigen confronts the wounds, illuminates the light, and helps us see the vistas that are there.

References

Aron, L. (2012). In M Eigen, *Kabbalah and psychoanalysis*. Back cover. Karnac.
Benjamin, J. (2007). In M Eigen and A Govrin, *Conversations with Michael Eigen*. Karnac.
Bloch, S and Daws, L (Eds.). (2015). *Living moments: On the work of Michael Eigen*. Routledge.
Bollas, C. (2009). In M Eigen, *Flames from the unconscious*. Back cover. Karnac.
Eigen, M. (1998). *The psychoanalytic mystic*. Esf Publishers.

Eigen, M. (2012). *Kabbalah and psychoanalysis*. Karnac.

Eigen, M. (2019). *Dialogues with Michael Eigen: Psyche singing* (L Daws Ed.). Routledge.

Fetting, M. (2018). Michael Eigen: rich impacts. In *Living moments: On the work of Michael Eigen* (S Bloch and L Daws Eds.). Routledge, pp. 177–95 (original work published 2015).

Grotstein, J. (2018). Foreword, *Living moments: On the work of Michael Eigen* (S Bloch and L Daws Eds.). Routledge (original work published 2015), pp. xxi–xxiii.

Harris, A. (2018). *Living moments: On the work of Michael Eigen* (S Bloch and L Daws Eds.). Back cover. Routledge (original work published 2015).

James, W. (1914). *Talks to teachers*. Henry Holt & Company (original work published 1899).

Mills, J. (2018). In *Living moments: On the work of Michael Eigen* (S Bloch and L Daws Eds.). Back cover. Routledge (original work published 2015).

Phillips, A. (1999) In M. Eigen (1999). *Toxic nourishment*. Karnac.

Part I

Breathing into life

Chapter 1

Rebirth

It's been around a long time

Michael Eigen

Rebirth is an amazing word in the English language, with reverberations of meaning going back to antiquity and before. My own exploration here is informal and associative, staying as close as I can to imaginative vision and everyday experience. We are made of so many capacities, including a felt, implicit sense (Gendlin, 1962; Eigen, 2014) opening nuances of worlds that form part of and exceed transformational "systems" throughout the ages.

I mention the difference between word and meaning, as meanings of rebirth far precede the English word, which was a latecomer dating to between 1200–1600 CE. Notions were in Sanskrit and likely Tamil at least 1000 BCE and probably earlier. Words are packed with meaning, and *samsara* is often linked with change, wandering the world, and may have earlier meant war. The Greeks spoke about a war between the elements accounting for phenomena, and it is no accident that part of the Western literary canon begins with an erotic theft that spiked and spiced the Homeric war, an Athenian version of exile–return. And it is no accident that Freud, a great reader of humanity, found in Eros a dramatic expression of war between tensions that wound and uplift.

What to do with the war between the tensions of our being? Freud (1985/1898) tells Fliess his work is akin to the ancient mysteries. The latter try to transcend change, war, our "lower" nature, and reorient our beings in its "higher" nature, changeless, blissful. Hence the term "sublime" – the sublimation of drives in creative effort. Freud does not pretend he has a utopian "solution." As he says in a recording (1938) near the end of his life, "And the struggle is not yet over." Nor may it ever be.

There are many ways to look at the transformation struggle Freud partly re-contextualized. So much philosophy reflects on qualities of our being that pull us in different directions and blend in with psychology's attempts at diagnosis, study, and remediation. It is easy to make a link between Socrates' depiction of himself as midwife and gadfly and today's psychotherapist. So often Socrates comes to a place where fictions of living fall apart and the unknown begins. At such a point he may resort to myth and again it is no accident that Freud called aspects of his metapsychology his "myth."

The virtue of creative waiting on the unknown can, at times, open up possibilities that are closed by war. Although William Blake depicted heaven as the war between all the voices of personality expressed to the maximum, each nourishing all. In this vision, an evolutionary challenge is how to build capacity to support experience in such a way that we partner experience and it us. Less a model of control or war than mutual nourishment, more a path than final result.

We assign so many circles of meaning to our experience, trying to express what cannot be pinned down, while at the same time managing to convey aspects of what touches us. On the one hand, rebirth has been associated with wandering, world, cyclic, circuitous change. On the other, it means to convey something new, new life, new sense of being and possibility. William James draws on spiritual traditions to speak of being twice-born: born again of the spirit. Rabbi Menachem Schneerson speaks of God creating the world anew in each moment, which in psychological terms can refer to a sense of being born anew from moment to moment. Can you find the place where you are born anew in each moment?

Perhaps one only means revival, a feeling of coming alive, renewal, reanimating, rejuvenating, awakening through sensation, feeling, vision. Images of dying out in agony and coming alive in wonder and joy are part of an expressive sense of resurrection, a rhythm in the psalms and life of Jesus. One of the basic concerns of the British School was loss–discovery, death–birth of feeling, and the growth of a more heightened sense of one's psychic reality, e.g. Balint's "new beginning." Coming into life with loss as a background, dropping into loss with life as a background.

In therapy, a little can go a long way. Little changes for the better can make profound differences in a life. We try to develop language for little changes that make a difference then fight therapy wars over formulations and realities touched. Are we learning to appreciate different therapy languages and approaches as we would different poets or composers, opening perception of ripples in emotional, attitudinal pools, shifting spectrums of affective attitudes?

I've been reading and thinking about Freud for over 60 years and appreciate him more today than ever. Not as a final frame but filled with suggestions that open psychic realities. At the moment, I'm thinking about his conjunction of resistance and permeability, a double tendency that is part of our makeup. For example, liquid and electrical images depicting the flow of psychic energy together with fixity, repetition, blockage, inertia, entropy, enduring patterns for better and worse.

It is, of course, a doubleness with many applications and forms. DT Suzuki told of his failure to achieve enlightenment while sitting in Japan at his meditation centre, no matter how strong his efforts. At some point, his teacher sent him to Chicago to help translate Buddhist sutras. His translation of the *Lankavatara sutra* can be found online.[1] While reading, he came upon the phrase "an elbow does not bend outward" and, in an unexpected moment, enlightenment was achieved. What kind of breakthrough can this be? And how much further mining and digesting will be necessary? But something happened, a shift of attitude that makes a difference in the way life is experienced and lived.

Bion touches a kind of parallel sequence when describing work with psychosis: breakup, breakdown, breakthrough. One might add break in, break out. The work of psychic digestion, in this case metabolizing aspects of our madness, is never-ending. An important question is what kind of beginning and nurturing can it have? As the Talmud says, we are not required to finish the task, but we are asked to begin it, to undertake the living and processing of our own existence. Bion speaks of a back and forth movement between breaking apart – putting together. Back to square one, patience, tolerating build-up of further reorganization. Back to square one again. But I suspect how square one looks and feels and tastes changes with experience. A question is not just whether you can step into the same square one twice, but whether you can step into it once. How to begin or begin to begin? Can one reach a point where beginning becomes a new old friend?

Suzuki remarks that once one crosses the river to nirvana, *samsara* does not disappear. Life goes on in all its dimensions, but nirvana opens a different attitude towards *samsara*. Again, a little goes a long way.

At a seminar I attended in 1977, Bion spoke of a patient who, after twelve years, wanted to leave therapy because nothing had changed, he was just the same as when he started. Bion reported asking him, "Do you mind telling me how you did that?" He laconically remarked to the audience that knowing how change does not happen would be a contribution to science. Well, there is change and there is *change*. It certainly would be a mystery if one could stop change since it is happening all the time. And yet it is also the case we can feel and do feel something constant; there are ways we do not change. Irrevocable pain that poisons a life. And for some, does life in.

During the seminar someone asked, "Don't you ever mention Freud?" and Bion answered, "Freud is great for when you're tired." Yet Bion ended the seminar on a positive note, calling attention to the "pleasure, the joy we feel going through something difficult together." He was referring to the emotional–intellectual hardships and challenges of the seminar itself, experiences we grappled with, calling for attention, going through, coming through. At some point, he wryly remarked, "At least you have a sense of what it would feel like to grapple with a patient like me."

Tearing down and building up has been a pairing with a long history, if not from time immemorial then from memorialized time. Anabolic–catabolic and symbolic–diabolic are just two sets of the longstanding pair undergoing shifts in use. The double tendency applies to physiological, physical, emotional, familial, social and spiritual processes. Freud's life drive builds unities, while through death drive unities fall apart, breakdown, entropy. He feels both tendencies are part of every psychic act. One sees both tendencies at work in children's play and adult activities in well-nigh ubiquitous ways.

Freud wondered which would win out in human life, building or falling apart or, in Biblical and mythical language, creating–destroying? Would the intertwining twins go on competing, opposing, fusing, juggling forever, or would there be, at last, a basic primacy of one or the other. Buddhism emphasizes basic goodness, and in a Kyoto temple I was moved by a sculpture with Kwan Yin on the top of a ladder of demons and Buddhas. Kwan Yin was a special Buddha who could only love and grant wishes. In this sculpture, she affirmed a kind of primacy of love and goodness that could channel and make use of all our demon traits and tendencies. Buddha nature as a conduit/transformer for demon nature.

Of course, the Biblical God is no slouch. He looked at his creation and called it good. So much goodness; then an explosion of evil. It took only the first siblings for murder to arrive. And if, as Alfred Adler describes, the whole human race are brothers and sisters, the problem is still with us, and we are still working with it. The Books of Moses ends with the question, which will win out, good or evil?

Kabbalah plants them both in the human heart: the left chamber evil, the right chamber good. Struggle between good and evil inclinations go on all life-long as part of the heart's transformational activities. Hindu saints speak of two hearts, the physical one on the left subject to evil, the spiritual one on the right pure. Felt tension between purity–corruption is a staple mythic theme and an ongoing psychological dilemma. Ancient mysteries depicted transformational processes enabling one to become rooted in an unchanging, pure, eternal self to offset change, corruption, and death.

A catatonic patient, hospitalized for 16 years, suddenly began snapping out of his catatonic state and becoming mobile. When asked what was happening inside him all these years, he said he couldn't tell whether life was basically good or evil and kept going back and forth: kind of like a roulette wheel, the spinning stopped, falling on good.

It is a question that has beset philosophy, religion and everyday life. There are dualisms in which good and evil are locked in eternal combat. Sometimes good and evil are divided between gods at different levels. One gets the impression that there is a tendency to feel a basic goodness, but it can be a close call and not always the case.

One wonders why the good Biblical God of creation enabled or allowed Satan to be the prince of this world. In many psychoses fusions and reversals, of God–Satan is a relentless, demanding, persecuting knot. Stories emerge in which Satan's rebellious energy becomes heroic, and God's judgements cruel. Satan is the master liar and God truth itself. But in real, human life, there are times that lies soften and save and truth kills. Bion distinguishes between truth-cruelty and truth-compassion. William Blake divides functions by seeing Satan as Energy and Energy as eternal delight, while Jesus is Imagination. In some ways, this division has links with Freud's id-ego.

There are theologians who want to validate the loving God and render power, glory, judgement, and cruelty to the human psyche. I would like to mention here someone I might call a psychoanalytic theologian, Matthias Beier (2006), who emphasizes the truth of love and offers a critique of the violent God. He amplifies the work of Eugen Drewermann. One wonders to what extent this is wishful thinking and to what extent deeply significant reality.

There are so many kinds of love. Bion speaks both of murderous love and *amor dei*, the latter similar to Spinoza or Meister Eckhart, a kind of deeper, higher frame of reference for the life of affect. Love can be toxic or saving, or both at once. In *Toxic Nourishment* (1999) and *Damaged Bonds* (2001), I tried to portray their fusions, oppositions, and oscillations.

There have been and still are groups that feel evil is secondary, less real than good. Only good is truly real. Evil appears as a lack, *privatio boni*, a privation of the good. It is interesting to trace this perception, dating at least from Saint Augustine and likely earlier, through its emergence in modern depictions of developmental deformations owing to deficit-deprivation of emotional nourishment. Of course, no formula covers all. Evil certainly can seem real in its own right, in certain situations horribly so. Many groups have argued for a well-nigh eternal struggle between good and evil, at the same time noting many various mixtures which play roles in love and creativity.

A capacity can be toxic or nourishing depending on its use. Linking evil with ignorance and good with knowledge may have uses but also serious limitations. As Saint Paul discovered when he bore witness to the predicament of not being able to do the good loved (affirmed), but doing the evil he hated (abhorred). A situation Freud elaborated in detail. Permutations of love, hate, their various qualities and dimensions, continue to be disclosed to this moment. As we know, there is suffocating love and liberating hate and vice versa, and combinations that keep shifting. Quality of capacities and our relationship to them is at the cutting edge of evolution.

The image "falling" has appeared a number of times above. Three times I mentioned falling apart, one time falling on good. A diagram Winnicott drew (2015) depicted a preponderance of bad objects in personality and a few good ones. A little good can go a long way. He added most of the personality is involved in psychic tyranny, only a small bit with psychic democracy. This reminds me of "the still small voice" within vis-a-vis the God of thunder, two faces/voices of our beings.

Falling can take us many places. Falling–rising often go together, oppose each other, form a contrast and counterpart, and form part of a rhythm of faith. Falling in love. Falling in love with life. Falling in love with death. Death has eat in it. As a traditional image goes, it devours our lives. No simple relation exhausts all possibilities. There are ways life feeds on death as well as the reverse. Death has nourished and played a role in stimulating so much poetry, myth, literature and science. It is a major character in the drama of life. Yet eating is associated with nourishing life.

Many have said that fall is their favourite season, when leaves burst into colour as they prepare to die. Falling is part of learning to walk, just as biting one's own mouth accidentally is part of learning to use teeth, self-injury part of the limits of our equipment. We liken tripping over our own feet or an unseen external obstacle to falling unexpectedly off a cliff. Or a moment's gap of loss of control as falling into an abyss or chaos. We swim in everythingness–nothingness. We swim in seas of pain. Even so, we may with the Zen master who falls off a cliff, spy a bunch of strawberries on the way down and murmur within our beings, "Ah, strawberries."

The physical fact of falling is part of our emotional and moral universe, not only touching the rise and fall of spirit and affect but our moral compass as well. There are so many ways to describe a fall from grace, falling from higher to lower planes of existence, which, paradoxically, open further dimensions of experience. Higher–lower is partly modelled on our upright posture and capacity to look around, a capacity for semi-panoramic vision which characterizes mental life as well, a work in progress.

I used to say if you can think it, someone is doing it. Action and thought stimulate each other. Thought experiments can have serious consequences, and action can transform thought. Lautréamont (2004/1969) tried to create a purely evil character in his fictional portrayal of Maldoror. What would pure evil, if that were possible, look like? It is not an unknown attempt in literary history; after all we have varied versions of Satan. Could good exist without evil? Is evil a moral growth of pain? To what extent did Lautréamont succeed and could any kind of success in this project be done by someone who did not have a mixed disposition? Since my mind is tainted (uplifted) by psychological thinking, I can't help wondering about Lautréamont's (Isidore Lucien Ducasse's) death at age 24 in a Paris hotel room, as some say at 8 o'clock in the morning. Suicide? Disease? Or his youthful frame dedicated to struggle with intensity simply could not take what it undertook, yearned for, needed to work with: raw materials of good and evil. It is not the first time someone struggled to see God and/or Satan and humanity and died.

We are used to change. There is something secure in night following day and day following night, which gives a relatively predictable change. We say some things change, and some remain the same, a theme in literature, myth, and life. Ecclesiastes and the Book of Changes are two of many attempts to express and explore this: Predictable–unpredictable, safety–surprise. I don't know what psychoanalysis would look like if literature had not been a core part of its background. In one way a science, but even more a form of literature.

★ ★ ★

Here I'd like to say a few words about Hercules, a stoic hero underplayed by psychoanalysis, yet raw ingredients for enlightenment are there. He is praised for loving wisdom and pursuing virtue in face of life's horrors and miseries. From his external actions it is often hard to see the work of wisdom. He lives by murder and fathers children, seemingly countless murders and children. At one point, consumed by madness he kills his own children by his first wife and perhaps her as well. However, often his murders have a heroic element, battling against great odds. He performs impossible tasks in impossible ways, endures through all manner of degradation and hardships. His courage does not die. How can he continue to affirm life through all he must go through? Is he and life affirming that murder is a necessary part of life?

He was one of many illegitimate sons of Zeus, who disguised himself as Alcmene's husband to plant the seed. Hera, Zeus's wife, was insanely jealous and tried to prevent the birth and failed but managed to fill Hercules's life with pain without end. One wonders what keeps one going in the face of boundless agonies. Yet Hercules's life was not without pleasure, triumphs and perhaps even love. If his fate was filled with trials, he embraced them, an example of not giving up in the face of challenges.

One could make the leap and see the whole story from the perspective of a single personality, one's own self and being, the multiplicity of tendencies and states that make one up, the climbs and falls of existence. Of course, none of us are as heroic as Hercules. Or are we? The tasks I've witnessed as a therapist, the struggles with themselves that people are called to undertake – there are ways that Hercules had nothing on them. I think of a macho man like Hemingway – of course, an unfair comparison – when facing depression as he began to age, he killed himself. Hercules, of course, was threatened by suicide but endured and came through, partly. It would appear that at crucial moments when facing madness, Hercules killed someone, sometimes compounding his difficulties. Murder as an antidote to madness. I suspect that could be one ingredient in the psychology of war.

Hercules, seeing the damage murder could inflict when directed at those he loved, would come to his senses, appalled and repentant, although his first impulse was self-injury. By comparison, psychoanalysis as a talking–writing cure seems eminently sane. An attempt to assimilate aspects of madness and murder through inner–outer dialogue, mindfulness building capacity for psychic experiencing.

And Hercules' death? Crossing a river with his second wife, Deianira, the centaur, Nessus, offers her a ride, then once on the other side tries to rape her. Hercules, using poisoned arrows dipped in Hydra's blood easily killed him. As the centaur died, he told Deianira that his blood had magic properties that would excite and bind Hercules to her. When the time came, Deianira unwittingly dipped Hercules's shirt in the poisoned blood and cleaned it so the blood did not show. A little like Adam eating the apple given to him by Eve at the serpent's behest, Hercules could not resist the poison and perished.

He perished by poison from his own arrows, which carried Hydra' poison. Neither men nor women have a monopoly on destruction. The blood on Lady Macbeth's hands stains the human soul.

There is no particular Trickster in this story, but trickery runs through it: Trickery and violence. Tricking in itself can work for good depending on how it functions. Sometimes one tries to trick a god to save a life. But in the end, for Hercules, it was fatal. One might see, through displacement, Hera's wrath finally being satisfied through Hydra's uncanny help. Of course, wrath is never satisfied. We are working with these psychic poisons today, trying to figure out what to do with our own destructiveness.

As an aside, Hercules was originally named Alcaeus (strength) but changed it to Hercules (Heracles) to show that through the trials of Hera he would grow, deepen and triumph. Persistence and endurance are necessary for survival and growth of heroic virtue. But isn't there more? Hercules certainly knew triumphs but also horrible defeats. His experience ranged from madness to divinity, traversing powerlessness and power, pleasure and agony, great extremes. I think of the Biblical David who went through everything but seemed to have a more human cast. His psalms are filled with longing. Alcaeus, too, was the name of a Greek poet, so a hint, if not penumbra, of warrior-poet touches Hercules as well. What kind of poetic spirit might it be?

Jesus, like many Biblical prophets, emphasizes the low as opening to the high. A child shall lead them. The humble shall inherit the earth. Humility as a path to God. And in his own way, Hercules was brought low over and over, despite his many exploits. Hemingway's "destroyed but not defeated" or Nietzsche's *amor fati* may have some application, but there is more. A piece of it as an ancient war between the sexes, Great Mother and Great Father, sexual betrayal and revenge, a theme that began the Homeric journey as well. A triangle that Freud filtered through childhood and applied to grown-up life with innumerable variations.

In one version, as he was dying, Hercules managed to reach a mountaintop and prepare a funeral pyre, where he lay himself down for his friend, Philoctetes, to light. And as is typical in ancient mysteries, his mortal remains turned to ash, but his immortal element ascended to heaven, lifted by Zeus himself as a reward for all his son went through and in some way came through. Remember Freud's remarking to Fliess that what he was doing was akin to the ancient mysteries. If not rebirth through the heavenly father in the face of decay in the earthly mother, then at least some kind of lifting of awareness to the elements of one's plight, and the tensions between capacities and the roles each may play in survival, creativity, and vicissitudes of growth. Struggles of war and peace within the personality and as Bion remarked, "making the best of a bad job."

Do I think we can do better? Yes, I do. Whether we will is another matter. We are at the cutting edge of our own evolution and must learn how to partner our capacities and they us. A partnership more than a mastery-control model. One of many things I get from Hercules is the necessity and perhaps even willingness (not always) to go through what one must, come through what one can. There are many agonies unto death and many modes of dying. In mythic terms, psycho-spiritual death is part of transformation processes, part of coming to life in new ways. We are born all life-long, partial deaths, partial births.

For the most part, Biblical disasters do not tend to be total, although they are bad enough. The flood meant to wipe out all of creation allows some to survive. The fire meant to wipe out sinful cities, allows some survivors to build anew. And so it goes. Over and over there is destruction, whether God's temper or our distemper, power, hunger, sexual, economic, vanity needs, and demands. One image that comes through is a good seed remains after all the destruction. A significant sub-theme is cleansing, something impure being cleaned, something bad being corrected. One can turn the kaleidoscope round and round and try to find one's own reality of the moment. One thing I come back to is God originally calling creation good, Buddhism's basic goodness, Socrates' love of wisdom and realness of the Good. We go through all the hells, purgatories and heavens we can and perhaps a little more, and the good seed touches us more deeply.

★ ★ ★

I'd like to make a little digression through Big Sister's giggles. Giggling is an important part of life, as are its cohorts on the whole spectrum of laughter. I've taken liberty writing Big Sister with lower case letters. In Bion's *A Memoir of the Future* (1990) it is written in capitals: BIG SISTER, as all the *dramatis personae* are.

She – if she is a she – makes a walk-on appearance in Book I Chapter 11 (I.11) after Robin's opening soliloquy. Robin in Hell, fusing God-Devil, so that "Lies and Truth are indistinguishable." All kinds of dimensions and moments of mind pop in and out. Robin's flow or flood of thoughts ends asking ARF! ARF! ARF! (one of Bion's names for God when he was a child), "Who are you?"

Big Sister answers, "I am someone you have forgotten." We can take the ball and run in many directions, but will select only a few here. Forgetting is a vital part of literature. The Biblical God keeps having to be reminded He is God. Ancient Greece has a river devoted to forgetting. Forgetfulness can be healing but can also unleash destructiveness. What is it we forget? Who we are? Aspects of identity? Important psychic functions? The otherness of the Other? Do we forget to reflect before succumbing to violent solutions for complex tensions? God says He is going to blot out His awareness of His sinful creation. Evacuate, get rid of, blot out, going blank in the face of trauma or its memory. Is it part of the life form we are to be "someone I have forgotten" or never knew? Is it part of our work and honour to be co-participants in the creative life of being our beings? Socrates and Freud had methods of remembering and more, learning to partner the work of discovery and creation in varied ways throughout life.

GOD EXHORTED-REPRIMANDED CAIN: "Why didn't you wait?"
CAIN: "I couldn't."
GOD: "You mean you didn't. Maybe you could have. Maybe you could have remembered or thought, 'This is one moment among many. God favors Abel now. At another moment he may favor me.'"
CAIN: "Anyway what's so great about being favored? Who needs to be tyrannized by favoritism? Why not wait and grow? Why didn't I? If I had it to do over again …'"

We are bigger than many moments. And Cain grew and became a builder of cities. Did he transcend his murder of Abel? Did he transcend murder as a solution to complex difficulties? He built cities where relationships might become still more complex. He participated in the building of psychic capacity.

The whole of *A Memoir of the Future* is an attempt to support the growth of psychic reality and reflect its failures. Psyche trying to be born, at the same time a mock-up of birth. There are ways of making fun of ourselves that are part of growing. There are lots of giggles, laughs, and psychic fun in *Memoir*.

Big Sister introduces giggling. As with Lewis Carroll's Alice books, identity, age and size slide around, there are shifts of subject, word plays and psyche play. In this little paragraph (p. 80), we have some trouble knowing who is who and what is what until we catch on and remember what we need to remember: psyche is playing. As far as I know, Wilfred had a little sister and he was big-bro. Here she is big and he is little bro. A little sister can seem big indeed. And being big can seem tiny. Alfred Adler's portrayal of a universal inferiority complex is partly based on our sense of tininess in the face of the amazing cosmos. Indeed, our tiny–huge sense of amazement in the face of our own existence. Why and sex meld as Little Big Sister feels her oats. Now she is walking in the dormitory of the boarding school that big-bro Wilfred was sent to in England at 8 years of age. He had to toughen and endure the cut of separation from those close to him and the land he lived in, India, which he never saw again. In magical psychoanalytic fashion, did he repeat this cut as an old man, leaving London for Los Angeles at 71 and separating from mortal life a decade later?

Big Sister may have been a little sister who asked big brother endless questions, "Miss Why-bro!" Bion calls her as he pens this volume in his 70s. His teeming mind bubbles with possibilities, already in Los Angeles, reminiscing about the time he was eight in England, cut off from those who sustained him in India. And the Little Big Sister within reminds him of how he would call her Sex-ton. Remember Freud linking sex with curiosity: Why? How? Sex and philosophy and mathematics and psychoanalysis, and … Big Sister, a character in Bion's waking dream, mind-building, a leg in outer and a leg in inner perception.

Not at the moment the thrilling passion of the saints, but let's keep that in mind. There are works in which Bion quotes Saint John of the Cross more than Freud, although he brings both together, counterparts and tendrils from a common root. For the moment it is Big Sister, down to earth, walking through the boarding school dorm, "little snivellers saying their prayers at the ends of the beds," Big Sister stepping on their "silly, pink little feet," saying "Ooh, Sorry! Ooh sorry! Ooh sorry! and giggle …" And what would happen? "Your damn god who couldn't see a kind and loving joke would go AAARF! ARRF!"

Does God simply lack a sense of humour? Little Big Sister stepping on kids' feet saying "Ooh sorry" and giggling, God Arf Arfing, not able to take a kindly joke? Action and response, stepping on feet, giggling, and the barking god. Well, it is funny for God to Arf instead of the horrifying threats and punishments in the Bible, myth and in our psyches. And more than sometimes in uncommonly everyday lived realities. Injury and response, barking gods don't bite? The reversal, fusion and opposition god-dog does not escape notice.

Little Big Sister makes fun of Big Little Brother, "Ever so funny you looked, scared out of your damned wits! And you didn't know whether to laugh or cry." Eight-year-old Wilfred alone in boarding school memorialized in the last decade of Bion's life, reviewing frights of existence. Bion is calling up an accusing sister in his mind who mocks him for not being good enough. Mathematics, sports, marksmanship blur. He feels like an Orphan! A being who can't start! Wrong again and again. "Better, better, but still wrong! Why don't you try, boy!" Is this what can't be remembered or can't be forgotten

We say good-bye to Big Sister teasing little Wilfred; a reversal of power or the play of different powers. Try and try again and underneath and overhead, the accuser. Does the accuser seek a comforter?

★ ★ ★

What do we do with the multiple tendencies that make us up? Maybe part of a beginning might be to notice them. World literature and religion has noted tensions between competing forces in our being. It is nothing for nature to destroy and bring into being; it is part of the continuous work it does. But once consciousness of life and death is born a sense of the catastrophic grows more prominent. Is it harder to live or die, which has greater complexity? Our relationships to life–death continue to grow. Spurred by the unsolvable, dimensions of existence keep opening.

Few psychoanalysts have been as self-deprecating in print as Wilfred Bion, who felt something wrong as a young man and remained haunted by something off in human life, possibly life itself. As fate would have it, he found his way in the psychoanalytic field at a time when a sense of being dead, vacant and depersonalized was becoming an important area of work in British therapeutic schools as well as existential literature of the day. What a word: existence! And what a fact! *Existere*: to stand out of, at once alive, arising, becoming and, in our case, both subject and object at the same time, being aware of being.

Some think this two-in-oneness, doubleness, separation–connection–fusion with oneself is a source of feeling something wrong. We are not at-one with ourselves, a gap part of our being. But the gap and relationship with our self-awareness can take on all sorts of emotional tones and attitudes. We may experience ourselves not just as dis-unity but toxic, beset by psycho-spiritual deformations, and aberrant. We are very concerned with the distortions of reality, our reality, as if a pure, clear, true way of being and relating are possible, awaiting us. Perhaps we mean that a less self-injurious way of being is worth seeking if only our experiential capacities are up to it. On this score, we are not done evolving and, I suspect, as long as there is life, more can happen.

Melanie Klein, Donald Winnicott, Wilfred Bion, Harry Guntrip, Ronald Fairbairn, and Marion Milner are some of the names linked with work on deadness and an aborted, deformed sense of aliveness, each in their own ways concerned with how psychical relationships can misfire. With what quality can we survive survival and open existence as it opens us in fuller ways? Not everyone survives themselves or survives themselves well. And there are those who prosper with deadness inside. One can come to life and die in many ways. This is not simply a matter of internal or external failure. There are people in high places who have had to deaden themselves to get there. As we know, Bion tells us he died in the Battle of Amiens, a sense that never fully left him, although there appear to be ways aspects of life came alive as he went on, perhaps through marriage and family and profession. I would not be surprised to learn that by trying to help others he was helping himself. And the sense of something wrong with him in his case made him more sensitive to what was "wrong" in others. It is perhaps no accident that a key interest for him included psychotic dimensions of being. The work of madness became for him a way of probing and opening existence.

I'm thinking of a person (P) who sought help because demons ruin his life. He is a gifted musician with no lack of work and appreciation. But he never knows when a demon will attack him and make it impossible to function without extreme dread or reduce him to paralysis. He suffered repeated hospitalizations before we began working and although he repudiates our relationship and attacks it, he has also held on to it for not so dear life. These demons are awful, but they are alive and feed on life. P sometimes says they keep him alive enough to feed on. He envies their energy and determination. They just enter his life as they wish and do what they want. He wonders how many other food sources there are in the demon farm he is part of.

It would take a long time to go into the details of our years of therapy. For the moment, I simply want to note that what heightens life can kill it and what kills life can heighten it. A bind P was in without knowing it, a knot (as RD Laing, 1972, might call it) with no solution. I suspect there are ways the whole human race is caught in such a knot, part of the challenge of being human. There are ways we are growing in a demon farm that keeps us alive for food. Perhaps, too, we are caught between learning how to be better demons and learning to help demons become better human beings. What kind of nourishment is needed for such tasks? We are now at work, trying to find out. The work itself is a form of nourishment, deeply humanizing work. A work we are still beginning and learning to begin, beginnings without end.

Note

1 See http://lirs.ru/do/lanka_eng/lanka-nondiacritical.htm

References

Beier, M. (2006). *A violent God-image: An introduction to the work of Eugen Drewermann.* Continuum.

Bion, W. (1990). *A memoir of the future.* Karnac.

Eigen, M. (2018). *Toxic nourishment.* Routledge (original work published 1999).

Eigen, M. (2018). *Damaged bonds.* Routledge (original work published 2001).

Eigen, M. (2018). *A felt sense: More explorations of psychoanalysis and Kabbalah.* Routledge (original work published 2014).

Freud, S. (1938). *Sigmund Freud: Hear the only known recording of his voice, 1938.* Open Culture, http://www.openculture.com/2018/09/sigmund-freud-speaks-hear-known-recording-voice-1938.html.

Freud, S. (1985). *The complete letters of Sigmund Freud to Wilhelm Fliess, 1887–1904.* (JM Masson, and Ed. and Trans). Harvard University Press.

Gendlin, ET. (1962). *Experiencing and the creation of meaning. A philosophical and psychological approach to the subjective.* Northwestern University Press.

Laing, RD. (1972). *Knots.* Vintage.

Lautréamont, Comte de. (2004). *Maldoror and Poems* (P Knight, Trans.). Penguin.

Winnicott, DW. (2015). *Human nature.* Routledge (original work published 1988).

Part II

Eigen in time

Chapter 2

Michael Eigen

A personal retrospective

Robin Bagai

In his book *Faith* (2014), Michael Eigen writes about people who were important to him and had a lasting impact on his life. He calls these "moments that count." Two of those moments were meeting DW Winnicott in London and Wilfred Bion in New York, when Eigen was just starting out on his career.

I want to begin with a story about my own first encounter with Eigen through a chance reading in a study group, and convey what mushroomed from there. After relating initial experiences of him in person, I will speak to the continuing impact he has brought to the psychology community here in the Pacific Northwest, as well as in my own life. I will also touch on a few of Eigen's themes as examples of why I feel his work is both significant and timeless. But first some history and context.

As a psychologist practicing in Portland, Oregon, for decades, I've been a life-long student of psychoanalysis, philosophy, and East–West spiritual traditions since my teenage years. Over those years, I've participated in all kinds of retreats, seminars, and study groups. In one of these collegial groups, there was a suggestion we read Michael Eigen's book *Eigen in Seoul Vol. 2: Faith and Transformation* (2011), a book transcribed from three days of seminar talks Eigen gave at the Object Relations Institute of Seoul, South Korea in 2009. This book was my first encounter with Eigen's work.

As I began to read *Seoul Vol. 2* – and I couldn't have been more than 10 or 20 pages into it – I was surprised to discover that my face had become wet with tears. I found myself unexpectedly weeping. Now I don't know about your experience, but mine is that psychoanalytic writing has not exactly been known for evoking tears! I was taken aback, and wasn't quite sure *why* I was crying, I just knew I was being deeply touched. The second thing I noticed: I found myself in a very quiet contemplative state, similar to what happens, if lucky, while meditating. I was startled by both the tears and inner quietude, and wondered: What exactly is going on here …? So I picked up a second Eigen book, this time *Flames from the Unconscious*, subtitled *Trauma, Madness and Faith* (2009). And much to my amazement the same thing happened: Meditative state, tears rolling down face. So now I'm very intrigued and curious. Who is this guy Michael Eigen and how does he manage to speak to my insides, affecting me like this? I told myself I needed to go to New York to meet him and find out. A feeling of necessity overtook me.

First, I attended one of Eigen's Tuesday seminars in 2014, and upon arriving found a warm host with twinkly eyes who met a group of us at the door with "Ahhh ... we have a stranger in our midst," smiling with a vortex of welcoming acceptance. This moment past in an instant, but has lingered.

My second trip to New York was a little embarrassing, at least in retrospect. Eigen had hosted a talk about Bion's unfinished movie at the National Psychological Association For Psychoanalysis, and had opened his office to visitors from out-of-town for an informal chat at the end of his long day seeing clients.

After some cordial greetings among the five of us, I told him with some combination of whimsy, trepidation, and drama that if I were a paranoid person, I might claim that he, Eigen, had been stealing my thoughts ... for years! But luckily, since I was not a paranoid person, I just figured we might be partly the same person, and I loved him for that. I was shocked at my own words. Eigen became soft and quiet ... with a deeply kind and quizzical look. A look-feel or a feeling-look that has grown in meaning over time. For one thing, it wasn't until many months later that I learned Eigen had accused the French analyst André Green of stealing his work, and apparently *without* any whimsy. For Eigen, meeting with Green was another of his moments that counted. Partly because of Green's graceful way of conveying at the end of their time together that translation from French into English took a long time. An indirect way of saying that Green's writing was his own and not lifted from Eigen. Eigen lauds Green for being able to respond humanely *and* analytically, not rubbing Eigen's nose in it (2016, Chapter 7).

After meeting with Eigen in New York a couple of times, what happened next basically changed the direction of my professional life as well as my inner life. I quickly realized there were many Eigen books and papers that came before those I had first encountered, and I developed a compelling need to try and teach Eigen's work. Partly because I wanted to understand it better, and partly because what the work stimulated emotionally, cognitively, intuitively, and spiritually felt so ecumenical and fertile. I sensed that Eigen's body of work was too profound not to immerse myself in it, and the best way to do this was to hold seminars in my office to study and explore with others. I posted an announcement on a local online list, and wondered who might be interested in joining such an exploration. The results were surprising and beyond what I expected. Eigen says some people are hungry for psyche-talk, and psychotherapy is one place to share psyche-talk. Perhaps study groups would be another? I tingled at the prospect of what a deep reading of Eigen's work might bring in the company of colleagues ... and dove in.

Continuously, since 2015, except for the summer season, I've led 90-minute weekly seminars on a dozen Eigen books, spending 10 to 12 weeks on each book (never enough), and after three years of the first group starting, there was enough interest to start a second concurrent weekly group. If you're wondering who comes to these seminars, it is not only psychotherapists. There are artists, poets, painters, a finance person, retired social workers, as well as two supervising and training analysts who are long-time members of the American Psychoanalytic Association. When I ask these senior analysts why they keep coming to my Eigen seminars, the response I get is "psyche feels alive in Eigen's work, and it is rare to find this kind of aliveness in much of contemporary psychoanalysis." The non-therapists tell me they benefit as well. Many report experiencing increased sensitivity and intimacy with their own inner process and emotional reality. Perhaps most poignant was one seminar member who simply said with a plaintive tone of appreciation: "We just don't get to talk like this anywhere else in life …"

For myself, I've found the effect of studying Eigen with others on a regular basis has been catalyzing and growth producing. I would encourage any reader who feels touched by Eigen's writing to discover what this can be like for yourself by starting your own group. Simply put, studying Eigen with others has deepened my own therapy practice, generating feelings of greater self-confidence, support from unconscious realms, and more resilience and spontaneity with clients than I have experienced in past years. Other psychotherapists tell of similar benefits.

From my little perch, Michael Eigen remains a largely unknown giant in the field, one whose writing stands on the shoulders of many other giants, among them Freud, Jung, Melanie Klein, André Green, Marion Milner, Jacque Lacan, Donald Winnicott, and Wilfred Bion. In my view, Eigen has taken-in and metabolized the work of these pioneers, along with many others, in such a way as to give this thing we call psychoanalysis or depth psychology an injection of new life, growing more branches on this remarkable tree. If these new tree branches continue to grow, as exemplified by programmes such as Ofra Eshel's radical independent track in Tel Aviv, then Eigen will ripple a little more widely in generative ways, while also receiving due recognition for his unique contributions.

But what about Eigen's work itself? What's the big deal? What can one possibly say about his more than 28 books? I often start my seminars each term with a simple paradox. I remind everyone that "doing justice" to Eigen's work is actually impossible. It is impossible partly because the depth and breadth found in his writing evokes unending amplifications and wide associations … and partly because his writing is often so lyrical and poetic that one must stop and pause … and pause again, to feel and digest the complex emotional–intellectual stimuli one experiences while reading it.

Eigen writes without technical jargon, thus stimulating the reader's own experience as much as providing new perspectives and understanding. One might even say that Eigen's work reflects a *rectification* of language, in that one does not need to learn any new terminology to be touched by it. His books provide readers a forum in which thoughts and feelings, felt senses and psychical tastes, intimations and intuitions, concepts and emotions all share the floor equally ... and begin to dance together in new ways. His work opens up so many different worlds and potentials that there can be no endpoint in realms of psyche and emotional reality he explores. Expertise is impossible because the psyche is always moving, always "becoming," never static. Psyche grows and is carved from infinity, moment by moment, and thus not even Michael Eigen can be an expert on Michael Eigen.

What I can say is this: By engaging and *staying with* the impossible feeling of ever fully encompassing his work, one opens up new channels and unexpected possibilities. Evidence for this can be seen in the variety of perspectives found in the anthology *Living Moments: On the Work of Michael Eigen* (Bloch and Daws, 2015), as well as this current anthology. Increased online interest in studying Eigen, as well as my own expanding office seminars also attest to these growing sparks.

Let me also tell the story of when I initially asked Eigen about my attempting to lead seminars on his work. I felt a little crazy even broaching the subject because I felt like such a newbie. But Mike's response was full of encouragement and generosity. He said,

> Robin, don't feel like you have to get it ... or get it all ... or get it right. Instead, take it your own way, and have fun with it ... use it in whatever way feels real to you ... have fun with it.
>
> (personal communication, 2014)

Take it my own way and have fun with it ... no one had ever said that to me before. What a joy and relief to hear, and what a sense of freedom it evoked. Soon after, I started the first group in 2015 studying *The Psychoanalytic Mystic* (1998) with about six others in the room. That first group grew into two weekly groups with 12–15 participants each. Given all that's happened thus far, I wonder what the future might bring?

If I could change one word in the title of this chapter, I would now change the word *retrospective* to *prospective*. Why prospective? Partly because I feel Eigen's work belongs to future generations. His level of complexity, like that of Winnicott and Bion, has yet to be fully acknowledged or widely assimilated. And, prospective also because his work valorizes the *importance of the unknown* ... an unknown that is always in front of us, even though invisible. Don't we all live within unknown future moments, living moments of psychical development that hold something for each of us, if we can access them? Major themes in Eigen's work often circle around mysteries of our psyche and body, their various mixtures within our emotional life, and how much aliveness we can bring to them.

Honouring psyche and complexity partly means paying close attention. And paying attention to inner process means not bypassing, shifting away, or deflecting, but *staying with* ... even when the going gets rough. Can we respect and uphold psyche and self by staying connected and in touch ... allowing our feeling-experiences to build and grow, rather than short-circuit or abort? Not always, of course, but maybe a little more? When this kind of honouring becomes an abiding attitude, it makes room for unborn potentials and emergent properties of psyche to arise spontaneously. Our relationship with unconscious processes become strengthened and facilitated through such an attitude, and partnering with unknown moments becomes more generative, and less threatening.

Staying connected and keeping close to our psychical, physical, and emotional life is hard work. It requires an abiding interest and devotion, but also a kind of trust or faith in self and the unknown. What does it take to have faith in the unknown?

I'm thinking now of Eigen emphasizing Wilfred Bion's shorthand: Faith (F) in unknown and unknowable reality (O) leading to transformations (T) in unknown and unknowable reality (O) (2014, p. x). All three of these signifiers point to something unknown. F in O facilitating or catalyzing T in O ... This one thread or "formula" woven into Eigen's work hints at gateways to more opening, similar to how one might practice or use a Zen koan. Ponder it and keep pondering ...

I think too of Winnicott's (1953) potential space and transitional space as part-mysteries of personality development, adding to the growth of experience and growth of psyche. I'm also reminded of a Hindu notion that within us we have something akin to "uncooked seeds" of emotional, psychological, and spiritual development. Seeds that are waiting for the right conditions in which to sprout and take root. Here I am trying to describe something ineffable ... yet also palpable to those who have experienced surprise at their own sudden spurts or pivotal moments of growth in life. Such notions touch forms of faith that live in unknown realities, a faith partly connected to our somatic substrate, our relationship with unconscious life, and our attitude toward both. Ideally, such relationships can be something like good dance partners, where no one part of us usurps or dominates, but instead where each is allowed to "lead" at times, and where all sides are listened to with care and respect. As Paul Tillich somewhere said, the first duty of love is to listen. Can we love and listen a little more to all parts of ourselves, even the unlovable ones? Is this another form of faith ... a being faithful?

At times, Eigen describes *faith* (2014) as a kind of fertile emptiness, embedded in our nature and life itself. A faith with many variations, including a quality of unconscious support, a living inner core of being, a hidden resource, an anchor that can sustain us in the face of traumatizing life circumstances, and a basic trust that receptively opens to life without excessive fear. Perhaps this faith is, at bottom, a sacred well of the human spirit that can never be killed or die. Faith as a living reality, but also a capacity awaiting our encounter, awaiting our further development and use of it. Faith as an attitude and approach to life and living that can make a difference in our very sense of feeling alive and feeling real … even though we cannot give these precise definition, formula, or words.

Unknown future moments are both exciting and terrifying. Do we *ever really know* what lies ahead, what's coming next? *Dare we* pretend to think we know, with our little egos peaking-out just above the waterline of Freud's structural iceberg? Is it not humbling to remember that most of our ego is also unconscious?

Do we think we know what force or power exists in this very moment to keep our hearts beating and breath circulating? Yet these are happening right now as you read this … can you feel them …? Think of all the hearts in many rooms at night, pumping silently, carrying-on these duties even as we sleep. Can we say what helps it all continue? Yes, we have our labels and guesses, we have our medical science and our belief systems, but we don't really *know* what keeps our heart muscle rhythmically contracting, or when it will decide to stop. I think of my mother saying something funny to me as a youngster; she said: "Robin, someday you'll realize that *you* are not breathing … you are *being breathed*." Isn't that more like it? Analogously, haven't you had the experience of not a year going by without discovering something new about yourself … something that changes you a little, or adds?

In a deep sense, life and development remain a mystery, and Michael Eigen honours this reality in its fullness … both as potentially terrifying and traumatizing as well as growth-promoting and full of promise, including a heart-smile that exists and can come through our worst screams of trauma.

How shall we meet the next moment … and the next? How will we encounter a new therapy patient or the next session? With what *attitude* shall we meet these? With what unconscious affective attitude do we routinely meet or encounter ourselves and unknowns within us? Eigen reminds us that our affective attitudes (often embedded and invisible) make a difference in the quality and feel of our lives and our relationships. Our attitude toward mystery tells us a lot about our own relationship to selfhood.

Eigen often says he is not interested in "solving" anything. He is more interested in *opening fields of experiencing* (2018, p. 130). For example, in psychoanalytic psychotherapy it need not be particular knowledge or insight that helps, important as these can be, but something else having to do with lived experience over time. In particular, experience coming out of accrued impact and response between the therapy couple. We cannot know ahead of time where these impacts will go, where they might lead. The *unknown* is part of psyche's birthright and constitution, out of which awareness unfolds. Our lives become co-created out of many partners and adversaries, poisons and nutrients, selves and others, inside us and out.

Eigen emphasizes an important difference between knowing and experiencing. Having certainty that we *know* something can run counter to our actual experience of it. Eigen writes: "It is difficult to overestimate the role omniscience plays in deadening one's capacity to experience. If one knows what is going to happen ahead of time, one does not have to experience it ..." (2004/1986, p. 320). Thus, "knowing" and our use of different kinds of knowledge can vary. There is a form of experiencing that allows receptivity to unknowns, and another form used as all-knowing foreclosure, a shutting-down or shutting-off. How any of our capacities function and how they are used makes a big difference.

Eigen portrays *opening* and *closing* themselves as rhythmic portals or doorways of the psyche and emotional life. There are psychical dynamics of opening and closing: Being more permeable, soft, receptive; and feeling blocked, hardened, stuck. Often there are mixtures. Can we think of opening and closing as a kind of therapy model? Opening as a path towards greater self-contact, life, and growth. Opening as an organic unfolding of psyche when not trapped or damaged by excessive trauma. This is not always possible. Things can go wrong very early in life and leave toxic residue hardened like clay within the soil of personality. Yet for any of us, opening to greater receptivity and experiencing takes growth of capacity, with ingredients like courage and daring, faith and trust, curiosity and sincerity, along with increased tolerance for what might unexpectedly arise in the future or be revisited from the past. Growth of capacity and growth in tolerating ourselves and our emotional realities become important in what psychotherapy can do and be, including all the benefits and hazards of a life more fully lived.

These days I sometimes see a generation of younger therapists trying to teach the bright side of psychic and emotional health, the joys of life founded in psychologies of optimism. Some are counsellors and therapists who coach and coax psyches of those in pain away from their suffering and toward happier worlds of achievement and self-esteem. But I'd rather sit with someone who knows deeply about emotional suffering as one better able to speak to genuine happiness and joy. That is, someone who has experienced and processed horrific screams of life, yet can still smile at the joy. Eigen writes, "the smile that grows out of the scream is not the same as the screamless smile, one that makes believe no scream is there" (2005, p. 51).

Why do I feel Eigen's writing is both timeless and important for our time? Because he circles unflinchingly around areas humanity needs most help grappling with: Sufferings of madness, trauma, destructiveness, and murder. Aren't these among our worst enemies? The very things that give us the most pain and hurt? The categories by which we continue to injure ourselves and each other? These are also areas that perennially frighten us, make us defensive and avoidant, even violent, while increasing suffering inside and out. And these are precisely the areas Eigen addresses and amplifies in his books and practice. At times, his writing soothes by adding lyrical psychic enzymes to help with emotional digestion around these difficult subjects.

Eigen's importance, and his gift, is precisely that he does not shy away from what is most difficult in being human. He has made it his business to struggle with the worst: Psychosis, emotional suffering, self-destruction, horrors of trauma … pains of life. Why does he do this? Isn't it partly because he has been challenged by such things, and wishes to help others survive themselves? In my imagination, Eigen goes further: Expanding our sense of being human and widening our capacity to be in life, without negating, denying, or covering over the very things that terrify us, deaden us, or storm through us, throwing our minds and bodies around like corks in the ocean.

Instead of shying away or deflecting, Eigen leans into these horrors. He explores, he suffers, he navigates, he learns, he teaches … and most remarkably, he does so with a feeling heart, a receptive and embracing heart, a listening heart.

To undergo the worst, to hang in there with what feels intolerable and impossible, and to come through, again and again … can this become a practice and a rhythm of emotional life that bears fruit? Not for everyone perhaps, but a practice I have seen result in patients' strengthening and transforming. Eigen himself has suffered the birth of some 28 books, and in doing so has allowed many of *us* to feel more real, more grounded, and more connected to our emotional life and psyche, helping to grow more inner durability and resilience as a result of developing increased capacities. Such work goes hand-in-hand with growing more tolerance for parts of ourselves and others we disdain.

And one last *prospective* rather than retrospective aspect that might help our individual and collective situation: Attempting to honour and embrace, rather than be frightened by the "otherness" of our diverse tendencies and alien feelings, so that instead of fighting (inner or outer) wars of domination or annihilation, we might begin to think and feel otherness as a potential resource. This is a more rewarding view of mystery-within-difference, when difference becomes mutually nourishing and cross-fertilizing, rather than injurious or to be feared.

Today, wars of difference continue everywhere around us. How might we learn to pivot to wars of inner and outer partnering? After all, psychotherapy and psychoanalysis have grown by engaging in wars as well as by partnering. The question becomes: What quality of war and what kind of partnering? Is it possible to engage both without serious injury? For example, in psychoanalytic history there have been warring languages of instinctual drives, and of object seeking and object usage; languages of insight and interpretation, and the power of unconscious relational effects. We have various one-person and two-person models from which to choose, and we also benefit from being of two minds.

Just 80 years ago there was war between Anna Freud and Melanie Klein for analytic dominance in England that gave rise to an independent group benefitting from both. How might we approach, enact, and use wars differently? Can we find better ways to fight with one another, to enrich each other through our diversity of theory and language, and do so with generosity and goodwill, widening our range and perspective with different-but-equal languages, signifiers, models? Can we acknowledge that each has something to offer? Or shall we continue to fight for supremacy, certainty, moral right-eousness, hegemony, and control? Shall we fight only for our own view and turf, our own perspective to the exclusion of others, or try to gain from part-nering otherness and difference? Such questions cut across therapy schools, ethnicities, religions, genders, individual psyches, and nations. I'll close with something Eigen said to an audience of therapists in Seoul, South Korea:

> We have so many languages and see things from so many perspectives. Scientific languages, faith languages, psychoanalytic languages, common sense languages, everyday languages. All of us have many languages and we're not sure how to reconcile them. Well, I'd like to say right now that we don't need to reconcile them. We need to use them. If there weren't faith languages, most of the art in the world wouldn't have happened. If there weren't science languages, we wouldn't be sitting in this building talking to each other this way right now. My feeling is that the human race needs to learn to stop the wars between different capacities, all the different languages, and begin to develop them, begin to develop each capacity as fully as possible.
>
> (2009, p.10)

References

Bloch, S and Daws, L. (Eds.) (2015). *Living moments: On the work of Michael Eigen.* Karnac.

Eigen, M. (2004/1986). *The psychotic core.* Karnac (reprinted Routledge, 2018).

Eigen, M. (1998). *The psychoanalytic mystic.* Free Association Books.

Eigen, M. (2005). *Emotional storm.* Wesleyan University Press.

Eigen, M. (2018). *Conversations with Michael Eigen* (Ed. A. Govrin). Karnac (original work published 2007).

Eigen, M. (2009). *Flames from the unconscious: Trauma, madness and faith.* Karnac (reprinted Routledge, 2018).

Eigen, M. (2011). *Eigen in Seoul, Vol. 2: Faith and transformation.* Karnac (reprinted Routledge, 2018).

Eigen, M. (2014). *Faith.* Karnac (reprinted Routledge, 2018).

Eigen, M. (2016). My Meeting With Andre. *Image, sense, infinities and everyday life,* Chapter 7. Karnac (reprinted Routledge, 2018).

Winnicott, DW. (1953). Transitional objects and transitional phenomena. *International Journal of Psycho-Analysis*, 34, 89–97.

Chapter 3

On the importance of time as a background object

Keri Cohen

> Do not now look for the answers. They cannot now be given to you because you could not live them. It is a question of experiencing everything. At present you need to live the question. Perhaps you will gradually, without even noticing it, find yourself experiencing the answer, some distant day.
> Rainer Maria Rilke, *Letters to a Young Poet* (2000, p. 35)

Michael Eigen has been sensing and holding time since he was a baby in the crib, using radio shows and hands on the clock as background objects of time to ground him, awaiting his mother's return from work (Eigen and Govrin, 2007, pp. 85–6).

MIKE: ... I still feel the rip of her leaving to go to work when I was eight months old. The feeling that she couldn't (didn't want to) be with me and had to get away ... I learned to tell time in my crib, putting together the hands of the clock in my field of vision with morning radio shows ... and realizing the time the talk show host announced dove-tailed with the position of the hands and numbers of the clock.

ANER: Why were you so preoccupied with the clock at that age?

MIKE: It was a recurrence, a correlation, a connection ... Clock, radio, mother's leaving and returning-all parts of an affective spatial-temporal emotional, cognitive field that clicked together. I suppose the radio voice was a kind of mother ... Later as a teen I listened to jazz when I went to sleep, and the jazz host told the time. Now I listen to ... a lot of classical music. Still mothering myself, not always in good ways.

In Eigen's Tuesday seminars, sometimes, he keeps time in the foreground, as he taps his feet to the musical rhythm of his words.

The way in which the analyst holds time in treatment becomes a para-doxical way for contact between the analyst and patient. Eigen, even as he ages, does not appear to be in a hurry. Time for him becomes part of the background object of what I call the incubation process of transformation and transcendence of the self. One moves from the object of the tyranny of the self to an object of welcome and desire.

The subjective appears in our everyday interactions. The objective appears in the therapeutic holding environment in its idealized form. Time, an objective background object, sits in silent reverie with the patient. Eigen helps the patient wait during the incubation process.

> The ability to wait on oneself is a missing function, just like ability to process emotional life is fast becoming a missing or damaged function (e.g. *Damaged bonds*, 2001b), on damaged emotional processing. Any little bit of waiting on or processing experience by analyst, Buddhist, Sufi, whatever walk of life, helps keep alive capacities that normative society is suffocating.
>
> (Eigen, 2016a)

Eigen's work with severely damaged patients beckons time to be used in unconventional ways. What do we do with time? Do we fill it with words, silence, action, and when? The silence of time becomes an element. What kind of time quality does one need? The timing of love, reverie, surrender, and what Bion espouses of being without memory, desire, or expectation is important. Can we hold time as a paradoxical contact background object in this spirit?

Part of Eigen's technique is to play for time. Playing for time allows for what Bion called *nameless dread* (Bion, 1984) to be held in a larger frame, thus helping the patient place dreadful traumatic events on the time continuum, a larger frame, taking up less room in the psyche. Time used as an objective background object by the analyst helps to soften the blow to the psyche.

Eigen becomes a creative artist using time, building an incubator for the patient's capacity to birth the psyche into an existence, welcoming a transformation for them to become their own background object, thus supporting their own developing life force. Eigen's use of time is really *a timeless presence*, one that nurtures transformation and transcendence, an ultimate surrender to the timeless difficulties of being human.

Eigen's use of time as a background object also holds the patient and suspends negative subjectivity. The ways Eigen envisions and uses time aids in the changes from quantity to quality (Bion, 1991) and helps the transformation within the patient from their own *obstructive object* (Eaton, 2011) to becoming their own internal *welcoming object* (Eaton, 2015). Eigen suspends time for transformations to occur. He slows the impact of time, so the catastrophe is not felt all at once, and the experience of negative subjective time becomes one used in the spirit of objective welcoming.

In *Under the Totem* (Eigen, 2016b), Eigen talks about gentle change as opposed to rapid change, akin to what a foetus may endure as it forms. Perhaps what we need is gentle change outside of the womb, where being immersed in the therapy womb incubator disperses gentle change over the time and space continuum (Cohen, 2016). Eigen's sense and use of time enhances his timeless presence in the face of the gentle change he forges in the therapeutic womb.

It is also evident that the way the analyst uses time in the session can be subject to an attack on linking (Bion, 1984). Likewise, the same can be said for how the patient uses time. Eigen holds and preserves time, when the patient does not have the capacity to use it fruitfully. Eigen plays for time, without attacking the link of time. He may play for time through the use of play or perhaps through being a container of the time continuum. When one thinks of playing for time, Eigen may use himself literally as a measure of time in the time and space continuum.

Eigen cites examples of asking the psychotic to tell him about their journey to his office (Eigen, February 2019, personal communication). How was the walk, the bus ride, the car ride; what did the patient encounter along the way? Did he see birds, trees, people talking? Here, time is used as a marker for how a capacity for daily life activities can be used in the present moment, suggesting daily meditation by staying in the present moment. The use of the time to the office invites a capacity to use the psyche in another way other than psychotic hallucinatory delusions. The analyst is in the position of teaching the psychotic how to play for time independently, both from an objective and subjective view. Overwhelming emotional fragments flood one short period of chronological time. In playing for time, one slows, stretches the time frame in order to process flooding with multiple variations and uses. The patient may attack this link of time or simply may not have developed the capacity to ground himself on the way to the office, yet the germination has begun.

Eigen's germination is across a time continuum, of present, past and future. It is not clock time. He shows the patient how to use time as a background object by using himself as an agency of time. It seems that Eigen uses Heidegger's link between the future and moving towards [the future] (Heidegger, 1962). For Heidegger, where we find ourselves on the time horizon is of importance. Eigen stays present and suggests a meditation practice as a seed to grow through time and space. Time here, is fluid, not past, present or future; like Heidegger, it is moving toward. The patient moves towards himself using capacities that Eigen plants as seeds in order to help the patient grow into himself. Subjectively, the patient's reality may be a hallucinated one, while objectively Eigen muses a path the patient may use towards a new subjective self-experience, if the patient can grow into using this new capacity. While clock time may be finite, emotional time is infinite: "The self is actually not just in time but of time. Self as process unfolds as time (experience) and space (memory)" (Eaton, personal communication, 2018).

Similar to Eigen, Bion also uses time as a background object. Bion's concept of O, the Unknown, serves the continuum of the Time horizon; unknown, unmeasurable, emotional unknown time. "'Past' and 'future' represent a realization related to another realization represented by the terms 'internal' and 'external'" (Bion, 1970, p. 42). Bion's notion of emptying the mind of memory, expectation and desire, serves to allow time to be free-floating, available to lend quality to fragmented psychic parts in wait of processing. The analyst tries to embody this state, or in some situations the patient may feel "imprisoned" by the analyst's wishes or desires, albeit nonverbally. This may parallel the imprisonment of the Psychotic or Obsessive. Eigen's notion is to help the patient germinate in the incubator of their relationship to the environment and within their intrapsychic self. He expands the pallet for capacities to make contact with their depths and relationships to and with others. If the background of time can be held in this spirit of O, the patient has freedom to move towards an internal future state of being that transcends and transforms his eternal self-state. Imprisonment moves towards a freer future state, opening a chance for contact with the depths of inner being. The analyst can use time to be at-one with the patient on the time-space continuum, thus providing the opportunity for internal transcendent deep contact. If time can be held objectively, the patient has a chance to subjectively grow. Conversely, the patient or analyst may attack the time experience. The link of objective time experience and its preservation are at stake. Eigen's graceful practice that Bion espouses, makes removing the imprisoned persecutory nature of time feel effortless, but it is borne of Eigen's lifetime of meditation, practice and contact with his depths.

Eigen draws deeply from Bion as both grapple with time and catching up to oneself, catching up to capacities unfolding over time. Herbert Read, in *Icon and Idea* (1955), speaks of fragmented images, art, or ideas taking time to mature into articulate words to describe experiences:

> One must imagine a constant force, a blind instinct, groping towards the light, discovering and opening in the veil of nothingness and becoming aware of significant shapes ... Before the word was the image.
> (Read, 1955, p. 20)

Read speaks of this happening over time, and the symbol becomes a link through time; symbol, meaning image, eventually language. All of these serve as links for consciousness to evolve into something tenable in the psyche that we can use to mitigate the severity of ourselves and our experiences. Eigen holds time in service to a constant background in wait of our capacities.

Over time, feelings can soften, harden, become rigid, even lead to psychic deadness. Eigen's use of time turns experience and feelings into more fluid capacities in a synchronistic way. Bion, too, highlights emotional fluidity from the point of many vertexes, reversals, and uses F in O (Faith in O, the Unknown) to shepherd one through the fragmented departed elements dissociated from the daily emotional field. Overwhelming emotional fragments flood one short period of chronological time. The quantity of fragmented increments transform into better quality and integrate into the psyche to birth new capacities.

Fragmented emotional experiences may flood the psyche, without any type of organized function. The feeling state may lead to a negative quality, such as distress, anxiety, depression, traumatic responses in daily living. Bion's character in *A Memoir of the Future*, Paranoid-Schizoid, speaks of

> reminiscences and premonitions ... as the same thing so long as a domain in which measurement of temporal and spatial time is proper to a constant conjunction of helplessness, omnipotence, idealization, embryonic sense of reality, embryonic sense of sense, transformed for use in a non-sensuous domain of thought without a thinker, from thoughts in which a thinker is itself the essence of thought.
>
> (Bion, 1991, p. 51)

Here, Bion highlights time collapsing in such a way that the quantity of experience floods the psyche while merging into one frame. The internal noise becomes amplified, obstructing the ability to digest the experience. Time persecutes and may seem subjectively obstructive.

Transforming the quantity of experiences and feelings into ones of positive quality may be tenable when time is held as a background object of quality. A sense of relief may accompany the feeling state in order to relax into a state of internal self-contact.

Over time, a traumatic emotional experience becomes dispersed, so that the same event is seen through many lenses. If time becomes a pressure point, this ability is compromised. If the patient or the analyst view an event as firmly marked on the time continuum, as opposed to spread out over the emotional time and space continuum, they miss the opportunity to spin it through the kaleidoscope of many views and capacities. Eigen nurses damaged souls to transform trauma in such a way that the self-reprocesses with a subjective experience borne out of compassion, welcoming a newly formed internal object into the time trajectory. Suspending negative subjective time opens room for this process to develop. Time held as an objective background support allows both patient and analyst to birth new psychic experience. Eaton speaks of Eigen as serving as a welcoming object (Eaton, 2015). Objective time merges with the background welcoming object of the analyst, thus allowing for the internalization of the patient's ability to transform into their own welcoming object. As a welcoming object of background support, the patient gains a capacity to hold time objectively as a background object.

To digest emotional fragments, Eigen works to slow this process down during chronological time. One way Eigen plays for time is by taking the patient's persecutory pressure point of time and *dispersing* it over years of work with the patient, thus enlarging the frame of emotional time. Eigen's use of time works to transform the quantity of dissociated fragments into better quality, recognizing time cannot be rushed or subjected to emotional psychological pressure.

Speaking to not knowing or O, Eigen remarks that,

> In practice, I often reach a deep point of not knowing, a kind of creative waiting, that shifts the ambiance in the room. As time goes on, a person with me begins to sense something further, perhaps a still point of her own that is a little freeing. It is less a matter of solving problems on their own terms as shifting the centre of gravity, allowing something more to grow.
>
> (Eigen, 2018a, p. 73)

Here, time is moved to the objective; subjective time is not used as a measure in which to complete some psychological mastery of oneself. Time is suspended, in order to reach a still point, in order to suspend moments in which the patient can move towards her future self. Time becomes a background welcoming object (Eaton, 2011), not an object of persecutory demands.

We need emotional time as a means to catch up to ourselves. In a 2018 Bion seminar, Eigen spoke of

> Creating a situation or condition to knock your homeostasis or status quo in order to transcend mortality and come into contact with the self-eternal and live it now. Eternity now! Many cultures have rituals and transformations of various kinds. The rituals have to do with transcending death and finding eternal self in time, outside of time, beyond time. In part, this has to do with transcending yourself.
>
> (Eigen, October 23, 2018b)

Here, Eigen is talking about welcoming time from the background into the foreground as a way to transcend the self and transform the internal self-state. This represents a welcoming of the function of time as a means for transformation, by "coming into contact with the self-eternal," becoming a timeless presence for the "self-eternal." In order to reach this state, time becomes a symbiotic object with the self, with the outside and inside world of the psyche. Time loses its persecutory function; it loses its essence of quantity and becomes time of quality. For Eigen, the question becomes, what quality can the fragment of time that is centred in transcending mortality, take in this moment? How many of the fragmented moments in one's life can be extracted and reformed, and how can these fragmented moments transcend into "self-eternal, live it now" quality? How does one practice the concept that inside is outside and outside is inside?

Time is held in the present moment. Eigen (2011, p. 20) quotes Winnicot's *Human Nature* (1988, p. 157), "In the most intimate contact there is a lack of contact." Eigen feels Winnicott is describing an alone state, that support can come from not knowing of the background support. The analyst provides this over time, provides support even in a state of aloneness. Winnicott (1988) mentions the unknown background support an infant has even in the face of feeling alone in time. The infant is unaware that the mother is in the background, but without the background support the infant could not thrive. In analysis, the analyst provides this background support for the patient to thrive, recover and eventually reach the "self-eternal, live it now" state of being with quality. "The essential aloneness we feel inside ourselves, the quality of our aloneness depends on the quality of support we've gotten. This plays a role in the quality of support we can give ourselves" (Eigen, 2011, p. 20).

Trauma over the lifespan damages one's ability to digest it. One may attack one's own processing ability as a way to dissociate trauma, or extricate it from one's field of vision. Eigen searches and points to peripheral vision as well; he plays for time for the patient to catch up with herself, to gently explore peripheral vision. He diffuses an attack on linking by waiting creatively. He is not in a hurry and understands clock time may be measured over a period of years, while emotional time begins to condense and congeal.

Eigen's Time holds the patient and suspends negative subjectivity. Emotional trauma fragments have a chance to incubate, grow and transcend the damaged self. Transformations gently begin to take shape.

The meaning of time as a background object as it relates to love, incubation and welcoming oneself as one's own background object becomes of interest to the patient. Eigen's sense of therapeutic time becomes an incubator for the psyche. As time, transformation and transcendence are embodied, I think of Eigen while giving his Tuesday seminars, saying, "every moment you are created," as he relishes and summarizes Rabbi Schneerson's words.

References

Bion, W. (1970). *Attention and interpretation*. Tavistock.
Bion, W. (1984). *Second thoughts: Selected papers on psychoanalysis*. Karnac.
Bion, W. (1991). *A memoir of the future*. Karnac.
Cohen, K. (2016, September 30–October 2). *Womb to womb psychic fetal growth and vitality*. The Bion 2016 International Congress. University of Milan. Milan, Italy.
Eaton, J. (2011). *A fruitful harvest*. The Alliance Press.
Eaton, J. (2015). Becoming a welcoming object: Personal notes on Michael Eigen's impact, *Living moments: On the work of Michael Eigen* (S Bloch and L Daws, Eds.). Karnac.
Eigen, M. (2001). *Damaged bonds*. Karnac.
Eigen, M. (2011). *Faith and transformation*. Karnac.
Eigen, M. (2016a). *Image, sense infinities and everyday life*. Routledge.
Eigen, M. (2016b). *Under the totem*. Karnac.
Eigen, M. (2018a). *The challenge of being human*. Routledge.
Eigen, M. (2018b). Eigen seminar. New York, New York.
Eigen, M. (2019). Bion seminar. New York, New York.

Eigen, M. and Govrin, A. (2007). *Conversations with Michael Eigen*. Karnac.

Heidegger, M. (1962). *Being and time* (J Macquarrie and E Robinson, Trans.) Blackwell (original work published 1927).

Read, H. (1955). *Icon and idea: The function of art in the development of human consciousness*. Harvard University Press.

Rilke, R.M. (2000). *Letters to a young poet* (J Brunham, Trans.). New World Library.

Winnicott, DW. (1988). *Human nature*. Free Association Books.

Chapter 4

Healing longing in the midst of damage[1]

Eigen's psychoanalytic vision

Loray Daws

Introduction

The clinical and academic work of Michael Eigen has touched countless clinicians in understanding the most challenging states of the human heart and mind. Starting a career[2] working with psychotic children and adults, even those deemed "unwanted," being the analysand of Dr Henry Elkin, and influenced by the supervision and/or personal communication with Donald Winnicott, Wilfred Bion, Marion Milner, André Green (to name but a few), Eigen's written and clinical works forges a unique, if not orphic, approach to our perennial disquiet. It is not possible to encompass all of Eigen's thinking in a single paper – his profound, poetic, and moving descriptions of *psychological impacts* as well as its *nourishing evolution(s)* evident in the therapeutic echo chamber. It may prove beneficial, given our task set out by the International Psychohistorical Association (2019) to accentuate some pivotal vertices evident in Eigen's unique psychoanalytic touch and vision. The reader is forewarned that such an approach to Eigen may read deceptively reductionistic and structural. Eigen's prose and writing style, creative psychoanalytic musings, and reveries, as well as technical approach, is difficult to approximate and remains an expression of his own soul music. Reading and savouring Eigen's work phenomenologically remains each reader's primary task.

In the beginning ... there was nourishment–trauma

Eigen's psychoanalytic songline and orphic sojourns into the primordial self see special attention given to both our nourishment and trauma registers. For Eigen, all psychological life as known, despite our best intentions, consists of painfully labouring the facticity of our nourishment ∞ trauma experiences, a *nourishment–trauma dialectic* in need of a psyche capacity allowing for its evolution as it is reflected within a *dual union–distinction* experience (Eigen, 1983, 1986, 1999, 2011a).[3] For Eigen all parental care reflects a mixed nourishment–trauma demand:

Thus love is mixed with a variety of tendencies, including anxious control, worry, death dread, ambition, self-hate. Parental love is not pure- it is mixed with everything else. Parents often view children as extensions of themselves, food for ego, stimulants for self. Parent-child boundaries are variable and fluid. The child must digest messianic expectations fused with everyday life. To an extent, we learn to use what psychic nutriments we can and avoid what is toxic. Often, we more or less successful, but not without casualties. In different measures, no one escapes toxic elements in nourishment secured.

(1999, p. xv)

More specifically, and lovingly furnished by the archetypal approach of Dr Henry Elkin (1972; Eigen, 1986, 1992, 1996, 2010, 2011a, 2011b, 2012, 2018), Winnicott's *Human Nature* (1988) and Bion's *Transformations* (i.e. F and K in O, etc.; Bion, 1957, 1958, 1959), Eigen's notion of the *sensitive self* tracks our autochthonous-being-in-the-world as primarily informed (if not transformed) by the pristine self's oceanic capacity as initial autistic-(proto-)being-in-the-world (pristine radiant awakening), the baby-mother of symbiosis and hatching as midwife to "primordial consciousness," the baby-and-mother of separation–individuation, as well as the triadic Oedipal drama as the commencement of primordial Selfhood. Within these autochthonous epochs, if not archetypal dramas, the internal and external self, and others are imbued with rich phantasy and imaginative potential that could facilitate psychological growth and/or entropy. Damaged bonds (Eigen, 2001) and toxic nourishment[4] (1999) sees a sensitive self (Eigen, 2004) labouring under too much or too little, suffering a poisoned mind-body-feeling self, necessitating psychic retreats, entombment, rigidity, fusional softness, nameless dread (Bion), and various primary agonies (ala Winnicott). Poetic Eigen states:

Something goes wrong as personality begins to form, at the onset of self-organization, so that birth of self goes awry. One suffers distortion or is blown away. One tightens oneself to get through, but self-tightening creates distorted casings around distorted insides, hardening and poisoning self. One holds vast areas of self at a distance, but poison spreads and there is no safe haven. Winnicott speaks of two kinds of persons, one who does not carry around with them a significant experience of a mental break-down in earliest infancy and those who do ... Therapy provides a place to embrace this double movement and develop a better rhythm so that the breakdown-recovery movement can be fruitful.

(2004, p. 23)

Psychoanalytically, and held in all its infinite psychosomatic variations and permutations, the loss of goodness in, and of, the Other's ministration serves as foundation to not only the loss of primordial consciousness (in need of

resurrection) but also to the primordial awakening of the destructive malevolent Other ("fear nucleus"), a destructive process only salvageable by the
merciful Others' continuous ministrations. The breakdown–recovery process
needs a merciful Other in countering stupor, various annihilation anxieties,
and the commencement of the psychotic self and its mind–body splits.[5] Eigen
describes the loss of goodness as follows:

> Loss of goodness mushrooms … From pristine radiant awakening to
> mental-spiritual agony and death, loss of primordial consciousness,
> a breaking of heart-to-heart, eye-to-eye, face-to-face contact. Simple
> radiant identification of primordial self with primordial Other tastes de-
> struction. In time the Other's ministrations take hold, and primordial
> consciousness is reborn. Or perhaps the infant experiences a spontaneous
> change of state, with correlative shifts of self-other feeling. The overall
> movement is a kind of death-resurrection sequence. However, with the
> rebirth of consciousness, the Other acquires new significance. The self
> experiences regeneration in consequence of the Other's raising it from
> death. Spirit has been fanned back to life with awareness of the Other as
> the eternal, numinous, Source of Being; that is, of light, or consciousness
> itself?
>
> (2004, pp. 19–20)

Registering and surviving, if nor holding and relating to what Eigen refers
to as *primary process impacts*,[6] sees the unfolding of archetypal rhythms such as
our birth–growth–damage–rebirth rhythms, trauma–nourishment rhythms,
nourishment as trauma rhythms, and healing longing in search of, for Eigen,
a unique rhythm of faith. The rhythm of faith as described by Eigen scaffolds the
distinction – union frustrations and traumas, enlivening the psyche's ability
and need towards autochthonous unfolding:

> Here I suggest that part of the rhythm Freud intuits has to do with a kind
> of psychic pulse, an opening–closing linked with death–rebirth (Elkin),
> breakdown–recovery (Winnicott), coming alive–being murdered–
> feeling all right (Bion) … For Elkin one is born through a *merciful Other*
> after suffering boundless horror. For Winnicott trauma breaks personal-
> ity as it forms, dread of breakdown persisting as an undercurrent associ-
> ated with new beginnings … For Bion it is as if one is murdered every
> time one tries to come alive.
>
> (2004, pp. 33–4)

Eigen, similar to Elkin and other archetypal analysts, holds that no primordial
experience is ever lost, that the "*initial* radiant self–other identification, inter-
mediate dread, rage, and stupor vis-à-vis a menacing Other, and culminating
faith in the divine Other's merciful love embrace each other, fuse, ebb, and

flow, *interpenetrate, threaten, support and feed emotional life*" (Eigen, 2004, p. 20, italics added). As described, Eigen's sensitive writing accentuates the facticity that this timeless interpenetration maps and limes the vicissitudes of the nascent self's continual struggle towards autochthonous living and expression, the infinite implications of entropy and psychic deadness, our deadening and hardening cores,[7] as well as our inherent vitality and sensitive self potentiality.

An analysand of mine stated it as follows; "I was rejected, I started to fear rejection, my parents ... I hardened myself, like a crab, hard shell, a too soft "inside." The soft inside feels too much, fears too much. I want to be numb, not feel, the feeling is for naught. Why feel if it is like this?" Another analysand; "Constant conflict ... my mind and thoughts are fractured, I cannot think. It is difficult to describe ... it is like sensory mayhem, sensory chaos, loud, pressure in my head, bursting – I cannot put anything together. The anxiety I feel in my stomach, my intestines, this is not it ... it's something else. It's frightening. I have to knock myself out with medication, re-boot myself ..."[8] Eigen gives special attention and articulation to these trauma artefacts, registers, signs, and signals – the "trauma globs" and "fright nucleus" (2001)[9] that remain in need of "transmutations" into "useable feeling/imagining/thinking flows" (1995, p. 113):

> [r]aw, unprocessed and unprocessable trauma globs [which], together with shards of aborted, deformed thoughts–affects (scraps of failed psychic movement), agglutinate and further block possibility of movement. One may depict this state as stagnant, as a graveyard or garbage heap – a dead or inert or wasted psyche. The psyche is at once dead and radioactive; its deadness takes on a poisonous life of its own, contaminating and destroying whatever comes near ...
>
> (1995, p. 113)

Also:

> However, we also know, partly explicit in Freud, that the unconscious, the psyche and the id can be damaged (see especially *Damaged Bonds*, Chapters 1–4). They can be deranged, they can be damaged, and if they are damaged, the primary processes are unable to play a proper role in beginning to digest experience. The psyche remains in a state of perennial psychic indigestion. The primary process is important to help initiate digesting experience. And if it's damaged, it damages experience that it's trying to digest; it adds to the damage. In psychosis, it's not simply that you go to a blissful inner realm – anyone who has worked with psychosis knows that it's not usually blissful. Maybe it's blissful for moments, but it's agonic. It's agonistic. Tormented, tortured. A tortured psyche, a tortured unconscious.
>
> (Eigen, 2019, p. 77)

To reiterate, the timeless interpenetration of the pristine/divine self–other (nourishment), as well as menacing self–other constellations (trauma globs, bad other, fright nucleus, tortured unconscious), serves as psychological soil to our psycho-spiritual growth (symbols), our capacity (or lack of) for soul care, as well as our damaged dream-work and the nourishment–trauma rhythms of our trauma registers (Eigen and Daws, 2019). Soul and psyche disaster (Dasein-icide) can be micro-traumatic (Brandchaft, Doctors, and Sorter, 2010; Crastnopol, 2015; Kafka, 2017; Khan, 1960, 1963, 1971, 1972) to apocalyptic (Laing, 1960; Miller, 1981, 1988, 1994; Shengold, 1999, 2011; Winnicott, 1945, 1974, Williams, 1998, Young-Bruehl, 2012), encasing, entombing, and encapsulating the primordial self:

> Nevertheless, a real disaster is being conveyed. A disaster as great as soul or self or world destruction, an apocalypse now, then, ongoing. A forever apocalypse. It is as if personality dies and comes to life semi-mummified, embalmed, semi-undead enough to keep on reporting (not bearing witness), saying over and over, repeating: something terrible happened to me and keeps on happening. It is sort of the reverse of Winnicott's "ongoing being," more an ongoing SOS, disaster in progress: I have become a crustacean or insect, an exoskeleton to live with it – and that is part of the disaster.
>
> (Eigen, 2004, p. 65)

Within Eigen's writing on the psychotic core and the psychotic self, painfully articulated by Judge Schreber (Eigen, 1986), the sensitive self continuously struggles to deal with a primordial injury. In comparing Schreber with a patient called Ruth (1986, Chapter 7), Eigen maps primordial injury, mind–body madness (corrupt body self-corrupt mental self), epistemological reversal, omniscience, unintegration, the containerless container, the point of no return (primal aloneness), as well as therapeutic coordinates that can be used to find a more meaningful, if not tolerable, relationship with self–other and reality (Eigen, 1986, pp. 306–12). The primordial disaster, the psyche's SOS (psychosis's basic language), finds a container worthy of transformation.

Eigen's later work also accentuates the clinical and lived reality that primordial agonies are not always obviously present.[10] The individual suffering various encapsulated variations of primordial agony and mind–body madness may be unaware of the problem(s) to be faced or have found tolerable compromises enabling some adaptation – usually at the expense of vitality, comfort, and a sense of feeling "real." Entropy and circumscribed numbness/deadness as a way of continuing a limited "semi"-aliveness may be evident:

SARAH: I am aware of my face, it was never perfect. Many operations to get it right. A face my mother wanted. I have to drink and eat carefully now as I have no feeling here on the left side of my mouth – a spot that has no feeling, it is numb. I am not aware of it, I rely on people letting me know there is something so I am not embarrassed.

LORAY: Mom's perfection, her "perfection" see-"ing" and making a perfect daughter numbed a part of your mouth-I-feel. Being aware that others are now the only ones to see the imperfection leaves you vulnerable to shame – their eyes, like mom's, the only coordinates to the resulting numbness … the perfection-numbness you constantly have to work with.

Conversion, psychosomatic pain, dissociation, time slippage, thought malignancies (thought "negatosis"), alexithymia, and other nuanced catastrophes beg analytic ministration: "In certain individuals, madness is obvious and the sense of unreality inescapable. In many others, it works silently; perhaps it is visible only in the gradual erosion of the quality of one's life and the deterioration of the capacity to generate vital and viable meaning" (Eigen, 1986, p. 331). Similar to oceanic dead spots, the impact craters of the moon, or buried scarring (similar to a psychic or emotional Chicxulub crater), toxic nourishment and damaged bonds can wipe out, if not obliterate, body-thinking-feeling-imagining-reverie potential, or leave scar tissue, emotional keloids,[11] even uninhabitable terrain (Eigen, 1977). Analysands would describe the latter as coming to terms with various anti-growth experiences called "thought negatosis," "emotional rigour mortis," "being socio-phobic," "being zombified" (dissociated), "ang-citement" (a mixture of anxiety and excitement that confuses), "a brain feeling botoxed," "optic rectomitis," "feeling fractured," "thinking-feeling-digestive tract diverticulosis," "emotional black lung," and much more. Such injury to the primordial self could even see the cultivation of a deep-seated pessimism (Eigen's cumulative injury rage), malevolent transformations, "faith"-less attitudes to self and the Other (even culture): "Cumulative rage helps nourish a pessimistic, depressive, semi-malevolent counter-part or undertow to one's official, happier self … chronic outrage over injury can eat at life like an acid and corrode psychosomatic integrity" (1999, p. 48). Eigen again mentions possibilities, that hydraulic and eliminative images may support and build the capacity to make use of such rage, although psychosomatic and mental poisons are challenging to process. Embryonic equipment, if not faulty equipment, haunts processing ability. At times, similar to radioactive wastelands, active distance and quarantine are the only mediums available in allowing dispersal. An analysand, Peter, mentioned in his very creative way that his interaction with his father remains limbic to limbic, violent, soul-destroying (shell shock to soul shock). Two nuclear powers perennially on the brink of devastating nuclear fall-out. *Waiting to begin and waiting as beginning* (see Eigen, 2019, Chapters 6, 9, and 10) may support processing ability, postponing an unthinkable emotional nuclear winter; "Explosive hate obliterates the self. Poisonous hate corrupts the self. One's efforts to rid oneself of explosive/poisonous hate backfire, so that the latter deforms the self that fights it, and the evolution of one's personality and life may miscarry" (1999, p. 48). This is certainly true even for our cultural self (see Eigen's Seoul volumes, 2010, 2011a). When caretaking others (parents) and we as citizens fail to serve as true psychic incubators for liberated futures, if we function predominantly as colonizers and instrumentalizers of self and other, only devastation follows. The dawn or age of psychopathy as described by Eigen (2006). Eigen's writing also describes various *toxic nourishment fall-out*[12] phenomena under headings such as being exposed to killers in dreams (2001, 2005), moral violence (1996/2004), being too good (1996/2004), experiencing an annihilated self (2007), suffering trauma clots (2007), experiencing empty and violent nourishment (1999), self-nulling tendencies (1999), needing a bug free universe (1999), experiencing the shadows of agony X (1999, broken X), needing soundproof sanity (1999), fearing madness (1999), and suffering the undreamable object (2001). All are meaningful signifiers to our psychotic, disorders of the self, and neurosis registers. Despite our psychoanalytic registers of damaged bonds, Eigen's notion of the ever-healing wound (Eigen, 2019), psychoanalytic Faith, rhythm of faith, and Faith's breath all provide much-needed *seelsorge*, that is, Eigen's presencing ensures an archetypal "coming alive" in an *area of faith* deeply honouring our nourishment–trauma dilemma and our divine spark (Eigen, 1981, 1985, 2009; Craig, 2008). A clinical example may illustrate Eigen's *felt sense*:

> Lily and I were stuck sitting with the broken x. Something broken that can't be fixed. I look at her and the feeling speaks, "I am broken". And she says, "I want to fix you". And I say, "I can't be fixed". I felt this true, from the bottom of my being and she weeps. I add, "Always trying to fix the brokenness that is part of life, our broken hearts. And in the center of our broken hearts there is a golden radiant point". In the next session, I can see a change. She felt better, freer, deeper, good again. We went through a sequence of crash and coming through. The trauma was not so severe as with past therapists, but it shares something of the same structure, the same formation.
>
> (Eigen, 2019, p. 51)

Eigen's welcoming and holding echo chamber

Whereas our modern tendency may be to *shrink*[13] from the psyche's lapsus (or *lalangue*, ala Lacan) and its immeasurable implications, Eigen has spent decades forging a language of vitality, of resurrection and redemption (*breakdown–recovery rhythm*) able to sustain contact "in" and "with" emotional storms (2005). Such a language and felt sense is of importance for Eigen as he rightly states: "The patient, in a way, reads himself in the therapist's being and vice versa"[14] (Eigen, 2001, p. 5). As previously written (Bloch and Daws, 2015), Eigen, akin to a medieval sin-eater, remains deeply partnered with the nourishment–trauma of the Other, relying on his unique psychic taste buds to sav(i)or the *nourishment–trauma dialectic* of the Other, allowing it into his own "psychic bloodstream" (participation mystique), nurturing the primary process impacts within his orphic rhythm of faith:

> In analysis the patient experiences the analyst variously as a traumatic force or wounding object, supportive background presence, vehicle of wisdom and stupidity, auxiliary dream-worker, *agent of faith*. The experiential arc described here constitutes a rhythm of faith. For Elkin faith evolves and is sustained as the primordial self is nursed through despair and stupor, quickening into life with the Other's help.
>
> (Eigen, 2004, p. 34)

Faith and serving as welcoming Other (Eaton, 2005) remains the product of good enough midwifery of the primordial self in despair. It is also good enough psychic midwifery that is expected, paradoxically, to *initiate* the "breakdown–recovery rhythm". Within the breakdown–recovery rhythm, there remains an inherent faith in the Other's ability to develop trust in the psyche's ability to not only come through the trauma–recovery sequence but ultimately to experience a unique inherent generative capacity. Symbolization of affective damage, the ability to "dream" the very catastrophe the primordial self has been exposed to remains very dependent on a receptive Other to be able to receive the SOS:

> A therapist may or may not get the message, but he tries to stay with the situation until it begins to reach him. To talk about reaching the patient before the therapist is reached can be premature. The therapist speaks from a place he is touched, which includes his own incomplete, ongoing bonding process, with its incessant dream-work ... As a therapist, it is necessary to go even deeper into strangulated states – not only to observe but to feel the closing in on oneself, collapsing, enduring mutilation, becoming aware of rotten, ruptured areas of one's own life ... [But] often one finds damage to self, tied to embedded damaged objects that are now part of self. It is not possible to remove the damage to self by removing the damaged object (e.g. residues of a depressed or psychotic or abusive parent): the damage is done. But one can help a person to open new channels to process the damage, enabling new states of self to evolve.
>
> (Eigen, 2001, p. 3–4)

Furthermore:

> The analyst's anxiety/resistance is about dreaming the patient, making the patient real, taking the patient in, making the patient's life and destruction part of one's psychic bloodstream. To constitute a living person within oneself is to constitute what is destroying this person as well.

The analyst must dream what destroys the patient's dreams, and since the analyst may or may not be much better at this than the patient, the analyst turns on two people becoming partners in evolution, doing work all humanity must come to do. In other words, part of the long term work involves becoming real to ourselves and each other and the profound ethic this implies.

(2004, p. 32)

Eigen's approach also mentions the presence of insoluble self–other–body binds, severe psyche-phobia, resistance to the real, sensitivity pain, Freud's soul entropy, and activity gone wrong – all in need of psychoanalytic incubation, allowing, despite its severity, the possibility of a *recovery–(re-)growth capacity*:

Inability to "solve" binds – often they are insoluble – may lead an individual (or group) to try to rid himself of the capacity that gives rise to endless knots. If we are sensitive to ourselves and the world we live in, unsolvable conflicts are inevitable. At times, the best one can do is wait, let problems be, turn them over this way or that and see what happens in time. Waiting on a problem builds waiting ability. Tolerating difficulties builds tolerating ability ... A psyche may attempt to uproot its own sensitivity as a solution to the pain it brings. That is, psychic life may try to cancel or undo itself, rather than be exposed to its own sensitivity. To *wait patiently* on what is bothering one may be a better solution than attempting to scratch irritation out of existence. When irritants involve tensions between one's own strivings, ridding oneself of disturbance can be costly.

(Eigen, 2004, pp. 68–9)

Elsewhere:

The ticking of the psyche goes on, although injury speeds, deforms, and magnifies it. There are all kinds of ways to partly abort and partly go through rebirth processes. The *quality* of *coming through* is hampered by our human limitations, fragility, rigidity and "necessary" compromises with evil and madness, whether materialistic or idealistic.

(2004, pp. 75–6)

Coming through activity gone wrong naturally sees postponement, our ridding adaptations (evacuation), evoking constriction, and pushing down techniques. Meeting the wounding–obstructive–obdurate object remains a developmental achievement as our capacity to work with its impacts remains embryonic.[15] It is this very embryonic nature that sees a desperate need for pain to be taken away, to be without the very thing that defines our complex experience and psychological soil. We *are* both, *exposed* to both, in need to work with both nourishment–trauma. Working with raw emotion will remain problematic, "dosage" in all things may not only contain but support us in sustaining and growing the psyche (rebirth) and nurture our embryonic capacity to come through catastrophes. In the therapeutic sense specifically, we are "practicing the basic rhythm of trauma-and-recovery in better ways" (Eigen and Daws, 2019, p. 130). Subverted psychic potentiality fuelled by both malevolent hypo- and hyper-transformations is part of living a very complex psychological and interpersonal life. Alterity usurps autochthony, fate overshadowing destiny. In a soulful book entitled *Fierce Attachments: A Memoir*, Vivian Grolnick describes Eigen's various dialectics in the most profound ways; the dual union–distinction and trauma–nourishment rhythms, hypo- and hyper-transformations, and the time needed for digestion:

> So this was her (mother's) condition: here in the kitchen she knew who she was, here in the kitchen she was restless and bored, here in the kitchen she functioned admirably, here in the kitchen she despised what she did. She would become angry over the "emptiness of a woman's life" as she called it, then laugh with a delight I can still hear when she analyzed some complicated bit of business going on in the alley. Passive in the morning, rebellious in the afternoon, *she was made and unmade daily.* She fastened hungrily on the only substance available to her, became affectionate toward her own animation, then felt like a collaborator. How could she not be devoted to a life of such intense division? And how could I not be devoted to her devotion?
>
> (Grolnick, 1987, pp. 15–16)

> [Grolnick reflecting on her mother and other women that served as surrogates:] Shrewd, volatile, unlettered, they performed on a Dreiserian scale. There would be years of apparent calm, then suddenly an outbreak of panic and wildness: two or three lives scarred (perhaps ruined), and the turmoil would subside. Once again: sullen quiet, erotic torpor, the ordinariness of daily denial. And I – the girl growing in their midst, being made in their image – I absorbed them as I would chloroform on a cloth laid against my face. It has taken me thirty years to understand how much of them I understood.
>
> (1987, p. 4)

Can one live without adequate processing equipment given the Dreiserian intensities experienced daily? Eigen remains sober and realistic yet sensitively hopeful, a sober hope, hopeful soberness – a psychic sobriety: "One can be alive with inadequate equipment. One can never adequately keep up with all that happens to one – and why would one want to? Therapy may help a person process injury/rage somewhat and help broaden one's response repertoire to the latter. Evolution in processing ability and response capability is a real achievement. But so is an evolution of ability to live decently with the vast un-processable, including wounds that never heal" (1999, p. 49). An analysand I will call Diane reflected on this as follows:

> As we talk about my experience I become aware of the fright I experienced. It was too much. I think ... no, *I know*, and this may sound dramatic, but I have to be born again ... It is even frightening[16] to see and become aware of the fact that I was frightened and exposed to a frightening event – frightening parents. It sounds strange ... I also know my parents won't change, they are who they are. I also know they see me a certain way, that may also not change. The question is who am I and who will I be for myself?

Elkin and Winnicott both provide, similar to Eigen, vivid and compelling descriptors of the dilemma between toxic nourishment, damaged bonds, and our need to make the best of what we have been given. In Eigen's own narrative:

> Winnicott touches another facet of this conjunction speaking about asthma and breathing. He seems to connect simple breathing in and out with a free flow of the true self. If something goes wrong so that you are afraid to or can't take in, free flow is hampered. You become afraid to breathe. You might be afraid of taking in toxins or something destructive and find yourself caught between being poisoned and suffocating. It is as if the true self no longer can work through the body tissues well. Whatever combination of somatic-psychic, you find yourself beset by destructive fears. The contagion can spread until you experience yourself as destructive, you yourself as dreadful. So what can you do? One alternative is to try to stop breathing. But you can't stop breathing and live. One's dilemma has similarities to a marasmic child, who may die from emotional starvation (Spitz, 1965).
>
>   Elkin gives an example of an infant trying to shut out the sight and sound of the mother in order to take in nourishment – in this case, nourishment tinged with emotional, psychosomatic toxins. If the infant were true to itself, it would starve to death. To live, it must take in what is available, what is possible.
>
> (Eigen, 2019, pp. 126–7)

Epilogue

The current chapter aimed to give a synoptic overview of various nodal reveries in Eigen's many works. Eigen's nourishment–trauma and distinction–dual union dialectic, psychotic core, sensitive self, and rhythm of faith are but a small sample of Eigen's creative psychoanalytic vision. Eigen's psychoanalytic faith in essence "stimulates cognitive-behavioral work that enables basic good-ness to circulate more freely in the psychic body. Better circulation of basic goodness supports more adequate (always partial) metabolization of emotional trauma and toxins (which are inevitable parts of every life)" (1999, p. 55). For Eigen our ability, individually and collectively, is to experience and digest destructive feelings rather than be usurped by it. Psychoanalytic Faith, as de-scribed and lived by Eigen, ensures the continuation of "living moments."

Notes

1   Title taken from an article published by Eigen (2008) in *Psychoanalytic dialogues*.
2   "I was privileged to work with autistic and schizophrenic children at the Reece School in Manhattan and the Blueberry in Brooklyn during the 1960s. I imme-diately felt at home with them, as if a mask had been torn away. I was given a chance to meet myself in a way that has remained decisive" (Eigen, 1986, p. ix).
3   "In sum, distinction–union tendencies enter into many kinds of relationships with each other, antagonistic, symbiotic, parasitic, nullifying, disconnecting, nourishing. We can always ask what one or other of these tendencies is doing at any moments, as both are always co-present. They implicitly characterize mind-body as well as self–other relations and can be read on many planes, adaptive, psychic, behavioral, individual, sociological, mystic. To be permeable and dis-tinct, connected and separate, in union yet distinct, is part of our plasticity and persistence, part of the mystery, difficulty, and creative challenge of our nature … Each strand of our being has a biography. Distinction has its history, so does union, as does their conjunction, their common fate" (Eigen, 2011a, pp. 15–16).
4   Eigen: "Emotional toxins and nourishment often are so mixed as to be indistin-guishable. Even if they can be distinguished, it may be impossible for an individ-ual to get one without the other. In order to get emotional nourishment one may have to take in emotional toxins" (1999, p. 1).
5   See Eigen's Psychotic Self concept, Chapter 8, in *The psychotic core* (1986).
6   "I keep my eye on shock and thawing" (1996, p. 141), and "[the] core ingredient … is the impact of the patient on the therapist. Impact is primary raw datum. It is the most private intimate fact of a meeting. *The therapist may hide yet secretly nurse the deep impact the patient has on him.* To put the impact into words too soon may spoil its *unfolding.* An impact needs time to take root and grow. It occurs instantaneously, but needs the analyst's faith, time, and loyalty in order to prosper" (1996, p. 143, emphasis added). "I must confess I am a primary process lover. In an important way, loving the flow of primary process meanings has made my life worth-while" (1996, p. 142) and "Micro-shot after micro-shot, as if burrowing into micro-moments and letting them speak, sometimes a quivering kind of speaking, often part of a lifelong scream, sometimes joyous" (Eigen, 2019, p. 67).
7   See "I am turning into a barnacle" in Eigen, 2019, Chapter 11.
8   I had images of a self-induced narco-therapy due to an inflammation caused by hundreds of wasps stinging her brain. The cerebral edema could not be accom-modated due to limited space. Given her background and maternal constric-tion, I also wondered, perhaps a bit dramatically, about an emotional Pfeiffer syndrome (a condition where a baby's skull plates join together earlier than usual.) and/or emotional craniosynostosis. Her mother's interpretations of her sensory, affective and emotional realities sounded in sessions frighteningly sim-ilar to the Type C communicational style as defined by Robert Langs (1976, 1977).

9 See *Damaged bonds*, 2001, pp. 24–8. Various fright experiences sees personality "congealed or collapsed around, or into the fright" (p. 24). The fright nucleus spreads throughout and permeates the psychosoma-somapsyche (e.g. adrenal fright infinitizes complexes, the intractable "Idea of Fright") and character of a person. The latter is difficult to undo and although most suffer from temporary breakdown, those that experience "broken" dream-work will suffer immensely as the object of fright cannot be processed sufficiently. It may be written as follows;

   The Mother/Father/the Other as Fright [somatic, adrenal shock as example] impacts the Idea of Fright. The Idea of Mother/Father/Other will be flooded by terror/fright which would in turn floods the Idea of fright (see Eigen's trauma statements, 1999, p. 145). The Eternal Idea (being infinitized) and External Reality may become cemented calling forth Archetypal Defenses. This is similar to Sullivan's self-system operations.

10 "The psycho-organism may respond by numbing, gradually deadening, obliterating, expelling – all manner of defensive organizations. You may, at some point, not even know you are traumatized. There is, too, the possibility over time of growing and, to some degree, meeting some of the problems that constitute us, adding to the pool of learning from experience" (Eigen, 2019, p. 124).

11 See the work Rothenberg, RE (2001). *The jewel in the wound: How the body expresses the needs of the psyche and offers a path to transformation.* Chiron Publications.

12 Also see the works of Paul Williams (2010) entitled *"The fifth element"* as well as *"Scum"* (2013).

13 See Eigen's "recoil on having another person" (1993, p. 21) as well as the many evocative and transformative works of both Dr. Ofra Eshel (and her concept of patient–analyst "with-ness", 2005, 2010, 2013, 2019) and Dr Annie G. Rogers (2006, 2016)

14 Eigen (1999, pp. 104–5) states; "When I was writing *Ecstasy* (2001), I wanted to give expression to what I felt was a core experience of mine, a positive experience of life, a sense of ecstasy in existence, a kind of credo – the ecstasy my alcoholic patient discovered, perhaps mirroring my unconscious without knowing it, and he mirrored it for me. A kind of unconscious sharing without knowing we were sharing."

15 "Capacity to work with raw emotion is fragile, undeveloped or damaged. Bion speaks of embryonic psychic capacities in search, in need of development. We keep on trying. This is the way to do it, that's the way to do it. But it's not so easy. I tend towards emphasizing helping someone come through a state, come through an experience. Going through, coming through, at least a little. A little can make a big difference" (Eigen, 2019, p. 124).

16 See Daws, L (2006). Charting the omega function: psychoanalytic thoughts on the quality of the internal object of eating disordered patients. *Issues in Psychoanalytic Psychology*, 28(2), 15–33.

References

Bion, WR. (1957). Differentiation of the psychotic from the non-psychotic personalities. *International Journal of Psychoanalysis*, 38, 266–75.

Bion, WR. (1958). On hallucination. *International Journal of Psychoanalysis*, 39, 341–9.

Bion, WR. (1959). Attacks on linking. *International Journal of Psychoanalysis*, 40, 308–15.

Bloch, S, and Daws, L (Eds.). (2015). *Living moments: On the work of Michael Eigen*. Karnac.

Brandchaft, B, Doctors, S, and Sorter, D. (2010). *Towards an emancipatory psychoanalysis. Brandchaft's intersubjective vision*. Routledge.

Craig, E. (2008). The "human and the hidden" existential wondering about depth, soul, and the unconscious. *Humanistic psychologist*, 36, 227–82.

Crastnopol, M. (2015). *Micro-trauma. A psychoanalytic understanding of cumulative psychic injury*. Routledge.

Daws, L. (2006). Charting the Omega Function: psychoanalytic thoughts on the quality of the internal object of eating disordered patients. *Issues in Psychoanalytic Psychology*, 28 (2), 15–32.

Eaton, JL. (2005). The obstructive object. *Psychoanalytic Review*, 92 (3), 355–72.

Eigen, M. (1977). On working with "unwanted" patients. *International Journal of Psychoanalysis*, 58, 109–21.

Eigen, M. (1981). The area of faith in Winnicott, Lacan and Bion. *International Journal of Psychoanalysis*, 62, 413–33.

Eigen, M. (1983). Dual union or undifferentiation? A critique of Marion Milner's view of the sense of psychic creativeness. *International Review of Psycho-Analysis*, 10, 415–28.

Eigen, M. (1985). Toward Bion's starting point: Between catastrophe and faith. *International Journal of Psychoanalysis*, 66, 321–30.

Eigen, M. (1986). *The psychotic core*. Karnac.

Eigen, M. (1992). *Coming through the whirlwind*. Chiron Publications.

Eigen, M. (1993). *The electrified tightrope*. (A Phillips, Ed.). Karnac.

Eigen, M. (1995). Psychic deadness: Freud. *Contemporary Psychoanalysis*, 31, 277–99.

Eigen, M. (1996). *Psychic deadness*. Karnac.

Eigen, M. (1999). *Toxic nourishment*. Karnac.

Eigen, M. (2001). *Damaged bonds*. Karnac.

Eigen, M. (2004). *The sensitive self*. Wesleyan University Press.

Eigen, M. (2005). *Emotional storm*. Wesleyan University Press.

Eigen, M. (2006). *Age of psychopathy*. Retrieved from http://www.psychoanalysis-and-therapy.com/human_nature/eigen/pref.html.

Eigen, M. (2007). *Feeling matters*. Karnac.

Eigen, M. (2008). Healing longing in the midst of damage. *Psychoanalytic Dialogues*, 15 (2), 169–83.

Eigen, M. (2009). *Flames from the unconscious: Trauma, madness and faith*. Karnac.

Eigen, M. (2010). *Eigen in Seoul Vol 1: Madness and murder*. Karnac.

Eigen, M. (2011a). *Eigen in Seoul Vol 2: Faith and transformation*. Karnac.

Eigen, M. (2011b). *Contact with the depths*. Karnac.

Eigen, M. (2012). *Kabbalah and psychoanalysis*. Karnac.

Eigen, M. (2018). *The challenge of being human*. Routledge.

Eigen, M. (2019). *Dialogues with Eigen: Psyche singing* (L Daws Ed.). Routledge.

Elkin, H. (1972). On selfhood and the development of ego structures in infancy. *The Psychoanalytic Review*, 59, 389–416.

Eshel O. (2005). Pentheus rather than Oedipus: on perversion, survival and analytic "presencing." *International Journal of Psychoanalysis*, 86, 1071–97.

Eshel O. (2010). Patient-analyst interconnectedness: personal notes on close encounters of a new dimension. *Psychoanalytic Inquiry*, 30, 146–54.

Eshel O. (2013). Patient-analyst "withness": On analytic "presencing", passion, and compassion in states of breakdown, despair, and deadness. *Psychoanalytic Quarterly*, 82, 925–63.

Eshel, O. (2019). *The emergence of analytic oneness: Into the heart of psychoanalysis*. Routledge.

Grolnick, V. (1987). *Fierce attachments: A memoir*. Farrar, Straus and Giroux.

Kafka, F. (2017). *Dearest father* (H Stokes, Trans.). Alma Classics.

Khan, MR. (1960). Regression and integration in the analytic setting: A clinical essay on the transference and counter-transference aspects of these phenomena. *International Journal of Psychoanalysis*, 41, 130–46.

Khan, MR. (1963). The concept of cumulative trauma. *Psychoanalytic Study of the Child*, 18, 286–306.

Khan, MR. (1971). Infantile neurosis as a false-self organization. *Psychoanalytic Quarterly*, 40, 245–63.

Khan, MR. (1972). Dread of surrender to resourceless dependence in the analytic situation. *International Journal of Psychoanalysis*, 53, 225–30.

Laing, RD. (1960). *The divided self*. Penguin Books.

Langs, RJ. (1976). *The bipersonal field*. Jason Aronson.

Langs, RJ. (1977). *The therapeutic interaction: A synthesis*. Jason Aronson.

Miller, A. (1981). *Thou shalt not be aware: Society's betrayal of the child*. Meridian

Miller, A. (1988). *Banished knowledge: Facing childhood injuries*. Doubleday.

Miller, A. (1994). *For your own good: Hidden cruelty in child rearing and the roots of violence*. Noonday Press

Rogers, AG. (2006). *The Unsayable: The hidden language of trauma*. Random House

Rogers, AG. (2016). *Incandescent alphabets: Psychosis and the enigma of language*. Karnac.

Rothenberg, RE. (2001). *The jewel in the wound: How the body expresses the needs of the psyche and offers a path to transformation*. Chiron Publications.

Shengold, L. (1999). *Soul murder: Thoughts about therapy, hate, love and memory*. Yale University Press.

Shengold, L. (2011). Trauma, soul murder, and change. *Psychoanalytic Quarterly*, 80(1), 121–38.

Willliams, G. (1998). *Internal landscapes and foreign bodies: Eating disorders and other pathologies*. Routledge (Tavistock Clinic Series).

Williams, P. (2010). *The fifth element*. Karnac.

Williams, P. (2013). *Scum*. Karnac.

Winnicott, DW. (1945). Primitive emotional development. *International Journal of Psychoanalysis*, 26, 137–43.

Winnicott, DW. (1974). Fear of breakdown. *International Review of Psycho-Analysis*, 1, 103–7.

Winnicott, DW. (1988). *Human nature*. Free Association Books.

Young-Bruehl, E. (2012). *Childism: Confronting prejudice against children*. Yale University Press.

Part III

Tasting the psyche through Eigen's writings

Chapter 5

Breakdown and recovery
Going *Berserk* and other rhythmic concerns

Louis Rothschild

Personal and clinical experience is drawn upon to explore the manner in which historicity and qualities of time and timelessness exist within Michael Eigen's (1999, 2012) conception of a breakdown and recovery rhythm as a basic quality of the human condition. Specifically, alpha function (Bion, 1994), fear (Bion, 1970), radical hope (Lear, 2006), and going *Berserk* (Davoine and Gaudillière, 2004) are utilized to illuminate experiential textures in the rhythms of Eigen's breakdown and recovery. Across each of these conceptions exists a grappling with a desire to feel whole and to work with variations of frustration tolerance that give birth to partiality and compromise, acceptance, and repetition.

Eigen's fictional therapist, Dr Z (Eigen, 2009, p. 114) asks, "Are poets suicide bombers? Are comedians?" When taken in the context of his writing, I find that such questioning in regard to traumatized and traumatic messengers points to other questions such as: How is it that psychological death occurs, how do we survive ourselves, and what may treatment afford in regard to the qualities of acceptance and survival? Words can shatter a speaker or listener, yet in the act of shattering there is a hope for something new. Maturity points to developing capacities to work with destructiveness in a constructive manner. To that end, I (Rothschild, 2011) have answered Eigen's character Dr Z with the poet Lawrence Ferlinghetti (2007) who writes that the poet may be considered a subversive barbarian at the edge of society who nonviolently challenges the toxicity found in the status quo.

Working with or challenging toxicity through poetry might be an important way to approach Eigen's clinically focused writing. Some (e.g. Jennings, 2010) have noted the manner in which he uses poetry and candour to describe the limits of our thought and in addition, our imperfect stance as healers which when made apparent and engaged with might foster growth. Eigen (2009) writes of poetry lust as a state if not a drive for holistic experiences that aid developmental integration. He (Eigen, 2009) also writes of poetry lust as a particular addiction that gives birth to experience. Eigen (2009) recommends a mindfully poetic attitude for clinical work, and also as a way to read psychoanalytic meta-theory. I take this to be an articulation that emphasizes play and simultaneously entails a radical respect for engagement with the coercive qualities of defensive structures that may undermine play. Eigen's (1999) conceptualization that toxicity and nourishment travel together places coercion and play in a uniquely audible register where tragic and lyric poetry do not so much co-exist alongside each other as intermingle.

The poet May Sarton (1997) writes of the soul being unencumbered in the pristine moment as a definition of poetry. Within psychoanalysis, some (e.g. Bion, 1970; Symington, 2012) have suggested that such conscious presence is a common factor of phenomenological encounters. Such awareness brings an important correction to observations that Western psychologists are tantalized by the flavour of immediate experience due to being dislocated from such experience as a result of being stuck within theories and conceptions of psychology as opposed to being with the psychological in the present (Trungpa, 2005). Knowledge can indeed be dangerous. In addition to dislocating one from the present, knowledge may also be used to defensively dislocate one from one's self. A poetic attitude can create openings.

Through Eigen we see that the road to decency or not being dangerous is no simple journey. He finds in the work of existentialist philosopher Paul Tillich the idea that greatness is obtained through a journey into the dissociated darkness of one's self (Eigen, 1993/2004). Additionally, Eigen writes of Wilfred Bion's psychoanalytic explorations as helpful when "barbed wire surrounds the soul and cuts into it" (Eigen, 2010, p. 40) in order to develop a capacity to sing "in the center of our gnarled selves" (Eigen, 2007, p. 92).

Following lines of fracture, Eigen consistently (cf., Eigen, 1981) points to experiences prior to early and coercive seduction, and finds what *pace* Donald Winnicott (1971/2005) he calls a primary smile and an early joy. Following the development of Winnicott's false self and Lacan's Imaginary, Eigen notes that soon enough, one may smile in bad faith. His attention to what he deems the loss of a spontaneous recovery rhythm fits with Blatt's (2008) focus on the science illuminating the interplay of relatedness and self-definition in the first few months of life.

Eigen's (2010) reading of Freud is one that highlights the manner in which the ego begins as a mad hallucinatory organ. Refreshingly drawing on the oft-cited example of a baby imagining a breast, he ventures into the lands of mysticism and psychosis. Moving beyond wish fulfilment, Eigen focuses on a trance or mad states as a way in which we become used to making ourselves disappear and reappear in order to survive ourselves. Here, ego may be an unreality machine that finds a way to appreciate limits. Eigen suggests that it is almost as if Freud asks how such a hallucinating machine can have reality testing.

Eigen has said (in Marchesani, 2003) that an adult is in a position to carry out the delusion of wish fulfilment with greater resources to produce havoc when compared to a child. In an age of psychopathic manipulation of the psychotic anxieties of splitting off out-groups – "they are bad" – Eigen (2001, 2009) writes that it is guilt that helps sensitize and bind. Simply, the capacity to bear guilt becomes an entrance to care – a psycho-spiritual wormhole (Eigen, 2009) – or trauma. Guilt may serve to bind our relationality, and Eigen (Chapter 1 in this volume) wonders if the biblical character Cain could simply slow down and consider not acting on his murderous tendencies.

Encounters

Eigen (2010) writes of himself as being a little less dangerous due to being transformed by love. Here, an ethics of sensitivity or care for weakness is being promoted.

The first memory to be explored in this chapter concerns a reading in which I was reminded of a time when I first learned of Eigen's work. In early 2007, I began reading Carlo Strenger's (2004) take on Eigen for a review of Strenger's work on the disorienting problems of postmodernism (Rothschild, 2007). Strenger's writing motivated me to pick up a copy of *Lust* (Eigen, 2006), and while reading I found myself remembering a paper given during an American Psychological Association film programme over ten years earlier (Eigen, 1995) just as I was beginning graduate school. In 1995, I deeply enjoyed the experiential quality of the paper, and was struck by Eigen as a thinker. However, I was about to be submerged in the New School for Social Research, and lacked a capacity to feel that there was space or time for engaging Eigen and his presentation following his talk. I placed my excitement in the fringes of limbo and a hopeful future. That night in 1995, I did not know who gave that paper. I worried that the joy I found in Eigen's weave of popular media, psychoanalysis, and critical social theory that playfully utilized language such as "Surfing along a patient's affect," would diminish my frustration tolerance for the rigours of graduate school. Fortunately for me, I survived, grew some, and Eigen's work returned.

In October 2008 while planning to write another review, this time of Eigen's work (Eigen, 2007; Rothschild, 2009b), I decided to contact APA's Convention Office due to my hope that the person who gave that paper in 1995 was the same person I was meeting in print in another century. In some sense, there was a test there: Did my reader's ego possess reality testing, or was I attempting a unification of memories and desires in some mad state? The American Psychological Association confirmed via fax that some reality testing was in my possession, and with this idiosyncratic certification, I pressed on as a self, writer, and clinician. That confirmation of not only the capacity to discern a tangible other, but that this particular other truly exists over time has been wonderful. Eigen's voice carries a recognizable consistency across the spoken and written word over decades. Not long after my review of Eigen's work was published, we began a correspondence. That second meeting via correspondence afforded an unexpected life raft as it provided a ground for me to reach out to Eigen in a moment of personal trauma when my son underwent emergency surgery (Rothschild, 2015).

Eigen turns to Winnicott's (1971/2005) idea of a dimension consisting of the dire if not irreparable aspects of traumatic history – a delayed reunion that in a Kafkaesque manner prevents reunion. Eigen (2009, 2012) eloquently works and reworks Winnicott's portrayal of a mother who is gone for a period of time beyond which a baby can bear, and subsequently – even upon a mother's mindfully relational return, the baby remains forever changed. A recovery rhythm is lost, and as a result a scream may become silent due to a loss of faith in the recovery of this shared rhythm. This dire and traumatic dimension is a change that Winnicott developed as a concept that he identified as a *Z dimension* (Winnicott, 1971/2005 in Eigen, 2009, 2011, 2012). In a manner that anticipates subsequent attachment research (cf., Blatt, 2008), Winnicott's Z dimension arises due to the lack of psychologically attuned holding persisting far beyond what can be tolerated. Due to such absence, a baby may become afraid of being held in the future (Shabad, 2004), and by extension also afraid of being creative. We may consider what is needed for a reunion to take place that restores faith in creative cries following such an absence. Here, I wish to bring attention to the manner in which Winnicott's mother may also be changed (we hope in a loving direction) upon recognizing that a marker of a Z dimension is part of her child. Each member of such a wounded and witnessing dyad may come to know each side of this breakdown and potential recovery matrix. Pace Winnicott, Mother is used as a gender-neutral verb applicable to acts of conscious holding (Winnicott, 1971/2005, cited in Rothschild, 2009a). Mother, which is to say holding capacities, may be traumatized. Through development and maturity, a baby may one day be capable of self-soothing, and a traumatized mother may be capable of good-enough holding. Psychotherapy and psychoanalysis may help what has been damaged and may also help to situate what is dead. An overarching rubric is that Eigen's work centres on working with what is damaged and often dead (a Z dimension) in a manner that reconstitutes joy.

To follow one of Eigen's (2007) metaphors, historically embodied cultural connectivity marks movement from absence in a time before teeth to a time in which teeth mark relational embodiment in a rich living history affording a good feed where we can learn to nourish what is vital and not destroy it. In such a world, my own Z-ness is not only encountered but also quite often, contained. Eigen writes of the impossibility to be consistently decent as an enacting of Z, that is a shattering within the therapeutic hour (Eigen, 2012). Sometimes, dead parts are the container, other times, the contained. Eigen (2012) considers that one may be alive and dead at the same time, and as it is with Chinese boxes, container and contained, of life and death may oscillate in regard to which is figure and which is ground. Encounters with decency then are encounters with grace, a fantastic moment occurring after one storm and before another.

Winter's silence

I began to know of a Z dimension in a different manner when my son underwent emergency surgery. That separation and subsequent reunion permanently changed me. The week that he spent as an inpatient led to difficult associations ranging from my identification with Demeter's rage in Persephone's absence as an explanation for the origin of winter to Odysseus' desire not only to return home but to have remained at home in the first place (Hamilton, 1969). In such stress and vulnerability, my own desire to deny fragility and separation was strong.

How I wanted to undo what has been done, to attack all links while simultaneously reaching out. I found a need to make space for the part of me that does not want to acknowledge space. I began to ask if separation always trucks with trauma (cf. Ferenczi, 1949) leaving a confused or confusing mark of the Z dimension, or is trauma simply hard to avoid? Avoiding trauma and Z certainly has a fantastic feel to it. A wish for union or an eternal sabbath in which one never shatters is also a wish for reunion, a wish to be whole. Eigen writes that we are partial beings who ache for total states (Eigen, 2009).

I had planned to attend one of Eigen's talks on Kabbalah and psychoanalysis in New York during the spring of 2012, but my plans were interrupted until I was able to hear him speak in the fall of that year. I emailed him from hospital lodging following a scream cry – not just crying not simply screaming – I found myself in Hades. In his contemporary Midrash about the potential sacrifice of Isaac, Bob Dylan makes way for Derrida's (2008) wonder in regard to what Isaac saw on Abraham's face:

> Oh God said to Abraham, "Kill me a son."
> Abe said, "Man, you must be puttin' me on."
> (Dylan, 2004, p. 178)

Z, a haemorrhage of reunion, marks an adventure most would not choose. In response to my email sent from hospital lodging, Eigen's heartfelt concern came across with his words that life is fragile. Indeed, even with our best care, haemorrhages occur. Eigen wrote then of sitting across from a playground, watching children play and weeping. Now, about seven years later a volatile 16-year-old challenges my stuck points, and I reflect that a few years ago he told me that Macklemore (Macklemore and Lewis, 2016) has advice on parenting as he knows breakdown to be ok. Indeed, what did Isaac see?

> They say boys don't cry
> But your dad has shed a lot of tears
> They say I should be a strong man
> But baby, I'm still filled with fear.
> (Macklemore, 2016)

Such awareness is an awareness that life is often simply too much. Laplanche (1999) writes of the excess that fills everyday moments. When to answer breakdown with a shrill call to life? When to sit quietly with breakdown feeling that metamorphosis is at work? Working with uncertainty in regard to direction, timing, and tact requires abundant faith in uncertainty. How does one discern a non-intrusive presence of optimal disengagement so that a home for curiosity may be found (Benjamin, 1988)? How does one have faith?

Eigen (1981) writes of an irony of radical sincerity in Bion's work, and this stance is maintained in Eigen's (2012) working with Bion's comment that Kabbalah is a frame for psychoanalysis. Kabbalah may be considered a broken container of trauma. This capacity to contain is illustrated by the timely popularization of Kabbalah as one response to the traumatic dislocation of the Inquisition (Patai, 1967). Therefore, Jewish mysticism may be considered another practice of working with the Z dimension. To work with Z through the ironic apprehension of dislocation also embodies something of what Tibetan Buddhist teacher Trungpa Rinpoche (Trungpa, 2005, 2009) aims at in his advocating of decency as compassionate containment. In that regard, like jazz, divergent traditions overlap on love (cf. Murray, 2016). Eigen (2012) speaks of a reading of the Jewish commandment that one love God with all one's heart as a commandment that one bring a loving attitude to all relational spaces. This is to say that we find our way through mad states and trance states by developing love.

Buddhist thought begins with the observation that pain is found in life, and the Shambhala tradition (Trungpa, 2009) considers the warrior one who occupies a raw space without skin. Armour is a product of the mind that does not facilitate but interferes with nakedness. In Shambhala as in psychoanalysis, special attention is given to the hard, internal edges that inhibit one's relating with a big heart. Fearlessness then is being ordinary and simpleminded – naked in encounters with obstacles, including fear.

The night before my son had surgery, I went to the bathroom in the paediatric intensive care unit while a boy in the next room was dying. There was a bustle of hopeful doctors and nurses with large implements moving around his body. In the hallway, his parents sat near the nurses' station. As I slowed near them on the way back to my room I felt as though the boy's father was vibrating out of his own skin. He was going *Berserk*. If only trauma were a hallucination or bad dream. I hoped I would not find myself so lost. The next morning, the other boy's room was no longer occupied. I remember the room, stark in its emptiness, as seen through some curtains, and I also remember my focusing on an unopened Monopoly game with the thought that it had not been left due to an oversight but was intentionally left because it would never be used.

A few years following that surgery, I learn that a childhood acquaintance from summer camp has lost her son, and maybe two years later that another high school friend, a social worker and a father discusses transplant surgery for his son, who later sadly died in surgery. My friend, the father whose son died following transplant surgery necessitated by cystic fibrosis also died the following year. Sometimes to bear hearing requires faith, as we cannot see. Sometimes hearing is too much. How is faith possible? Eigen (2011) recommends an attitude of beginning that allows for bearing witness to Z in order to see if faith is possible.

Breaking into being

A client says, "I want to be able to hide – to not disappoint."
Another, "The transition lasts forever."
In a case of severe trauma, "Someone has to die."

Over the course of a month a patient who I had been with over a year begins to scream in my office. First, he tears at a pillow on my couch. As though he is a monster who is feeding, he utters, "I am death." I struggle. I know his history: A brutal father, gynaecomastia that led to him being beaten by fellow students, and taunted with names such as "knobby." Surgery, years later, inpatient hospitalizations, sadomasochistic sex. A few weeks later, the screaming begins again, "Someone has to die." In the language of Davoine and Gaudillière (2004), he has become a reified monster who is trying to break into time and beckons the clinician to approach the bridge linking different temporalities in order to be free of reification.

In this shared struggle, I am reminded of the genocide that marked the colonization of North America and motivated Sitting Bull to challenge Chief Plenty Coups to fight together in response to the destruction of their cultural symbolic order (Lear, 2006). In thinking of Plenty Coups refusal to fight as a vehicle in and through my own anxiety, I say to my patient who also likes to write, "The pen is mightier than the sword." My client's face softens, and we begin to speak. For the moment, homicide and suicide have been averted.

In an essay on Lear's work on hope, the philosopher Charles Taylor (2007) writes that in the wake of culturecide that thick descriptions – Lacan's symbolic – are lost, and that if one is fortunate to have the courage to walk in uncertainty, then radical hope may be utilized to build new meaning – thin descriptions to use Taylor's language that may grow over time. This is akin to working with haemorrhage so that life may continue.

With trauma, destruction is not found to be creative. Creativity is hopefully found *apres coup*. With trauma, the inside/outside distinction is confused. The inside/outside distinction may be restored though work in the aftermath. However, confusion may bind, and create what Eigen (2007) calls trauma clots. Jessica Benjamin (1988) suggests working rapprochement around Winnicott's awareness that destruction provides a chance to distinguish inside and outside (cf., Winnicott, 1963 as cited in Eigen, 1981). Eigen (1981) focuses on the manner in which Winnicott highlights the creative aspects of destruction and therefore moves from guilt to joy. When the other survives, and is recognized as one who can survive or be grieved, joy is possible.

Thin descriptions found through breakdown and recovery may be considered a meta-cognition that is consistent with Bion's concept of a faith in openness that one can accept and work with catastrophic feelings.

Following a Shakespearian distinction between genius and power, Keats (2014) considers *negative capability* to be the capacity to tolerate uncertainty without reaching for fact or reason. Bion (1991a) links literature and physics by calling Keats's negativity an uncertainty principle. In real life, working with such a principle demands much: A fear of letting go – when holding interferes with living with (and in) rhythms of distinctions and mergers – may unexpectedly be encountered. Such a dread causing constipation has been compared to a fear of total incontinence and a fear of finding a loss of good-enough or that a work is not as beautiful as what had been imagined (Eigen, 1993/2004). Such fear is a marker of the Z dimension.

Experience can be challenging, and in the land of Rorschach inkblots, I find that in regard to bad form, poor integration has been considered to be due to experiencing a passivity in being struck in a manner that thwarts integration (Schachtel, 2001). Colour shock. Shell shock. Ernst Schachtel adds that an individual may not consciously experience this helpless attitude. John Rickman, a Quaker and conscientious objector who was Bion's analyst in the 1930s used the term "nameless horror" to convey the rekindling of an experience already lived in a stage in which the mind was still immature (Civitarese, 2011; Roper, 2012). As Michael Eigen (2004) writes, haemorrhage expresses injury to thinking and feeling processes.

When we speak of faith, we speak of working with a thinking and feeling process that is not always optimal. Haemorrhage happens. Clotting occurs. Faith is entering into a paradox in which injured thinking and feeling process are harnessed to heal injured thinking and feeling processes. This is an uncertain journey; faith is a willingness to take another breath and see.

Bion (1994) considers working with qualities of thinking through his additional concept of alpha function, a description of variation within human performance as a characteristic of the reality principle. The ego can work, and hallucinatory capacities may be engaged.

Thinking processes fluctuate, and Bion considers raw sense-impressions that Eigen (2011, p. 65) has referred to as "impact globs", which may overlap with feeling or other perceptions; along Kantian lines they are experienced like a pre-cursor to Winnicott's transitional object – as a thing rather than phenomena. For Bion, these globs are beta-elements. Beta-elements may be evaded or converted into alpha elements, and Bion (1991b) adds that this process may either be conscious or unconscious. Alpha function then is a modification and storage (cf., Eigen, 2011) process that entails a searching for durable and familiar sense-impressions (Bion, 1991b, 1994). To that end,

Alpha function is required for creativity (Brown, 2012). Alpha is about how a capacity is being used, as one may have alpha intuition at times and not at others (Eigen, 2004). This has been considered a type of thinking that shapes the thinker (Williams, 2010), and Bion turns to celestial navigation as a means to measure time in order to pursue questions as to if a self holds ideas or if ideas hold a self (Bion, 1991a).

Jazz musician Wynton Marsalis is thinking along these lines when he intimates that jazz improvisation is an associational and transitional process found and created after slavery (Murray, 2016). Yet creative jazz is not all that is found in the aftermath of slavery. As Marsalis helps depict in the recent film *Bolden* (Pritzker, 2019) where he wrote, arranged, and performed the music; social and cultural breakdowns of prostitution and bare fist fighting for sport are markers of trauma. For Bion, such breakdowns are moments when alpha runs backwards, that is – flow backs up into a hubris of gang violence and alienated passion that is differentiated from negative capacity by destructive violence and a thirst for power as opposed to the genius that is secure enough to have faith in uncertainty where thinking along loving and creative lines may become possible. This is to say that alpha running backwards presents as a mindless and dissociated enactment as opposed to the flow of functioning alpha that breaks with the repetition compulsion. Therefore, alpha running backward in a repetition compulsion is an enactment of the Z dimension.

As with André Green (1999), Eigen speaks of an integration process where there is an acceptance of being shattered; that one is never whole. Sometimes part of our mind is dissociated or outside of time, other times we associate feeling as though our mind is engaged and awake, firing on all cylinders. As with repetition, dissociation may be appreciated through Donnel Stern's (2010) heuristic whereby mild dissociation easily results in a reply of "my bad," while more severe dissociation is marked by a denial of anything that is off or missing in regards to the self. As shown in *Bolden* as well as our consulting rooms, finding a way to sing in the aftermath of trauma is no simple matter.

Françoise Davoine's and Jean-Max Gaudillière's (2004) use of the Norse word *Berserker* emphasizes a breaking out of a dissociated timelessness. Timelessness characterizes Stern's framing of dissociation and what Eigen has referred to as a trauma clot that has qualities similar to Winnicott's sense of falling forever in the aftermath of Z.

Davoine and Gaudillière write that Bion's statement that he died in the First World War is not to be treated as a metaphor. This consideration of the literal quality of death is found again in treatment given to Chief Plenty Coups's comment that after the buffalo disappeared, nothing happened as a means to illuminate the challenges of moving forward into uncertainty without symbolic guideposts (Lear, 2006). Here, alpha stutters and sputters. Going *Berserk* is an attempt to re-enter time, and with time, meaning. The *Berserker* acts out of a state in which integration, direction, and goals are uncertain. One's aim cannot be conceptualized when alpha backs up. Bion (2015) writes of using his compass as a tank commander in the First World War not because he thought the coordinates would save his life, but because the cognitive press needed to find coordinates allowed him to focus on something other than his terror. Bion shows that in breakdown there are tendrils that may be harnessed toward faith in recovery, a radical hope that is screamed into existence by going *Berserk*. Sometimes tendrils are quiet, and hard to perceive. Derrida (2008) wonders what Isaac saw when he looked into Abraham's face. What do we find upon perceiving that we are dropped and lost? Are Abraham and Isaac intact when they walk home? How do we survive when witnessing breaks down (Benjamin, 2018)?

Conclusion

In surfing along with this chapter, a reverie took hold from a moment in high school. I was in fencing garb, and turned to see my first best friend from early childhood standing in his football uniform. My old friend had finished practice and was on his way to the locker room. He stopped to look. As told by our uniforms, our paths had separated. Across that distance, some sort of silent approval passed between us. Years before that quiet we had gone *Berserk* together. What I have labelled "A butter incident," took place at a Jewish camp in Mississippi during the late 1970s. We were about 9 years old, and it was our first Shabbat away from home. The sabbath prayers afforded no container to hold us as the meal began. Teetering without faith in a tether we began a frenzied table side oscillation of tit-for-tat with butter squares. Pads of butter were used as hair gel in an exciting breakdown that led us straight to the camp directors table. The head of camp sentenced us for our transgressive breakdown: We were told that we would be unable to shower that evening and would therefore go to sleep with the butter in our hair. Such punishment did not prevent an alcohol-induced regression a few years later at the New Orleans Jazz Festival.

Someone had sold two latency age boys beer outside our parent's gaze. Going *Berserk* is an assertion that may be read as a confession. This time, in view of our parents, and again amidst fits of laughter, we attacked each other's arms with crawfish claws. Physical sutures were not needed to mend those embodied scratches. Whatever psychic haemorrhage led to that outburst remained unregistered by the proverbial parental gaze. In each incident we were I think attempting to say a lot with very little brain to work with the excess (Laplanche, 1999) that marks our lives. We did not know that we were outside of time until we broke down. Little did we know what we felt deep in our bones. Over time, capacities develop, and we consciously enter time. We learn how to slow down a bit more in awe. Eigen's master surfing is helpful here.

References

Benjamin, J. (1988). *The bonds of love: Psychoanalysis, feminism, and the problem of domination*. Pantheon Books.

Benjamin, J. (2018). *Beyond doer and done to: Recognition theory, intersubjectivity and the third*. Routledge.

Bion, WR. (1970). *Attention and interpretation: A scientific approach to insight in psycho-analysis and groups*. Tavistock.

Bion, WR. (1991a). *A memoir of the future*. Karnac.

Bion, WR. (1991b). *Learning from experience*. Karnac.

Bion, WR. (1994). *Cogitations: New extended edition* (F Bion, Ed.). Karnac.

Bion, WR. (2015). *War memoirs: 1917–1919*, second edition (F Bion, Ed.). Karnac.

Blatt, S. (2008). *Polarities of experience: Relatedness and self-definition in personality development, psychopathology, and the therapeutic process*. American Psychological Association.

Brown, LJ. (2012). Bion's discovery of alpha function: Thinking under fire on the battlefield and in the consulting room. *International Journal of Psychoanalysis*, 93, 1191–214.

Civitarese, G. (2011). Towards an ethics of responsibility. *International Forum of Psychoanalysis*, 20, 108–12.

Davoine, F and Gaudillière, JM. (2004). *History beyond trauma: Whereof one cannot speak, thereof one cannot stay silent* (S Fairfield, Trans.). Other Press.

Derrida, J. (2008). *The gift of death, second edition and literature in secret* (D Wills Trans.). University of Chicago Press.

Dylan, B. (2004). Highway 61 revisited. *Lyrics, 1962–2001*. Simon & Schuster (originally Released 1965).

Eigen, M. (1981). The area of faith in Winnicott, Lacan and Bion. *International Journal of Psychoanalysis*, 62, 413–33.

Eigen, M. (1993/2004). Psychopathy and individuation, in *The electrified tightrope* (A Phillips, Ed.). Karnac, pp. 9–20.

Eigen, M. (1995). Discussion of the Film *Nell*. Annual Convention of the American Psychological Association, 12 August, New York, NY.

Eigen, M. (1999). *Toxic nourishment*. Karnac.

Eigen, M. (2001). *Damaged bonds*. Karnac.

Eigen, M. (2004). *The sensitive self*. Wesleyan University Press.

Eigen, M. (2006). *Lust*. Wesleyan University Press.

Eigen, M. (2007). *Feeling matters*. Karnac.

Eigen, M. (2009). *Flames from the unconscious: Trauma, madness, and faith*. Karnac.

Eigen, M. (2010). *Eigen in Seoul, Volume One: Madness and murder*. Karnac.

Eigen, M. (2011). *Contact with the depths*. Karnac.

Eigen, M. (2012). *Kabbalah and psychoanalysis*. Karnac.

Ferenczi, S. (1949). Confusion of tongues between the adult and child. *International Journal of Psychoanalysis*, 30, 225–30.

Ferlinghetti, L. (2007). *Poetry as insurgent art*. New Directions Publishing Corporation.

Green, A. (1999). *The work of the negative* (A Wells, Trans.). Free Association Books.

Hamilton, E. (1969). *Mythology: Timeless tales of gods and heroes*. A Mentor Book (originally published 1940).

Jennings, P. (2010). *Mixing minds: The power of relationship in psychoanalysis and Buddhism.* Wisdom Publications.

Keats, J. (2014). *Selected letters* (J Barnard, Ed.). Penguin Classics.

Laplanche, J. (1999). *Essays on otherness.* Routledge.

Lear, J. (2006). *Radical hope: Ethics in the face of cultural devastation.* Harvard University Press.

Macklemore and Lewis, R (Writers/Singers). (2016). Growing up (Sloane's song). *The unruly mess I've made.* [Record Album]. Macklemore LLC, ADA.

Marchesani, R.B. (2003). Vulgar links: Up, down, all around: An Interview with Michael Eigen. In EM Stern and RB Marchesani (Eds.), *Inhabitants of the unconscious: The grotesque and the vulgar in everyday life.* The Haworth Press, pp. 99–110.

Murray, A. (2016). *Murray talks music: Albert Murray on jazz and blues* (P Delvin, Ed.). University of Minnesota Press.

Patai, R. (1967). *The Hebrew goddess.* K'tav Publishing House.

Pritzker, D (Writer). (2019). *Bolden.* [Motion Picture]. Abramorama.

Roper, M. (2012). The "Spear head of an advance": Bion's wartime letters to Rickman. *Psychoanalysis and History,* 14, 95–109.

Rothschild, L. (2007). Book review of: C. Strenger, *The designed self: Psychoanalysis and contemporary identities. Psychoanalysis, Culture, and Society* 12, 94–7.

Rothschild, L. (2009a). Finding a father: Repetition difference and fantasy in Finding Nemo. In B Reis and R Grossmark (Eds.), *Heterosexual masculinities: contemporary perspectives from psychoanalytic gender theory.* Taylor & Francis, pp. 217–30.

Rothschild, L. (2009b). Review of the book M. Eigen, *Feeling Matters. Newsletter of Division 39 of the American Psychological Association.* Winter, 18–19.

Rothschild, L. (2011). Review of the books M. Eigen, *Eigen in Seoul, Volume One: Madness and murder* and *Flames from the unconscious: Trauma madness and faith. Division Review: A Quarterly Psychoanalytic Forum,* 1 (2).

Rothschild, L. (2015). Sensing the mustard seed: Defense, awakening, and fragmentation. In S Bloch and L Daws (Eds.), *Living moments: On the work of Michael Eigen.* Karnac, pp. 307–22.

Sarton, M. (1997). *Coming into 80.* W. W. Norton & Company.

Schachtel, EG. (2001). *Experiential foundations of Rorschch's test.* The Analytic Press.

Shabad, P. (2004). Through the mind's eye: The problem of Self-Consciousness and the need for reality. In J Reppen, J Tucker, and M Schulman (Eds.), *Way beyond Freud: Postmodern psychoanalysis observed.* Open Gate Press, pp. 156–72.

Stern, DB. (2010). *Partners in thought: Working with unformulated experience, dissociation, and enactment.* Routledge.

Strenger, C. (2004). *The designed self: Psychoanalysis and contemporary identities.* The Analytic Press.

Symington, N. (2012). The essence of psycho-analysis as opposed to what is secondary. *Psychoanalytic Dialogues,* 22, 395–409.

Taylor, C. (2007). Review of *Radical hope: Ethics in the face of cultural devastation* by Jonathan Lear. *The New York Review of Books,* LIV (7), 4–8.

Trungpa, C. (2005). *The sanity we are born with: A Buddhist approach to psychology* (CR Gimian, Ed.). Shambhala Publications.

Trungpa, C. (2009). *Smile at fear: Awakening the true heart of bravery* (CR Gimian, Ed.). Shambhala Publications.

Williams, MH. (2010). *Bion's dream: A reading of the autobiographies.* Karnac.

Winnicott, DW. (1963). The development of the capacity for concern. *Bulletin of the Menninger Clinic,* 27, 167–76.

Winnicott, DW. (1971/2005). *Playing and reality.* Routledge.

Chapter 6

Reading the works of Michael Eigen

Artist of the invisible

Shalini Masih

> To have a successful dream is not just to feel better, to succeed in wish-fulfilment, but to nibble on what is bothering one a little more. Nibbling on what is bothering one sooner or later brings one to a nameless irritant built into life, an agony that remains invisible no matter how one names it. Exploding dream bubbles challenges us to become artists of the invisible.
>
> Michael Eigen, *Feeling Matters* (2018a, p. 28)

In this chapter, the author as an apprentice of Eigen for many years, nibbles on Eigen's work with his patients in a bid to meditate on the unconscious wisdom guiding the thinker's clinical work where he emerges as an "artist of the invisible." Clinical moments are picked up where Eigen uses his astute clinical sensibilities to capture those invisible aches engraved on the walls of his patients' inner home leaving them haunted. The author also reflects on her own sessions with Eigen and how reading his works has informed her own clinical work with clients in India.

What would be a befitting tribute to Eigen, or Mike as he's addressed lovingly by his students? How can one possibly capture the depth and range of his ideas? How could I possibly write about how his ideas have shaped and saved me? Like a firefly mind fluttered from one thought to another, as another part of me frantically tried to catch it. I found my anchor in Mike's wisdom – our ability to produce states will always be ahead of our ability to process them: Something settled.

When this chapter was taking form within me, I was struggling with a male patient who brought his intense erotic feelings towards me. I felt them as intensely towards him as he towards me. I often caught myself fantasizing about being intimate with him. It disturbed me. I worked with his fantasies about us while remaining guilty of having similar fantasies of my own! I sat in sessions struggling to sustain thinking while being alive to waves of pulsating sensations across my body. My memory of reading about Mike's work with Ruth and Cynthia nudged me to write to Mike for guidance. How to escape love so powerful and haunting? – I asked Mike. How did he survive the love of his patients? Mike, at his cryptic best, responded: "How'd I get through it? Just lived through it. Endurance? Enjoy the loving feeling and keep on keeping on … keep on being and working … Time is important."

Making time for time

Mike's responses were scarce and cryptic. Like a midwife for thought that struggled to be born, Mike left room for more. At first, his response created an irritation. He was inviting me for creative waiting rather than succumbing to intensities. I sat in sessions, permeable to intense feelings, with no way of thinking through them or evacuating them in reciprocal action. Mike reminds us, "How the clinician relates to realizations of his or her own permeability (and of the patient's) is crucial in determining the direction of defensive operations in the therapeutic partnership" (Eigen, 2018b, p. 183). I could sense I was oblivious and an "invisible ache" resided in the gap between mind and body. Like a ghost, it crept in through the cracks in awareness, in my intense, haunting, and unthinkable love for my patient.

Mike helps take notice of how the body morphs around psychic malaise and psychic health. His work emphasizes the contribution of mind and body and "seeks to release their evolution and interplay." He considers tuning into body self and mental self as an indispensable part of a useful clinical encounter. In Mike's own words, "In a sense, my work is a kind of biography of body self/mental self in heart-to-heart, mind-to-mind encounter" (Eigen, 1992). How did Mike hold the tension of passionate and agonizing intensities in his clinical work while his patients remained oblivious to them? It is as if that which lies "invisible" in psyche makes its reverberations felt in the intensities that haunt the clinician. What about moments which drove Mike to the edge of experiencing, until he clinched the invisible ache in his patient emerging as an artist of the invisible, a master clinician, and an ascetic of desire.

One pertinent case from Mike's early years comes to mind. Dee was one of the first cases Mike worked with. "A vegetative pubertal girl, epileptic and schizophrenic," remotely interested in her surroundings, spending most of her time watching television and occasionally masturbating, dependent on others for her care. She was believed to be suffering progressive brain deterioration. To Mike, she seemed most alive in her seizures, "her skin had colour: Her body filled out, and she became a mass of explosive movement" (Eigen, 2018b, p. 186). Although she seemed to be unconscious throughout these episodes, Mike sensed a presence:

> I was stunned at believing I saw staring through her eyes a devil, a malevolent core of consciousness at the heart of her apparent oblivion. It was a searing look, pure hate, a mocking laser. As I looked more closely, I believed I saw malicious glee and ghastly suffering combined, but also something regal and haughty and even prankish, as though the devil were

sticking his tongue out and defiantly saying, "Okay, let's see what you can do." At the same time this presence was walled off and electrical … One day, as Dee started a seizure and flashed her spiteful leer, I found myself screaming, "You bitch!" The grand mal instantaneously stopped, and she glowered. I believe her real progress with me dated from this episode.

(Eigen, 2018b, p. 187)

The wall of mutual invisibility came crumbling down. Mike made space for himself in her perceptual field. She began to notice him, trying extra hard to blot him out. Despite her fierce "walled-offness," Mike could also see longing and suffering, her seizures as a baby's helpless fit, recurrent SOS signals using the body to break into visibility. He had a dream:

I dreamt that Dee was underwater without knowing how to swim. I was trying to teach her. Her parents held her under each time she tried to surface, yet refused to let her either swim or drown. She already showed signs of decomposition but quickly reached out to me.

(Eigen, 2018b, p. 187)

Beaten down by impingement from parents, the Dee in the dream was not without hope. The dream carried Mike's own capacity to strive for building adequate psychic processes. Yet he wondered if she were not in some way using his capacities to create an image she needed but lacked the resources to create herself. Faced with slyness in actual Dee, Mike wondered if she was deriving pleasure in "making herself known in unseen ways." Dreaming continued in reverie as Dee and Mike continued to converse, unconscious to unconscious.

Mike wrote,

I conceived an urge to put my hand in her mouth … I was well aware of its hostile and sexual connotations as well as its impatient and possibly defensive mothering. I also felt it was a linking gesture, however negative … At first she did not seem to notice, and I simply waited. For an instant I experienced her like the proverbial woman who smokes during sexual intercourse. She eventually turned her head to look at me with dismay, the most direct and empathic look of recognition I had yet experienced from her. She tried to collapse and ignore what was happening, but I continued thrusting my fingers into her mouth. Almost without warning she reared to full height, stared at me with outrage, and screamed. I maintained my hand in position as best I could without choking her, and she bit me. I could tell she was biting me with all her might, but I could not feel any pain. I felt only joy. She rose up in indignant majesty and beat me to her heart's content, pummelling any part of my face or body she could contact. She looked righteous and queenly and radiant, a mixture of imperious incredulity and chagrin: "How dare you affront Her Majesty!" It was the first physical exercise I had seen her take outside of her seizures.

(Eigen, 2018b, p. 188)

Her seizures began to diminish. She was alive, her skin acquired a glow, her speech improved, and she began to help herself. The change was slow and was reflected in a dream Mike dreamt for both himself and Dee:

A man's face, simply there, a pure resonant passivity expressively waiting. This face had an unintrusive look one could trust; evoked by the change in Dee, it doubtless reflected a quality that had informed my work all along but of which I was unaware. I suspected it also mirrored what was most positive in Dee's mutilated passivity. The dream heightened my awareness and made me more appreciative of a very valuable kind of passivity, a most precious capacity indeed (possibly Dee's lasting contribution to my sense of self).

(Eigen, 2018b, p. 188)

A second moment from recent times was when nervous about my first meeting with a luminary like Mike, I walked in his office. I stood wide-eyed, facing the stacks of Mike's works in his waiting room. I had stumbled upon a treasure. Mike's voice broke the spell. In his toddler-like aliveness, he said "*Shalini! You found my jelly beans!*" I chuckled. The toddler is curious, and unlike the infant, he is in touch with the ground, humble, greets the "new" with "awe" and excited with the ever-growing capacity to use his limbs in ways not imagined before. Mike, the toddler eased something in me.

I opened the session with a dream which was like the previous day:

ME: I landed in NYC in early morning hours. My aunt picked me up from the airport and took me to her place. I was jetlagged, so I decided to sleep for a bit. I slept. My sleep was interrupted with sounds of gunshots, bombings, and people screaming. A loud thud suggested that someone had broken in my aunt's house. She must have been in the living room. I heard her scream. There were some gunshots. Then she stopped screaming. I knew there were terrorists in the house. Perhaps, I will be shot too because I was Indian. Footsteps approached the bedroom I was in. Somebody opened the door. I saw the terrorist standing on the threshold, and the dream ended.

M.E.: What did the terrorist look like?

ME: I don't know. His face was covered with a black cloth. He wore black.

M.E.: *You* are wearing Black.

Insight is violent. Mike heard the SOS signals from the terrorized and ter-rorizing parts residing in the depths of my being. Little did I know, I was the terrorist I needed to dream. Mike's contribution to the discipline of psychoa-nalysis lies in situating his works in "excess," in intense agonies and ecstasies and the "invisible ache" that feeds them, and in meeting the challenge of our ever-evolving make-up.

What enabled Mike to "sense" the invisible, whether it is the demonic and/ or terrorist part playing hide and seek. It was as if Mike had a multisensory self at work, allowing him to possess a 360-degree vision as well as a scotopic vision. The former lets him see and share various vantage points while the latter makes it possible for him to adapt his vision to the bleakest clinical mo-ments. Perhaps it is these two features of his clinician self that let Mike convey that he will give time to *time* for some "knowing" to be arrived at. Rumi-nating on the face from Mike's dream – "a man's face, simply there, a pure resonant passivity expressively waiting" – and surrounded by Mike's works scattered on my desk like a toddler's jelly beans, I think of two spindles – Shame and The Maternal. It is as if around these two spindles is woven a multisensory self which can help cultivate psychic sensors to facilitate a vision for those invisible aches that plague the psychic constellations we deal with.

Shame

Reading Mike as an artist who clinches that which thrives in invisibility, I was gifted with a reverie by the many gods that surround me in Indian soil. The reverie is a story from *Ramayana*. Many dreams ago, in a forest there lived a sage named *Gautam* with his beautiful wife *Ahalya* who was once a nymph. Her beauty was unparalleled in the three universes. Even gods could not escape being held captive by her radiant beauty. The king of gods himself, Lord *Indra*, suffered pangs of passion for *Ahalya* wishing to attain her by trick-ery. The omnipresent god became a stalker. One day, in the absence of sage *Gautam*, *Indra* approached *Ahalya* in the guise of her husband. They made love. The real sage *Gautam* found out and cursed *Indra* to have a thousand vaginas all over his body. Ashamed, Lord *Indra* went into hiding. Concerned, the gods intervened and appealed to the sage *Gautam*. He agreed to reduce the extent of the curse. The thousand vaginas all over *Indra's* body were trans-formed into a thousand eyes. This myth can and has been interpreted in many ways. For instance, Wendy Doniger (1999) has written a detailed discussion of this myth. For the purpose of this chapter, I shall use the image of a "body with thousand vaginas transformed into thousand eyes" to help us understand the fate of failed appetites that turn into invisible aches, the immensity of desires leading to Shame and the transformation of Shame into the function of "psychic sensing" in a clinician's self.

In *Madness and Murder* (Eigen, 2018c), Mike draws from Freud's wisdom and reflects on "psychic sensing." Alluding to Freud's idea about ego as an organ of psychic sensing, he wrote, "Part of a model for work … is that because of our ability to sense the psyche, a kind of psychic sensing, we may spontaneously at times unveil for patients senses that they didn't know they had."

In order to cultivate this "psychic sensing," the therapist is required to undertake the journey suggested by the myth. Mind, like the sage *Gautam*, aims for infinite boundlessness. While body, like Ahalya, longs to touch aliveness. Eros, notorious like *Indra*, tantalizes the body with a promise of fusion with the mind, their union is a sure shot at a fuller experience. At times patients make relentless efforts at experiencing body aliveness through many sexual experiences. Each time the illusion of such a fusion shatters, the mind becomes further distant from the body. Result – a cursed, stupefied, numb body, a state of depersonalization.

Two crucial moments from Mike's journey stand out. Meditating on Shame (Eigen, 2018e), Mike recalls a moment from his childhood when he was 7 or 8 years old. His father would threaten to hit him, and he turned into steel. Mike wondered, "Did my father induce shame and something in me refused it? A steel won't." To steel or to become opaque is to deprive the other of the satisfaction of leaving an impact on oneself. Tables turn. Passivity is mutilated because becoming passive becomes associated with Shame. But the possibility to grow out of other's impact also gets foreclosed. Being permeable or steeling oneself, both feed Shame.

Just like for Indra's body covered with a thousand vaginas, in Shame the other is experienced as penetrating through many entry points but without exit. Mike's steeled off self unfroze into a raging scream. I wonder if the scream screamed was the one withheld by steeling one from father's beating. Ushered by Winnicott's wisdom which saw scream as a link between psyche and soma, it is as if, the steel armour of Shame could be shed, and one could taste raw vitality. Mike wrote, "Screaming … got me in touch with my body, open body self in new ways … My heart was a vagina opening … Raging scream and vaginal heart, strange twins in the shock and thrill of self …" (Eigen, 2002). Elsewhere, Mike recalls:

> As a young man in a bio-energetic class, the leader tried an intervention in which I lay over his back, back on back, and he pulled me up, off the ground, and bent slightly forward, so that my back stretched and arched, a bow. I did not expect what happened. When he asked what I felt, I said, "Like a vagina." My whole body became a vagina. You might say, an imaginary vagina. But at that moment I was filled with ineffable sensation that brought me to another reality. I am tempted to use a Bion notation and say, I got a taste of O-itself, all through my body, which opened dimensions of experience I did not know before…
>
> (Eigen, 2018d)

These anecdotes bring to mind Pollak's (2009) ideas on the frontal spine.

> The frontal spine links up the processing and organizing of sensory perceptions (the head); the stabilizing rhythmic continuity of sucking, breathing and uttering (the chest); filling, emptying, digesting, internalizing, projecting and transforming (the stomach); and controlling and organizing purposeful movement between inside and outside (the lower orifices). It can be fully realized only in the context of object relations … On turning your back on someone, the motivation is "frontal" – protecting bodily soft parts, avoiding eye-contact or communicating withdrawal from object relatedness.

One wonders if the anecdotes shared above opened up mind–body to an active relatedness with its functions of seeing, verbalizing, or communicating.

The heightening of perception becomes part of one's repertoire in Shame,

> a heightened sense of being or being in jeopardy. It can bring to bear capacities that contribute to the feeling of being me, making me self-aware through heightened self-consciousness. It is also in touch with another's awareness, particularly the other's perception of me, real or imaginary. An acute sense of the other's subjective view of me can grow to encompass realisation of my effect on the other … A heightened concern with my own reality can evoke awareness of the sensitive centre of the other as well …
>
> (Eigen, 2018d, p. 77)

Coming through Shame by giving space to hidden screams could open up pores in the self that one did not know were closed. It is as if, the many passive vagina-like-openings transformed into heightened sensing (many eyes or I's or selves) and make way for a *pure resonant passivity expressively waiting*, a capacity that Dee made Mike aware of. Mike "dropped deeper into body and self-sensing unending nuances of what it feels like to be alive" (Eigen, 2002).

The experience of being permeable to an other's perception is only too familiar. I once walked around with a haunting sense that my words will be judged. In other words, my mouth ought to elicit gold. I remained silent in group situations, fearing that I will not make sense. When my efforts were met with mockery, it only heightened Shame. I shut myself further in. Like a shaman, Mike gave me a mantra to chant for a little while, "Mike says I can't do anything wrong" (Eigen, personal communication, June 28, 2014).

Something shifted. Instead of a sense of grandiosity, a sense of responsibility dawned upon me. I felt responsible for Mike, who now took room inside me. The reckless internal critic took less space. The body which spoke thoughts had to be mind-full. Psyche and Soma had to come together to make sure that I did not fail Mike's belief in me. If Shame focused my perception outwards, the purpose Mike propelled turned it inwards. What others would think of my thoughts became less important. Mike had become a vitalizing object. In his chapter on Shame (Eigen, 2018d), Mike reflects,

> I sometimes tell people to think, "I can't do anything wrong." Say it over and over, live with it like a mantra. Far from stimulating grandiosity, the opposite often occurs. Humility and assurance grows, shame shrinks, takes up less room, is less gripping and overpowering. It doesn't go away in defeat, but finds its place in the larger whole, tempers but does not obliterate.
>
> (Eigen, 2018d, p. 86)

The Maternal

I was visiting NYC for the second time and was looking forward to seeing Mike for a session. A friend asked me what fee I paid Mike. Fee? It hit me then that my sense of entitlement had blinded me enough to even be curious about paying him his fee! Shame returned. How did it not occur to me that I was to pay for the sessions Mike offered? I was prepared to pay him but also to discuss this major lapse from my end. I walked into Mike's office in October 2017. As I sat I could feel my cheeks and ears were flushed. Something in me couldn't meet his eyes. Mike began the session.

M.E.: What are you hiding?
ME: [Had he noticed the blush?] What thrives in hiding?
M.E.: You are very talented.
ME: No. I am ashamed.

Mike invited me to talk more about my Shame, and I went on apologizing for a few minutes. How could I be so greedy? With greed so blinding, how could I ever imagine motherhood? Being a mother would mean to shrink in order to make room for another being. And I had only begun to express my appetites. Mike interrupted my rant,

M.E.: Why are you so starved?

Starved? Before this, I had heard that I have been deprived. The "deprivation" logic led my perception outwards. The sources of my deprivation were outside. It helped only temporarily. Mike's words, the ("starvation" logic) sharpened the perception inwards. My appetites were internal, so were my inhibitions. I fumbled to respond and repeated something about remaining starved to nurture the imagination of motherhood. Motherhood would demand that I practiced restraint on my appetites. Mike challenged.

M.E.: Well, enjoy them!

Until this point, I had not thought of motherhood including a licence to indulge one's appetites. What kind of mother would I become if I did not value my own desires? Was it possible to be a mother and be oneself? Something shifted. I came back to India. Months later, there was enough ease in me to conceive the idea of motherhood.

The first trimester of my pregnancy was a period plagued with palpable anxieties. A nightmare, like a colicky infant, kept me awake. Each time I tried to fall asleep I dreamt of a 6- or 7-year-old girl, standing on the threshold of my bedroom door, waiting for me to fall asleep so she could possess me and replace my baby in the womb. This nightmare persisted. Until one night during the nightmare there was an auditory dream, a male voice said, "You should keep your grandmother close." It was most bizarre. I was close to my grandmother, but never ever did I think of also reflecting on her capacities when I was still doing my doctoral research. She could see ghosts, talk to them, and relay messages from them to their grieving family members. As a child, I felt I would disrupt something in her if I asked whether these ghosts visited her her or if she created them. She would receive the ghosts with a maternal attitude. Sitting in the next-ness to the memory of my grandmother's easy being, I found myself floating from one room to another in my house, helping myself to food and humming *La vie en rose* to myself and the life growing in me. Love was growing.

The nightmares stopped, and I shared this movement with Mike. He responded,

> To be maternal even to ghosts!!!! Motherly to what is scary. This has application to baby too, who at times can be too much, scary, demanding, needy, and so much more and else we have no words for. And yet being in this position forces us to grow in ways we were unable to before, perhaps didn't even know about.
>
> (Eigen, personal communication, May 27, 2018)

Yet again, Mike was alluding to the "invisible" and a maternal attitude to approach it with. The ghost was a nightmare, a damaged dream, a dream aching to be dreamt like an alive baby, kicking to be born. Psyche froze in the face of aliveness.

The invisible ache that one encounters in Mike's clinical work as an "artist of the invisible" is perhaps like the jabs of the unborn embryonic parts of the self. In his recent work, Mike notes, "Throughout our lives we are pregnant with our lives, pregnant with unborn selves and psychic babies, including thoughts, feelings, attitudes, modes of experiencing. A pregnancy that never stops, no matter how many births. Gestation does not end" (Eigen, 2018d). As mother-to-be, I felt at ease by Mike's and my grandmother's maternal attitude, to "sense" the movements of my baby. Approaching my pregnancy with the attitude of extending the maternal even to what scared me, opened me to love I had neither known nor thought I was capable of. It was the love towards someone I had not even met or seen yet, it remained invisible but whose movements, even contours of whose ever-growing and forming body I could feel. In addition to opening to faith and traversing through Shame, during pregnancy I felt a sharpening of my perceptual organ as my innards groped in the darkness of my womb meeting this unseen life, with each meeting knowing a little more about it and in turn being known, lovingly so. Psyche sensing psyche. Body sensing body. Perhaps I dreaded the aliveness of my baby which would have possessed me ruthlessly, throwing me in a state of unbearable mutilated passivity. The maternal attitude to that which terrified made it possible for me to be passive – resonant and expressively anticipating the birth. As a mother, and by extension as a therapist, I am learning to acknowledge my own desires and appetites, so my daughter (and patients) learns to acknowledge her (and their) own and to be okay with being an imperfect ordinary mother (and therapist) who does not always know what to do but falls back in faith on her own intuition and makes time for time that gestation of thought demands. On some days I break down, I get angry, I cry, but mostly I and my daughter are growing together in loving embrace.

Beginning again

> We are bees of the invisible. We madly gather the honey of the visible to store it in the great golden hive of the invisible.
>
> Rainer Maria Rilke (1996)

In his clinical encounters, Mike seems to be perched in darkness, like an ascetic on the edge of his desires or heightened emotional experience, his fantasies always on the verge of coming true. On this cliff his harness remains a "blind faith, that whatever happens, good would come of it." "Faith in the process." Eigen (1973) distinguishes daily living with psychotherapy on the axis of heightened truth-freedom that bypasses acting out and compromises of all kinds. To his patients' desire for him, he would respond with a life-affirming no, validating feelings, something that he also picked from his own experience of having similar feelings for his analyst Dorothy Bloch. Not only do feelings matter, but they also demand that one "makes time" for feelings. Communication in therapy is affectively charged; the juices of Eros are always dripping and seeping in to make the soil of therapy fertile. Analytic experience then remains the closest approximation to "experience proper."

Green (2005) wrote about analytic speech that it takes mourning out of language. It is palpable with affective intensities. Giving primacy to faith in time renders structure to intensities of ecstasies and agonies, challenging the therapist and patient to stretch their capacities. The psychoanalytic ethic then lies in giving primacy to the opening of psychic reality. The tension between lure stemming from our carnal nature and the call of this psychoanalytic ethic is held along with the pulsating anticipation that accompanies it. In therapy, it becomes possible to tame the recklessness of affective intensities in the service of opening one's psyche.

The body-ego's propensity towards fusion and explosiveness coupled with a mental-ego propelled towards megalomania forms the patterns that one encounters when working with aspects of the baby self. Thinking about his clinical encounters with patients, Mike reflects on the "Age of the Baby." When working with very damaged self-feelings, Mike would ask:

> "What kind of baby is here now? What is the baby doing now, and now, and now?" The therapist always asked: "What image or reconstruction of the baby fits this moment most effectively? What kind of baby must be envisioned so that the complex feelings and behaviour now arising can be most usefully understood?" Felt reverberations that often characterize mother-baby experience were imaginatively reworked to crystallise into an inner methodology that made therapeutic contact work …
>
> (Eigen, 2018b, pp. 206, 207)

I think of my daughter when she was only a few months old: In one instance, she saw me at a distance and moved her arm in the air to grab me. Realizing that she could not touch me but could see me, she increasingly became irritable. Her vision made her mind believe that she could touch her mother. However, her body was limited. Her frustration said that her body could not reach where her vision could. I had to remain alive to these subtle moments and help her mourn the distance between the flights of her mind and the limits of her body. This reverie and tolerance for the baby's aliveness helped in return of thinking in my work with the patient I fell in love with. The excess of feelings I felt for him also spoke of his expansiveness that I failed to sense before. As I stayed with these feelings he went on to talk about his vision for his life – to be a therapist, a musician, earn a lot of money, travel, to learn to play every musical instrument. He then sighed and touched frustration.

S: There is so much to do. What do I do?

ME: Perhaps you suffer because your mind makes you see so many things you could do, but you still have to be where your body is.

It hit home. Gradually his mind began to work towards things he *can* do.

That which is different feels excessive and terrifies us. The mother receives the difference in the baby with love. Mike's work helps us to see therapy as a space like the one shared between mother and child, marked by a maternal attitude towards what scares one the most, a space for feelings, for intensities to be held with a faith that whatever happens will open psychic reality. It is this "pause" that is becoming increasingly absent from our world today. Emotional capacities are stunted. Psychic democracy, an easy relationship between pluralities that make the self and by extension make a nation, is under threat. The thoughts I have tried to share on Mike as an artist of the invisible may be crystallized into this one image from Mike's dream – "a man's face, simply there, a pure resonant passivity expressively waiting...an unintrusive look one could trust ..." Mike makes me wonder what would it mean to allow oneself to be passive and receive the other, to wait in the dark, like an ascetic who is perched at the edge of the cliff, his fantasies always on the verge of becoming true. He carries a maternal sentiment with which to welcome that which is terrifying. One hopes that this chapter, as an ode to Mike, has been able to offer a successful dream, to offer something that can be nibbled and gradually constitutes one's blood and bones.

I end with gratitude towards
the stars above immigrant Jersey town of Passaic
reflected in the twinkling eyes of a 2-year-old Mike
to the sweet wetness of the first kiss at the age of 17
indeed like in dreaming and later in dreamlike sessions,
stars could be seen in broad day light
to Plato for basic goodness
to Socrates for love of Truth
to Cummings and Joyce
for plasticity of words
that let self breathe easier
to endless conversations with God
to the radiant face of Rabbi Kellner
to Sports for augmenting Body Sensing
to Vivaldi and Jazz improvisation
to Jung &
Freud & Winnicott,
Bion & Buber
Elkin & Rilke
to Ruth, Dee, Smith, Cynthia
& every other heart
to Mike's heart that split open
to light that shined through
to discovery of heart within heart within heart
for giving us Mike.

References

Doniger, W. (1999). *Splitting the difference: Gender and myth in ancient Greece and India.* The University of Chicago Press.

Eigen, M. (1973). The call and the lure. *Psychotherapy: Theory, Research and Practice*, 10, 194–97.

Eigen, M. (1992). *Coming through the whirlwind: Case studies in psychotherapy.* Chiron Publications.

Eigen, M. (2002). *Rage.* Wesleyan University Press.

Eigen, M. (2006). *Age of psychopathy.* Retrieved from www.psychoanalysisand-therapy.com/human_nature/eigen/pref.html.

Eigen, M. (2018a). *Feeling matters.* Routledge.

Eigen, M. (2018b). *The electrified tightrope.* Routledge.

Eigen, M. (2018c). *Eigen in Seoul: Madness and murder.* Routledge.

Eigen, M. (2018d). *Image, sense, infinities and everyday life.* Routledge.

Green, A. (2005). *Key ideas for a contemporary psychoanalysis: Misrecognition and recognition of the unconscious.* Routledge.

Pollak, T. (2009). The "body-container": A new perspective on the "body-ego." *International Journal of Psychoanalysis*, 90, 487–506.

Rilke, R.M. (1996). "Letter to Witold von Hulewicz." *Selected Letters 1902–1926.* Cited in *The Inner Eye* by Marina Warner. National Exhibitions/South Bank Centre.

Chapter 7

Chasing the uncatchable

Mystery and metaphor in the work of Michael Eigen

Sean Harrell

I first came into contact with the work of Michael Eigen while training as a pre-doctoral intern. Adrift in a foreign place, working for the first time with deeply disturbed patients in an intensive psychoanalytic therapy setting, I was eager as ever for some voice to help me make sense of the difficult work I was trying to do. I was looking for clarity, in truth certainty, a theoretical dogma that I could rest in like a safe ship amidst a sea of psychosis. Instead, I found Eigen's *The Psychotic Core* and it was unbearable to me.

I remember a feeling like I was reading about madness from the inside. A structured text but with a wildness about it. Associative and authoritative, as if written from someone fluent in the native tongue of psychosis, the depths of human experience. It was a kind of reading that strained me immensely.

I was looking for a creedal formulation and found a mystic; looking for a ship safely above the *waves* and found someone signalling me to dip into the waters. I stopped reading him, only to be led back a few short years later, this time by means of a new hand, that of my analyst. Another hand to guide me into the waters perhaps. I remember lying hour after hour on my analyst's couch, gazing up at titles like *Rage, Lust, Ecstasy, Toxic Nourishment, Psychic Deadness*: The language of experience, a call that grew louder and louder.

Soon, I waded into the first few titles, *Rage, Lust,* and *Ecstasy.* In *Rage* (2002), Eigen begins with an imaginary dialogue:

> "I'm right, you're wrong," says Rage.
> "No, *I'm* right, *you're* wrong," says Rage.
> "We're right, we're wrong," says the Yearning for Something More.
>
> (no page number)

In *Lust* (2006) he shares his childhood stories of being a sick child, of kissing girls, and of masturbating endlessly, day and night.

Early on in *Ecstasy* (2001) he laments a therapeutic misstep, bemoaning his encouraging words forming where silence would be better: "How Pollyanish, corrupt. To say it would spoil everything. In the end, I'm like all therapists, like all parents, wanting something to come of it. In spite of myself, the words push out" (p. 16).

These were honest books, psychoanalytic books of poetry, coupled with theoretical and clinical wisdom, well digested and ready for use.

In a way, I needed to find Eigen's work to find something of my own voice. I am grateful, and am still reading him; still following threads he presents, leading me to others of my own, which of course lead to new paths, new threads for myself and for my patients. I focus less on the reaching, take more pleasure in the searching. After all, as Eigen has said, "One works with the uncatchable" (Eigen, 2016, p. 23).

★ ★ ★ ★

With remarkable breadth and depth, Eigen draws widely from the history of psychoanalytic thinking. However, the double influence of Donald Winnicott and Wilfred Bion runs like a neon thread throughout all of his work – at times explicitly stated, at other times, implied. In this chapter, I want to focus specifically on his use of Winnicott and Bion. More specifically still, I want to focus on two aspects of this double influence – Mystery and Metaphor. By this I mean Eigen's unique use of Bion and his concept of "O" to deepen the sense of the mysterious, the unknowable, the searching within psychoanalysis, and his use of Winnicott's play-centric, creative, and metaphorical therapeutic language.

In exploring mystery and metaphor, I will orient my thoughts around a brief clinical vignette of Eigen's work with a patient. I chose this particular interview for a couple of reasons: First, it was, and remains, deeply moving to me in ways that I cannot fully understand. Like other portions of Eigen's writing, I recalled attempting to read this session aloud to a colleague, only to suddenly become unexpectedly choked with tears, moved but in ways still mysterious to me. As such, I was drawn to the interview time and time again. Second, as I continued to return to the interview, sharing it with others, I was repeatedly impressed by the variety of responses and reactions. Some found it profound, moving; others expressed confusion at a bizarre encounter, something perhaps difficult to categorize or recognize as "therapy." *However*, each time *I* returned to the interview, something new stood out me: A fresh observation, association, question. And the interview naturally became, in my mind, emblematic of Eigen's unique voice and rich contributions. He was, once again, showing me a way of swimming in tumultuous waters.

★ ★ ★ ★

Before moving on to the interview, a brief word about Winnicott's play and Bion's O.

Winnicott proposed that play is universal, and that psychoanalytic experience be thought of as a variety of play. More than a simple analogue, Winnicott (1989) told us, "Psychotherapy takes place in the overlap of two areas of playing, that of the patient and that of the therapist. Psychotherapy has to do with two people playing together" (p. 38). The profundity of this notion may be too easily lost in its simplicity. It is a fundamental recasting of the vision of the psychoanalytic experience. Psychoanalysis is still, of course, a talking cure and our play is in the realm of the verbal, but Winnicott offers us different ears with which to hear. He says,

> I suggest that we must expect to find playing just as evident in the analyses of adults as it is in the case of our work with children. It manifests itself, for instance, in the choice of words, in the inflections of the voice, and indeed in the sense of humour.
>
> (Winnicott, 1989, p. 40)

The play I want to attend closely to today is Eigen's choice of words, often metaphorical, playful, improvisational language that, together with his patients' words, create a shared scene, like a child with a doll house, within which they act out various versions of reality.

What is meant by O? At times O is Bion's notation for all unknowable reality: Phrases like "ultimate reality," "fundamental reality," "the thing-in-itself," "infinity," "ultimate truth," and even "the godhead," are often used. In the context of a psychoanalysis, however, we may begin to narrow O to the O of the session, that is the immediate emotional reality of the session, the psychic depths which can only be intuited, grasped at, never fully apprehended by the senses. This is important. O cannot be "known" in the way that sensory data can be known, through seeing, hearing, and so on, but only intuited[1]; one's experience of O is not knowing O, but "becoming" O.

James Grotstein (1997) has said of O, "One cannot know 'O'; one must resonate with it in a transformation or evolution in 'O'" (p. 13).

Eigen (1981) reflects, "this is paradoxical: An unknowable is to be the focus of our attention" (p. 423). From another angle, Joseph Aguayo (2019) has said,

> [Bion's] fundamental presumption is: "I am missing something." ... Bion was more preoccupied with what was absent than what was present in the clinical situation. Bion did not treat any insight, however hard gained and temporarily illuminating, as a final resting place ... What matters is what happens next.
>
> (p. 43)

It is this presumption of *more*, the continuous chasing of the mysterious un-known that I want to, together with Winnicott's play, explore in the clinical interview below.

★ ★ ★ ★

The interview is presented without context. Eigen only described the inter-view as "A few moments dialogue in a session with a man who has not had to return to hospital since we began speaking" (personal communication, May 25, 2018). The patient begins:

D.N: I am turning into a barnacle.
M.E: So there is transformation, at least change going on.
D.N: You must be kidding. You can't mean it.
M.E: You detect a note of irony?
D.N: I fear sincerity. Sincerity is a cage.
M.E: So you live in water without being caught?
D.N: I am made of shells within shells.
M.E: Yet …
D.N: Yet my sensors are growing inside you. I am inside you.
M.E: Absorbing nourishment with your sensors?
D.N: Quietly. You can't feel me, see me, hear me.
M.E: But we are talking …
D.N: I mean my sensors inside you, quietly feeding …
M.E: Do I mind?
D.N: You will vanish without knowing. Only a shell will be left.
M.E: Did someone feed on you? Eat your insides?
D.N: But my sensors are still here. I still have my sensors.
M.E: You are eating my insides. Am I eating yours?
D.N: You backed against a wall.
M.E: I don't think I meant to take away your room. I'm sorry if I did.
D.N: You reach me when you say things like that. No one talks to me that way.
M.E: And how do *you* talk to you?
D.N: I feel you know there is a monster that turns me into a shell.
M.E: Thank god for sensors. How is it possible they survive?
D.N: That's a mystery. Shells with sensors, sensors with shells.
M.E: We are very sensitive. We are almost pure sensitivity.
D.N: Even with shells.
M.E: Sometimes shells make us more sensitive.
D.N: I'm afraid we are running out of time, and I haven't told you how awful it is to be eaten by a monster inside the sensors.

M.E: Everything is in jeopardy.

D.N: Yes, everything.

M.E: I feel like making a psalm for the living sensors, even with monsters within.

D.N: Have you felt worms inside your head?

M.E: Bad thoughts?

D.N: No, more. Worms.

M.E.: Like in a corpse?

D.N.: You're getting closer.

M.E: Closer to what it feels like being you?

D.N: Yes.

M.E: All the time?

D.N: Almost all the time. Once I would have said yes, all the time. But it is not all the time now.

M.E: Thank God.

D.N: Not sure whom to thank or how – moments of life.

M.E: With all the monsters, shells, and eating oneself alive.

D.N: With all the worms eating my insides.

M.E: And mine. I am thankful for some better moments wherever they come from.

D.N: I am thankful too, even if they come and go. Something comes up. I want to say thank you.

M.E: Thank you too. It sometimes is good to be together.

D.N: It can be.

(Eigen, 2018b, pp. 1–2)

What have we just read? What is happening in this exchange? Surely more than could be unpacked in one hour, or one day's time. These words paint a profound picture of the human condition, of trauma, of human relatedness, and of the psychotherapeutic endeavour.

"I am turning into a barnacle."

An amazing statement! Surely there are any number of ways one might respond, or not respond, to such a statement. As stated above, Winnicott (1989) told us, "Psychotherapy has to do with two people playing together" (p. 38). I think Eigen's initial response shows us, among other things, what therapeutic play might look like in action. "So there is transformation, at least change going on," he says.

What is crucial about play, in the Winnicottian understanding, is that neither party ever asks, "Is this real or is this make believe?" for to do so would be to collapse the transitional space, the play space between one's mind and the outside world, and would shut down the game. Like Winnicott's squiggle game, a game for two wherein a line or a mark is made on paper by one, and then elaborated into something unexpected by the other, Eigen selects one aspect of the patient's communication, one part of the initial squiggle, and follows it, elaborates it. It seems worth noting that what he does not do is challenge the "reality" of his patient turning into a barnacle, or question why a barnacle, but rather accepts it and accentuates part of the emotional reality: "I am turning into … I am transforming." Here we may detect echoes of Bion's emphasis on transformations present in Eigen's words as well.

What is transforming? We don't know. The patient says he is transforming. I wonder if Eigen hears this as an expression of O – transformations in O. I suspect so. The patient speaks at the level of ontology, being: "I am." And in turn I am reminded of Bion's concept of Faith. Faith in O, denoted by capital F in capital O. For Bion, and for Eigen, Faith as *the* psychoanalytic attitude or posture. Not a religious faith, but a psychoanalytic faith, a deep and profound openness to being moved, carried along by the process.

★ ★ ★ ★

Eigen has written a great deal about Faith. He has said,

> What is faith? Not a question I can answer, but I am poor at answering many questions. How can I write about something without knowing what it is? Without being able to say what it is? Yet it is, at least, so I feel. But faith is more than feeling, at times not even feeling. A felt sense, but not just a felt sense. A mode of cognition? A mode of experiencing? Part of the atmospheric condition of psychic being that helps support the work of other capacities? Premonition? Intimation?
>
> (2014, p. xi)

To all of this we could probably say "yes, and more." This is part of the mystery.

But because every faith, at some eventuality, is tested, there is always danger of a collapse of faith. Collapse into what? Doubt? Eigen is concerned less with doubt resulting from a crisis of faith – or as a defence against faith – and more with omniscience – the quality of knowing all there is to be known.

Eigen cautions, warns, moves endlessly against omniscience. In the language of religion, omniscience is an attribute of the divine. More specifically, it is one of God's incommunicable attributes, that is, is an attribute that belongs to God alone, that cannot be communicated to, shared or participated in by humanity. It is a quality reserved for the divine, denoting fullness and perfection. However, as an attribute of humanity, omniscience is a deadening illusion, maintained by the unconscious, that functions as a barrier between oneself and experience of the outside world. In *The Psychotic Core*, Eigen (1999) writes:

> It is difficult to overestimate the role omniscience plays in deadening one's capacity to experience. If one knows what is going to happen ahead of time, one does not have to experience it. The individual scarcely realizes he is inured in omniscience. In effect, he lives from omniscience without knowing it.
>
> (p. 320)

As a person of religious faith myself, and having academic training in the field of theology – where omniscience is common parlance – it did not initially occur to me that, unlike omnipotence, omniscience is a far less common concept in the psychoanalytic literature. I began to wonder how and why Eigen came to focus on this religiously tinged word in his writing. Omniscience is often associated with immutability and impassibility, other incommunicable divine attributes, equally loaded theological language: God as all-knowing, unchanging, and unsuffering.

While considering omniscience, the story of the Garden of Eden, in the early chapters of Genesis comes to mind – another story contrasting Faith and omniscience. As the serpent says, seducing humanity away from Faith, "when you eat from the tree you will be like God, *knowing* good and evil" (Genesis 3:5, New International Version), yet rather than a pronouncement of divinization humanity received a pronouncement of death.

In a similar vein, Eigen, following Bion, warns of a kind of "psychic deadness" (1996) that follows from too much knowing, or rather the presumption of too much knowing – false omniscience. As quoted above, Eigen links omniscience with an inability to experience: If one knows all there is to know, what is going to happen, one does not need to experience it; if one doesn't experience, surely one can't suffer, and can't change: Impassibility and immutability. Like Eigen's patient: One might become made of shells for pain, attach like a barnacle, cease movement, avoid sincerity because one *knows* sincerity is a cage.

Was the story of the Garden in Eigen's mind, I wonder? Perhaps in the background? Pursuit of too much knowing, or the wrong kind of knowing, or knowing at the wrong time risks deadness. But, as Eigen (2016) has said, "Wait in the unknown and further transformation will occur" (p. 2).

★ ★ ★ ★

So, returning to the session: "There is a transformation, at least change going on." We don't know what kind of change, what kind of transformation, good, bad, or otherwise, but a transformation in the process is noted, which means, if nothing else, the patient is not completely stagnant or unmovable, a far scarier psychological prospect. Where there is transformation, there is still life; there is potential for growth, movement, maybe toward health. Eigen's play keeps things moving.

The patient responds with shock, "You must be kidding. You can't mean it" (Eigen, 2018b, p. 1). Not, I don't think, because Eigen got it wrong, but because he *grasped* something of the emotional reality of the moment and that is *always* a shocking experience. For a person who has known trauma or madness, it may be even more so. As Eigen's patient says, "I fear sincerity. Sincerity is a cage" (Eigen, 2018b, p. 1). Yes, indeed. Bion warned,

> A certain class of patient feels "possessed" by or imprisoned "in" the mind of the analyst if he considers the analyst desires something relative to him – his presence or his cure or his welfare.
>
> (Bion, 1970, p. 42)

That is, for a traumatized person, or a psychotic person – and often the two go together – to be close to another is often a terrifying prospect. Sincerity, a desire to cure, concern – all potential cages to be trapped within.

I wish I had learned this from Eigen sooner. During my pre-doctoral training, while working with a young schizophrenic man, I learned this lesson with startling clarity. During one session, while my patient was describing a memory of watching a particular movie with his family, he asked if I had ever seen the same movie. I replied that I had, that I too used to watch the movie with my own family. I had intended to communicate something warm, a shared humanity, shared experience. However his eyes soon glazed over, and I eventually asked what it was like for him to hear that he and I had that in common, and he replied with wide eyes and a distant gaze, "It's cool; it's like our brains are glued together." He then immediately hallucinated a man in the office whom he described as searching for a pair of scissors in my desk and stated that the man wanted to stab one of us with the scissors. Sincerity and closeness linked with literal fusion (brains glued together), which prompted fear and hallucinated violence, perhaps as a defence, to restore separation (scissors, perhaps also to cut us apart?),[2] perhaps retaliation for my taking over his mind, perhaps both, and more.

"I fear sincerity. Sincerity is a cage" (Eigen, 2018b, p. 1). Again Eigen plays with his response, saying, "so you live in water without being caught?" "I am made of shells within shells." "Yet …" (Eigen, 2018b, p. 1).

Linking the patients earlier use of the barnacle metaphor with the cage metaphor, Eigen offers something new, in the form of an interpretation, yet as a question still pointing toward the further unknown. Playing with words and with possibilities.

★ ★ ★ ★

In Bion's theory of thinking, thoughts, senses, feelings must be linked one to another, and this is a difficult and frustrating psychological work, a capacity that cannot be taken for granted. At times, because of internal emotional turmoil, environmental catastrophe, or both, the links that hold elements of experience together are attacked and severed. Eigen begins implicitly and experientially forming, or re-forming, the links for his patient: Sincerity is linked with emotional closeness, emotional closeness is linked with fear, fear is in turn linked with turning into a barnacle, i.e. perhaps, petrification, de-humanization, immobility, hardness, shells, hiddenness.

In Eigen's interpretive question, we see the "ethics of the unknown" that guides much of his writing. As he says in *Under the Totem*, "one guesses, constructs, tries out. The whole enterprise (i.e. therapy) is more hypothesis making than answering … it is not clear that knowing or knowledge is the main thing at stake, as much as open-ended exploring, asking" (2016, p. 21).

Eigen is with his patient, fully I think. The exploration is a joint one. Two men on a path, poking, prodding about, searching and testing possible "samples of the truth" to use Winnicott's (2018) phrase.

The interview continues, and the patient says, "Yet my sensors are growing inside you. I am inside you." Notice this is another statement like the first, "I am …" No as-if quality, no safe symbolic distance. This *is* reality for the moment; this *is* the game to be played. And Eigen again stays in character as he questions, "Absorbing nourishment with your sensors?"

"Quietly. You can't feel me, see me, hear me." A moment later, "Do I mind?" The patient tells Eigen, "you can't feel, see, or hear me." One way of hearing this again links up with Bion's concept of O, as something that is beyond the reach of the senses, can only be intuited and known by the senses after it undergoes a psychic transformation. Again, "it is not a matter of knowing O, but of being O" (Eigen, 2018a, p. 73).

Is the patient speaking at the level of O, something that takes place deeper than our physical senses? A kind of immediacy of contact – mind to mind, O to O, perhaps Eigen might say, soul to soul?

★ ★ ★ ★

At times, I am awestruck at the concept of O. At others, filled with scepticism. O feels like too much for me, too unwieldy. Not that I think the truthfulness of a concept depends on my ability to comprehend it. Sometimes there is necessarily a broad cavern between theory and application; sometimes the trek from one side of a cavern to another is the point, a task that must be arduous to be effective. The journey is an essential part of the experience. Still, when I again begin to feel O's unwieldy weight, straining my abilities, it is good to have a guide like Eigen to help illuminate the path.

★ ★ ★ ★

Next, Eigen follows with a question that again "samples the truth," from completely within the play of the session. He offers himself as an object for the patient's use: "Do I mind?" I've always been struck by this question, both what it is and what it is not. He doesn't ask the question in a perhaps more familiar therapeutic style, something akin to: "I wonder if ..." but directly, from the *inside*, "Do I?," as if to say "you write the script; you dream this out loud as you go; I'm playing along; I'm fully available, the breast present, use what you need, how you need it."

Also, in the question "Do I mind?" I hear Bion's famous injunction: "Without memory or desire" (1967). As if Eigen, following Bion, has divested himself of desire, explicitly in this moment: "Do I mind? Maybe I do, maybe I don't; I don't know, we don't know. You make another mark and we'll test that out, follow it."

★ ★ ★ ★

Our patients need us to be particular ways at particular times. They attempt to dress us up as familiar people from their past; too often I am woefully slow to recognize whatever they would have me wear, and when I finally realize it, it is difficult to not resist it. I don't like being cast as a sadist, a voyeur, a weakling, passive and mute, or an aggressor full of judgement and condemnation. Eigen's patient dresses him as an emotional meal, and perhaps a retaliatory cannibal: Someone on whom the patient feeds, and who may in turn feed upon the patient. As the patient fears he will eat all of Eigen's insides, leaving him depleted and empty, only a shell ("You will vanish without knowing, only a shell will be left"), Eigen intuits the patient may fear the same will be done in response, perhaps this has already been done to the patient: A character from a traumatic game played long ago in the patient's memory.

Again, Eigen asks from the inside, suspending his own knowing: "You are eating my insides. Am I eating yours?"

It seems to me that metaphorical questions like these are most fully recognizable as play in the Winnicottian sense of the word. Questions that are asked from within a cycle of assumed projective–introjective identifications, one moment object-relating, another moment object-usage. Slipping back and forth between developmental modes of being. Winnicott, in *The Piggle* (1977), draws a distinction between "playing at" rather than "being in" the situation, identifying "playing at" as a way of maintaining more control over the moment. Eigen demonstrates here a way of being "in" the situation, "surrendering" to it (to use Emmanuel Ghent's elegant expression), moving along with the developmental current of his patient's associations. Again, Faith.

In Eigen's question I am also reminded of Winnicott's emphasis on the link between destruction and creativity. As Eigen (1981) has said, "For Winnicott it is the subject's dawning awareness of the *limitations* of his all out destructive attacks ... that creates the experience of externality as such" (p. 415, italics mine). That is, the subject must experience his own destructiveness and experience the Other's survival of his destructiveness, in order to recognize the

Other as a real, separate subject in her own right. And that is, it seems, what the patient is engaged in here, in this session; the patient is saying, "I am eating you, feeding on you; I am destroying you, yet here you are, here we are. My omnipotence and destructiveness are crashing against your reality, and we're both surviving."

This is Winnicott in a Bionian key. Playing and not knowing.

It combines the interpretive questioning style of Winnicott, as one might encounter in texts like *The Piggle* (1977) or *Holding and Interpretation* (1972), but with what strikes me as a more impressionistic style, more like a jazz musician than I feel in Winnicott; Eigen riffing on Winnicott's original melodies, recognizable but distinctly embellished.

★ ★ ★ ★

The session doesn't go on for long without talk of survival returning again to death in the form of worms and corpses. Dying out, surviving, dying again. A cycle, a pattern in their work together perhaps. I wonder if Eigen noted this in the moment but chose to stay in the immediacy of each line, focusing on the detail of each tree as it were, rather than pulling back and describing the shape the forest. It took me reading many times through the session to notice the movement back and forth from death to life, but when I did I was reminded of Eigen's words from *Under the Totem* (2016),

> My emphasis tends to involve coming through. Over and over, we come through difficulties and mishaps of our personalities in particular situations. We survive ourselves, at times with decent quality. Therapy, as so much of life, is practice in survival and quality of survival. Coming through the muddle, at times the worst. It is an ancient model, destruction and rebuilding of the holy temple, death and resurrection, rebirth rituals.
>
> (p. 6)

Coming through is a difficult task; like a prolonged and repeated birthing process, but a grace when compared to the alternative.

★ ★ ★ ★

The patient asks,

PATIENT: "Have you felt worms inside your head?"
EIGEN: "Bad thoughts?"
PATIENT: "No, more. Worms."

I think this was a kind of miss. Eigen begins to move in one direction, and his patient alerts him that suddenly he feels further way. It reminds me of the childhood game Marco Polo in a way; also like a frequent metaphor of one of my own patients, that of echo location. As if the patient is flying in the dark, aware that something is there, a feeling perhaps, but he needs help to discern its details.

Of course, worms, in this case, are thoughts, or feelings, but "bad thoughts" are a higher transformation of O; the patient is not at that register, and he signals Eigen away from thoughts back to worms, as if to say, "No, stay with me, don't decode this! Worms are worms, and they are inside of me, and it's awful. *Living things* have thoughts; I have been eaten and am *dead* and have worms. Be in the death with me."

And Eigen adjusts, realigns within the play,

"Like in a corpse?"
"You're getting closer."
"Closer to what it feels like being you?"
"Yes."
"All the time?"

Question, question, question, one after the other: A relentless pursuit; the echo location pinging of this experiential contour and that, bringing both therapist and patient closer, a little further down the path.

Again, this is a chasing of the O of the session, the emotional reality. In this moment, the emotional reality is death, yet in contacting it, it is undergoing a change. For Bion, and I think also for Eigen, the reality of death does not need to be interpreted, at least not in a more traditional understanding of that word, but contacted by both therapist and patient; it is likely unfair and inaccurate to draw too firm a dichotomy between understanding and experiencing, surely both are involved to some degree, but the emphasis here is on experiencing. The patient has *become* death, and for Eigen to be helpful, he needs to become death in a way as well. "It is not about knowing O, but becoming O ..."

To Eigen's question, the patient responds,

"Almost all the time. Once I would have said yes, all the time. But it is not
    all the time now."
"Thank God."
"Not sure whom to thank – moments of life."

Moments of life, in death. Brief bits of nourishment the patient finds; perhaps through his feeding on Eigen, through "eating his insides," the patient is regaining his own life blood. The image of a vampire comes to mind, but that is perhaps too pathological. An umbilical cord seems better – moments of life and nourishment are beginning to flow again in a near-stillborn situation.

Eigen soon says,

"I am thankful for some better moments, wherever they come from."
"I am thankful too, even if they come and go. Something comes up. I want
    to say thank you."
"Thank you too. It sometimes is good to be together."
"It can be."

Words like "sometimes"; "can be." Imperfect goodness, but goodness still.
Touched but not fully grasped. This is chasing the uncatchable.

Notes

1   I think, at least within the interpersonal dimension of contacting O, this
    kind of intuiting in some ways bears resemblance to Freud's idea of "thought
    transference."
2   It occurs to me as well the possible significance of hallucinating scissors, some-
    thing which cuts apart – as opposed to some other potential weapon – as po-
    tentially related to a concrete, hallucinated "attack on linking." After all, to
    paraphrase Bion, the most fundamental problems with linking involve links be-
    tween people.

References

Aguayo, J. (2019). Wilfred Bion's Los Angeles seminars (1969): One gateway to con-
    temporary Kleinian technique. In A Alisbhani and G Corstorphine (Eds.), *Explo-
    rations in Bion's O: Everything we know nothing About*. Routledge, pp. 41–50.
Bion, WR. (1967). Notes on memory and desire. *The Psychoanalytic Forum*, 2 (3).
    Retrieved from http://braungardt.trialectics.com/projects/psychoanalysis/bion/
    bion-memory-desire/.
Bion, WR. (1970). *Attention and interpretation*. Rowman & Littlefield.
Eigen, M. (1981). The area of faith in Winnicott, Lacan and Bion. *International Journal
    of Psychoanalysis*, 62, 413–33.
Eigen, M. (1986). *The psychotic core*. Jason Aronson.
Eigen, M. (1996). *Psychic deadness*. Karnac.
Eigen, M. (1999). *Toxic nourishment*. Karnac.
Eigen, M. (2001). *Ecstasy*. Wesleyan University Press.
Eigen, M. (2002). *Rage*. Wesleyan University Press.
Eigen, M. (2006). *Lust*. Wesleyan University Press.
Eigen, M. (2014). *Faith*. Karnac.
Eigen, M. (2016). *Under the totem: In search of a path*. Karnac.
Eigen, M. (2018a). *The challenge of being human*. Routledge.
Eigen, M. (2018b). Fragment of a session published in The International Society for
    Psychological and Social Approaches to Psychosis, United States chapter newslet-
    ter Winter/Spring 2018, 17(1), 1–2.

Grotstein, J. (1997). Bion's "transformation in O" and the concept of "the transcendent position". Unpublished paper, digital edition. Retrieved from http://www.sicap.it/~merciai/bion/papers/grots.htm.

Winnicott, DW. (1972). *Holding and interpretation.* Grove Press.

Winnicott, DW. (1977). *The piggle.* Penguin Books.

Winnicott, DW. (1989). *Playing and reality.* Routledge (originally published 1971).

Winnicott, DW. (2018). Interpretation in psycho-analysis. *Psycho-analtic explorations: D.W. Winnicott* (C Winnicott, R Shepherd, and M Davis, Eds.). Routledge.

Chapter 8

Michael Eigen and evolution of psyche

Robin Bagai

I ask the reader's indulgence for the presumptuous title of this chapter. Why do I say presumptuous? Because evolution of psyche is always on-going … it never stops, whether we call this a continuous form of birth, a process of becoming, or simply a developmental unfolding. Psyche, like physical life, never stops circulating and being in motion. Whether we look to society at large or inside ourselves, we know that development and growth are anything but smooth. Instead, we find erratic rhythms of all kinds – progress and regress, growth, and decay, leaps, plateaus, and stasis … at times all going on simultaneously. Extremes often sit side by side highlighting large divides, like rich and poor, healthy and ill. But what of their mixtures? This chapter highlights textured ways of thinking and feeling whereby Michael Eigen opens doors and pathways for psyche's growth and evolution.

Sometimes one needs to paint a picture using large brush strokes. In order to convey even a little of Eigen, whose embrace of psychical and emotional life is wide and deep, some very large brush strokes mixing primary colours are called for. Can one convey more than words can say? Eigen writes:

> It is part of emotional life that we can express or narrate or convey only a bit of what we feel. We do not know the whole of it. There is always some frustration built in. It is like swimming in the ocean. We can never take in the whole ocean all at once. But we do swim in part of it and the water we swim in, while not the whole ocean, is real water.
>
> (2011, p. 124)

Eigen's work is like that ocean. My attempt here will be to shake some drops of "real water" onto you, water absorbed from swimming in various parts of his ocean over the last several years.

The development or evolution of psyche, as I mean it, refers in part to changes in our self-concept as a species. I begin with some well-known psychological pivot points that have changed how human beings view themselves in psychical and historical mirrors.

Consider this from Freud:

Humanity has in the course of time had to endure from the hands of science two great outrages upon its naïve self-love. The first was when it realized that our earth was not the center of the universe, but only a tiny speck in a world-system of a magnitude hardly conceivable; this is associated in our minds with the name of Copernicus, although Alexandrian doctrines taught something very similar. The second was when biological research robbed man of his peculiar privilege of having been specially created, and relegated him to a descent from the animal world, implying an ineradicable animal nature in him: This transvaluation has been accomplished in our own time upon the instigation of Charles Darwin, Wallace, and their predecessors, and not without the most violent opposition from their contemporaries. But man's craving for grandiosity is now suffering the third and most bitter blow from present-day psychological research which is endeavoring to prove to the ego of each one of us that he is not even master in his own house, but that he must remain content with the veriest scraps of information about what is going on unconsciously in his own mind. We psycho-analysts were neither the first nor the only ones to propose to mankind that they should look inward; but it appears to be our lot to advocate it most insistently and to support it by empirical evidence which touches every man closely.

(1916–17, pp. 284–5)

With these three pivotal insights and insults to our self-perception from Copernicus, Darwin, and Freud, we might say that two things are happening at the same time. This is a first example of what might be called *double-sided* thinking: There is simultaneously a constriction and an expansion occurring. The constriction is that we cringe and contract when, to use Freud's term, our "naïve self-love" or grand idealizations come under attack. But at the same time, we also expand our understanding of where we are in the universe, where we come from in the animal world, and what we're made of psychologically. We are encouraged by Copernicus, Darwin, and Freud to "take back our projections," gaining from increased humility. We are not the same as our wishful projected images. And if in the vernacular psychotherapists and psychoanalysts are sometimes called "shrinks," we are also mindful that one aspect of therapy is to "expand" psychological health and psyche through more opening to life and aliveness. Shrinking and expanding, opening and closing as conjunctions, doubles that go together.

Double-sided, conjoined, and paradoxical thinking-feeling runs through the work of several analytic writers, perhaps most prominently in the works of Donald Winnicott, Wilfred Bion, and Michael Eigen. Such an approach and perspective has gone by many names and phrases: Dialectical, double-sided, two things at once, paradoxical, interwoven, conjoined. Mixtures of all kinds. One of Eigen's books, titled *Toxic Nourishment* (1999) speaks to this paradoxical mixture. James Grotstein's book *But at the Same Time and on Another Level* (2009) does the same. There are also phrases like *two-in-one, one-in-two* (Eigen, 2015). And another variant might be *each-within-the-other*. What if we pair psyche and soma as spirit and flesh, then mix them together? In Eigen's language this becomes *inspirited flesh and enfleshed spirit* (2005, p. 2). For a pictorial image of *two-in-one, one-in-two*, one might view the familiar Taoist Yin–Yang symbol.

Eigen captures many forms of doubleness and paradox with his *distinction-union* formulation, a structure that is also a process. It becomes a bit dizzying to try and see or think things from more than one perspective at the same time, but then aren't we always more than we can know at any given moment? We are more than simply seeing and knowing creatures. We think, we feel, we listen … we sense, intuit, dream, and sometimes even draw from the future, not just the past. As the poet Whitman intimated, we are multitudes (1855, Part 51).

DW Winnicott (1971) implored us *not* to try and solve or dissolve paradox using rational thinking or the intellect, but instead to hold the value inherent in the tension of doubleness. For example, what value would irony or metaphor have if they did not juxtapose or interweave two things at once, portraying their own unique forms of doubleness? To be sure, it's often much simpler to think in terms of either/or, this or that … one thing at a time. Science and formal logic have made good use of such approaches. But in realms of psyche, feeling, and emotion, it becomes a measure of collective growth to begin to appreciate psychological worlds with more inclusiveness: Not just *either/or*, but also, *both/and*.

Can we go even further? Why lean solely on one pair or the other? Why make a full stop at either distinction or union? Why separate either/or … from both/and, when in our psychical and emotional lives it is their combinations and exchanges that feel truer and make things more interesting. Like toxins and nourishment combined. Eigen explores mixtures and interactions among our various tendencies and capacities, while reserving lots of room for the unknown by valorizing mystery. Can domains of the unknown and unknowable become regarded as something useful, even precious? The poet John Keats coined the phrase *negative capability*: To stay with the tension of not knowing, to patiently wait in the unknown instead of "irritably reaching after fact and reason" (2002, pp. 41–2). Irritable reaching is often meant to avoid uncertainty and maintain a sense of control and mastery. What happens if we stop reaching?

Another example of double-sided thinking: Human beings as both the same and different simultaneously. We humans are all the "same" in that we have the very same body parts: Two eyes, ears, organs, same number of bones, etc. But equally, we are all different in that we each have distinct combinations of lineage, temperament, ethnicity, personality, family history, and so on. Sameness and difference together, distinction and union as conjoined.

Eigen continues further. He has us consider a rhythmic component to our emotional and psychic lives, rhythms that reveal many kinds and qualities of interaction between our tendencies and capacities. Some possibilities include merger and fusion alternating with antagonistic breaking apart of connection; or reversals that swing and oscillate, like love turning to hate, marriage to divorce; and also forms of co-union: Symbiosis, mutual nourishment, creative synergy. Eigen writes:

> Distinction–union tendencies enter into many kinds of relationships with each other, antagonistic, symbiotic, parasitic, nullifying, disconnecting, nourishing. We can always ask what one or other of these tendencies is doing at any moment, since both are always co-present. They implicitly characterize mind–body as well as self–other relations and can be read on many planes: adaptive, psychic, behavioral, individual, sociological, mystical … To be permeable and distinct, connected and separate, in union yet different, is part of our plasticity… part of the mystery, difficulty, and creative challenge of our nature. Can we make room for ourselves? What quality of partnership with our beings can we work out?
>
> (2011, pp. 15–16)

Can we in the twenty-first century make room for Eigen's complexity … a complexity that offers a potential step in psyche's growth?

Shakespeare's work offered increasing psychological complexity, perhaps highlighting another pivot point in psyche's evolution. Eigen cites the literary critic Harold Bloom and Bloom's notion that Shakespeare "invented the human" (1998). What could be meant by this? Eigen speculates that Bloom is referring, in part, to the development, expansion, and exploration of what we call character or personality, found in increasing complexity in Shakespeare's plays, where personality and psyche are brought to new levels of self-reflection.

Complexity itself reflects developmental levels of responsiveness, feeling, and sensitivity – not just cognition. Shakespeare's complexity draws our attention to inner worlds of agony and increasing self-doubt, showing conflicted states and urges within characters as they suffer their desires and ponder their circumstance.

With Shakespeare, we find more emphasis on attention to conflicts *within*, as a way to come to terms with circumstances in outer life. With Freud, our inner world expanded further with his theory of unconscious conflict. In Shakespeare, we remember Hamlet's famous question, "to be or not to be" in the face of unsolvable pain and conflict. More importantly, Hamlet's *pausing before acting*, his pondering and his ambivalence about whether to proceed with retaliation and revenge killing, that strong force attached to family honour and lineage, evoking the age-old question of whether to adhere to tradition or rebel against it. Eigen cites Hamlet as pausing, waiting, pondering, reflecting, agonizing … rather than immediately moving into murderous revenge expected by his tradition (2002, p. 3).

The ability to wait, to think, to reflect, to agonize … to feel one's way into conflicts, and then be able to interpose word or symbol between impulse and action – these are developmental accomplishments and perhaps also evolutionary steps (though never vouchsafe from regression and undoing). Even though Hamlet eventually succumbed to the pull of his murderous revenge tradition, there is a sense that his pausing to consider the futility of vengeful destruction, knowing full well the damage would continue to ricochet into the future, is a step. Hamlet's pause itself, as Eigen relates it, can be seen as a gift to us, even as Eigen jokes that Hamlet wasn't being Hamlet *enough*, i.e. he did not pause or wait long enough for further developments or perspective to occur. The same could be said about the ending of Romeo and Juliet. Tragedy born from an inability to wait, or not waiting long enough, for more to emerge and unfold.

Aren't we still blinded by impulse and inability to wait, tangled-up with intolerance of our emotional life? Perhaps we are blind from birth, and remain partly blind throughout life, limited in our ability to see more fully. Isn't this one of the lessons from Oedipus? We are blind to our unconscious blind spots, and blind to our destructive and self-destructive makeup.

Freud, Klein, Winnicott, and Bion, among others, all proposed variants of a destructive force, an aggressive-destructive drive embedded within human life. Astronomers and physicists tell us the universe was formed and began violently with a big bang. I sometimes think of such destructive forces as being on a grand continuum: From explosive emotions like rage or a baby's scream when born, possible echoes of the big bang of the universe … all the way to the silent power of entropy: As if the universe has an inherent sense of needing to de-cathect itself. The question becomes one of whether we must succumb to and be ruled by destructive forces that cause grave injury and wounding. It is naïve and simplistic to try and destroy destruction, to think we can completely "get rid of the bad stuff" in our nature. Psychologically, it has never worked to get rid of anything. What gets denied, overlooked, unprocessed, or repressed eventually returns, and can reappear strengthened.

Winnicott's *use of object* formulation (1969) and Eigen's embrace of emotional complexity remind us that our aggressive and destructive nature can also be thrilling and enlivening. Aggressive and destructive impulses are part of aliveness, whether it is a child gleefully demolishing sandcastles and towers of blocks, or the violent aliveness of extreme sports and contagion of war, or destructive apocalyptic movie thrillers that never lose popularity. The title of one of Eigen's papers expresses this conjunction succinctly: *Life kills, aliveness kills* (2018, Chapter 8). This conundrum is not solvable, but *can* have different outcomes depending on how we use these destructive forces. Eigen wonders if we might do a little better than re-channelling or sublimating, important as these can be. One suggestion is to wait-out the destructive impulse, an attempt at "creative waiting." Another might be developing forms of "creative destruction."

Can we somehow build more resilience and practice in accepting wounding or even "murdering" each other emotionally, but then come to feel all right again, as Bion proposed? Our current situation seems to be a regressive conjunction of extremes. On the one hand, there is a call in some educational settings for a mandate and guarantee to feel safe emotionally, where potentially injurious language is flagged ahead of time, and diligently avoided. At the other end, blatantly crude and prejudicial language has never been more pervasive, aggressive, and hurtful in social and political settings. We have wishes for invulnerability and immunity from "hurt" coupled with aggressive injurious attacks, side by side. A conjunction of opposite social responses and attitudes.

Patience and waiting are also double-sided. There are times when we need to act quickly and decisively, as well as other times when we act too precipitously rather than giving time for further development and perspective to occur.

To wait rather than act ... to stop and reflect rather than immediately evacuate ... to digest and metabolize difficult feelings and emotions rather than project these and hurt others or ourselves ... isn't this a more difficult but more sustainable path ... signifying growth of capacity ... and a potential step in the maturity of our species? The evolution of psyche comes about, in part, from changes in self-perception, in how we view ourselves and what we do with these new perceptions of who we are and what we're made of. Perhaps deeply acknowledging destructive and self-destructive impulses as part of who we are is repeatedly necessary, since each generation must arrive at this insight for themselves and struggle with it.

Eigen's work addresses many important areas of our psychological future. Foundational is his emphasis on the enormous power of our feelings, urges, drives, and wishes (as well as their absence), and how these impact our lives. Eigen increases our awareness of complexity in emotional life, and it is our emotional life that remains the greatest challenge to the quality of our ongoing existence. Human emotions and what we do with them are among the most important of our "final frontiers." Not outer space, not the ocean depths nor climbing the highest mountains ... no, our emotional reality and how we use it – this is our most daunting final frontier. Because if we cannot navigate and grow collectively using the currency of our emotional life, we will remain at its mercy, and it won't matter which other planets we might colonize technologically, because the problem of ourselves will go with us wherever we venture.

More complexity: Emotional reality is so difficult because it is so vast. Our feeling life and sensitivities involve whatever psyche, body and spirit touch, including things unknown and partly known, like subliminal sensations, raw feels, vague intimations, dream life, imagination, myriad forms of sensing, along with common labels like anger, fear, sorrow, and joy. In spite of such emotional abundance, it remains an open question whether or not one's emotional reality is noticed, and then actually *experienced* by someone. Just as there are thoughts without a thinker (a Bion phrase [1970, 1994] that Mark Epstein [1995] used), feelings and emotions can exist without a person present and able to experience them. It's an odd but relevant notion to consider that we must develop and grow into ourselves in order to experience ourselves. How far can we venture, and how much experiencing can we allow ourselves, how much can we take? Raw awareness is often beyond words and representation. Metaphorically, as wordless reality is like an older sibling to words, we can be struck dumb and wordless at times by the superior strength of our feeling-meanings.

Consider the last time you awoke from a dream and were completely lost for words. *Something* had just been experienced, but it was impossible to say anything coherent about it. Perhaps there was a mood, something sensed, remnants of a vague atmospheric feeling, or an unclear image. Perhaps just amorphous jelly or a hodgepodge of sensuous impressions. Such experiences are very *real*, but our ability to depict or describe them is limited. Our ability to experience ourselves experiencing … and to experience more fully, is a capacity requiring lifelong practice.

Eigen emphasizes what we may know intuitively – that emotional reality and our experiential awareness are always more than we can grasp, always more than we can sustain, and always more than we can fully experience.

> The impact of reality is far greater than our ability to process it. We can't take too much reality. Our equipment simply is not up to it. If we are lucky, persistent, patient, hungry enough for the real, our equipment grows into the job, building more capacity to work with what is. Nevertheless, we are always behind the impact of the moment, at best able to process crumbs broken off from the whole. But those crumbs can be rich indeed!
>
> (2004b, p. 8)

Likewise, Eigen writes that our technology products are always ahead of our ability to assimilate their full scope and make good use of them. Our products run past and ahead of our ability to know what to do with them. This seems as true of nuclear energy as our use of social media and so-called smartphones. Ironically, it may be that smartphones are making us dumber, thinning us out, making us more emotionally isolated from one another even as they provide instant forms of contact. Eigen emphasizes growth of capacity as an ongoing challenge:

> I was saying that we don't yet have psyches – psychic capacity that can support the intensity of the thoughts and feelings we have. We do not know what to do with our mental or emotional productions. We don't know how to bring them together. So many feelings, so many thoughts,

but how to process them is another matter. Our psychic means of production outstrips our capacity to assimilate what we produce. Psychic and mental digestion must always be incomplete, but maybe we can do a little better. And since our psyches are not well developed, not really up to what feelings and thoughts demand of them, we get overwhelmed. We give up on the task of growing psychic capacity that can do a better job and turn our attention to other things, like raping the environment, making war, bullying ourselves and each other ...

(2016, p. 136)

Look at pain as a kind of negative example. If the psyche is too weak or underdeveloped to work with that pain, and if it is unwilling or unable to wait on its own development, it may just try to make the pain go away one way or another. It may even try to make itself go away in order to rid itself of experiences it cannot support ... often violence is an attempt to make the pain of one's life go away ... But the pain does not go away or stay away. It gets worse and the means to make it go away get stronger.

(2016, p. 137)

Such predicaments feel timeless and perennial. We try to get rid of pain, as if it is possible to destroy suffering, rather than grow more capacity to process and use it, both in our intra–psychic world and vis-a-vis others. We try to make the pain go away instead of addressing it, acknowledging it, leaning into it, welcoming it, and learning from it. Can we listen for what emotional pain might be trying to tell us? I think of the Sufi poet Rumi (2004) who challenged us to honour our inner "guesthouse" of psyche, to honour our emotional life by respecting all variety of feelings and emotions as visitors who arrive and present themselves. All emotional visitors have something to tell us, to teach us. Rumi asks that we welcome these guests and hear what they have to say, experiencing and considering their messages, rather than denying, avoiding, fighting-off, or looking the other way.

As psychotherapists, we welcome whatever our patients bring to sessions, listening to ourselves listening to them. Rumi's guesthouse can be a therapy model that, like Eigen's call for growth of capacity, offers an important path for development. Growth of capacity arrives most durably a little at a time, in baby steps, day by day ... session by session.

To extrapolate from individual psyche to the collective is hazardous, yet where does psychological progress and collective maturation come from if not pioneering individuals like Eigen? Can we grow a little more into our emotional lives ... can we grow into acknowledging our complexity ... can the heightened aliveness of our destructive nature be both contained and used in ways that are not so damaging and injurious ...? We don't know. We don't know if our psychological development and emotional maturity will be enough to sustain us, or keep us safe from ourselves. What we do know is that tolerating differences, along with greater tolerance for our ability to wait rather than act on impulse – these are in short supply. To wait in the unknown for further transformations to occur – this capacity utilizing Eigen's notion of Faith (2014) needs more patience and practice.

Emmanuel Levinas (1999) is one who writes about the power of waiting together, maintaining a "proximity of persons" when faced with conflicts and insoluble problems, whether in the consultation room or among "Others." The value Levinas places on waiting leads me to a final conjunction. I want to compare two broad and general approaches to psychotherapy, each of which can be valuable in its own right. In the following sketch, I use the terms top-down and bottom-up as shorthand.

Top-down models apply a set of protocols using theory and technique to try and effect change in the patient. For example, one could think of *in vivo desensitization* for someone with a phobia. Apply the protocol and technique, practice it, and measure the results. We could also think of various psychoanalytic techniques as being top-down, as when transference interpretation to elicit insight and understanding is privileged as a curative factor. In top-down models, one is trying to "get somewhere" using a pre-determined method, theory, language, and technique. Often the goal or destination is pre-determined, and the model has a hierarchical trajectory.

Perhaps Freud too was hierarchical, a kind of "id conqueror" when he proclaimed, "where id was there ego shall be" (1933, p. 79). Domestication of the id through usurpation by the ego was proposed as a higher level of societal achievement. Melanie Klein (1957) thought that patients should progress to the *depressive position* (D), an advance in development from the less mature *paranoid-schizoid position* (Ps). In such models, there are ascending hierarchies of better and worse, health and illness, under-developed and more mature states. Such approaches have a trajectory and goal from the start, and the clinician's job is to help move patients higher up the ladder. The vertical hierarchy tries to uplift or transcend a lesser or lower one, rather than valuing each capacity (Id and Ego; Ps and D) for what they can offer. An alternative view considers benefits to be gained from all parts of ourselves, as when horizontal exchange and partnering of capacities is practiced, rather than vertical "transcending."

I'm using top-down approaches as a kind of foil, even though top-down can be very useful with some patients. By contrast, bottom-up models of psychotherapy rely on what is not known, a trust in unconscious process. Bottom-up engages an organic unfolding of unconscious rhythms that have their own timetable of development, their own idiosyncratic progression, their own logic, their own pace, their own uneven trajectory, and perhaps ultimately their own wisdom if given enough time to develop and grow.

The bottom-up process often feels like working in the dark, without map or template, an uncharted territory without handholds or anchor points. Yet bottom-up approaches presume a good deal of knowledge and accrued experience as a foundational backdrop. Bottom-up is a practice that requires its own form of patience, time, and maturity, including trust or faith, ongoing self-critique, as well as persistence and durability in the face of unknowns. It's not for everyone, yet there are patients for whom nothing else will do.

Bottom-up models rely on something much less certain and definable than top-down. Let's call it a kind of trust in unconscious processes, or faith in support from deeper layers of psyche. And if this support in the patient is lacking or too damaged from early trauma, the therapy must rely on the therapist's own unconscious processing as a support surrogate. As Eigen (2001) puts it, the therapist must become like an "auxiliary dreamer" or mid-wife of unconscious support for the patient's psyche.

Bottom-up approaches are filled with dangers and uncertainties. They require forms of merger and melding between therapist and patient while simultaneously maintaining firm and compassionate boundaries that adequately hold steady the therapeutic frame or container. Such combinations allow for the possibility of durable growth in the patient's psyche, rather than grafting pre-made solutions that may or may not "take." One might say bottom-up requires a full measure of one's subjectivity with another human being, a form of *distinction–union* that is fluid and unique to each therapy couple. Perhaps it goes without saying that blends using both top-down and bottom-up approaches occur more frequently than not.

Eigen emphasizes the value inherent in partnering the flow between any two polarities, tendencies, or capacities. Here he contrasts horizontal flow with vertical rigidity:

> One of the great contributions of modern cultural history is to question the basis of traditional hierarchies, perhaps the very meaning of hierarchy (top–bottom). In psychic realities, double arrows are placed between traditional oppositions. What a relief to be able to flow back and forth between antagonistic currents and not pit one against the other. One takes and learns from each. Each contributes to the growth of self. Without polarities life would be poorer, but we do not have to be trapped by polarities.
>
> (2004a, p. 266)

In sum, I have outlined a few aspects in the development and evolution of psyche that offer new challenges, challenges posed by psychological complexities inherent in the work of Michael Eigen. Hierarchical control models are contrasted with partnering our different capacities as co-equals. One could go even further by reversing hierarchy, and "letting the horse lead the rider," i.e. letting unconscious spontaneity and creativity lead, rather than ego control and mastery. However, if used rigidly, this too might become another hierarchy, and miss the benefits of back and forth flow cited above.

I will end with a brief quote from Eigen that captures an additional important element, an *aesthetic element* in psychotherapy and in life that should not be overlooked. Eigen copied me on an email as part of our separate responses to a mutual colleague's painful life crisis, writing: "What we go through in a lifetime ... so much shock and grief ... if we become nothing else, we come closer to being artists of the pain of existence" (2019, email communication).

Artists of the pain of existence ... what a profound expression, and how true it feels. Can we become artists of life's inevitable sufferings ... or try to? Emotional suffering is part of psyche's existence, a home where we must live. As psychotherapists, we try to help open more inner contact and resource as palettes for psyche's brush strokes that paint life. My hope for all who practice psychotherapy is that you will be blessed to find or construct such an inner artist for yourselves, as you persevere in doing this difficult but rewarding work with our fellow beings.

References

Bion, WR. (1970). *Attention and interpretation*. Tavistock.

Bion, WR. (1994). *Cogitations* (F Bion, Ed.). Karnac.

Bloom, H. (1998). *Shakespeare: The invention of the human*. Riverhead Books.

Eigen, M. (1999). *Toxic nourishment*. Karnac.

Eigen, M. (2001). *Damaged bonds*. Karnac.

Eigen, M. (2002). *Rage*. Wesleyan University Press.

Eigen, M. (2004a). *The electrified tightrope* (A Phillips, Ed.). Karnac.

Eigen, M. (2004b). *The sensitive self*. Wesleyan University Press.

Eigen, M. (2005). *Emotional storm*. Wesleyan University Press.

Eigen, M. (2011). *Contact with the depths*. Karnac.

Eigen, M. (2014). *Faith*. Karnac.

Eigen, M. (2015). O, orgasm and beyond. *Psychoanalytic Dialogues*, 25, 646–54.

Eigen, M. (2016). *Image, sense, infinities, and everyday life*. Karnac.

Eigen, M. (2018). *The challenge of being human*. Routledge.

Epstein, M. (1995). *Thoughts without a thinker*. Basic Books.

Freud, S. (1916–17). Introductory lectures on psycho-analysis. *Standard Edition of the Complete Psychological Works*, 16, 284–5. Hogarth Press.

Freud, S. (1933). New introductory lectures on psycho-analysis. *Standard Edition of the Complete Psychological Works*, 22, 79. Hogarth Press.

Grotstein, JS. (2009). *But at the same time and on another level: Psychoanalytic theory and technique in the Kleinian/Bionian mode*. Karnac.

Keats, J. (2002). *Selected letters*. Oxford University Press, 41–2 (original work written 1818).

Klein, M. (1957). *Envy and gratitude*. Free Association Books.

Levinas, E. (1999). *Alterity and transcendence* (MB Smith, Trans). Columbia University Press, 87–9.

Rumi, J. (2004). *Selected poems* (C Barks with J Moynce, AJ Arberry, R Nicholson, Trans.). Penguin Books.

Whitman, W. (1855). *Song of myself, part 51. Leaves of grass*. Self-published.

Winnicott, DW. (1971). *Playing and reality*. Basic Books.

Winnicott, DW. (1969). The use of an object. *International Journal of Psycho-Analysis*, 50, 711–16.

Chapter 9

On not knowing Michael Eigen

Alitta Kullman

Introduction

If WR Bion's "psychoanalytic attitude" is being without memory, desire, understanding, or expectation, Michael Eigen's psychoanalytic attitude can be thought of as the boundless openness and curiosity that emerges out of his willingness to not know. Eigen embodies Bion's famous plea, to approach humanity and humanness without pre-conditions, to wait for and welcome what emerges, to recognize and embrace what we cannot know, to allow things to grow, develop, and flourish. For me, Michael Eigen is a verb, a spiritual and psychoanalytic attitude, a presence, a process, an evolution. Freeing himself of the burden of needing to find answers or pretending to know, he offers us a seemingly endless capacity to mine the inner and outermost elements of human experience.

Michael Eigen's psychoanalytic attitude of "not knowing" embodies an openness, a humility, a curiosity; a celebration of the imagination and of faith as well as a generosity of spirit. Eigen's works are steeped in references, explorations, and dissections of the words and works of others: The thoughts, ideas, and musings of Freud, Winnicott, Bion, Milner, Elkin, Moses, Jesus, Buddha, philosophers, mystics, prophets, patients, and of God Himself. Immersing himself deeply within and beyond what they might have said or what their intent might have been, Eigen allows the mighty and the meek to infuse his thinking while he wrestles with meaning itself. He makes space for others to touch him, to stir his soul – and in so doing, invites us, his readers, to allow our own souls to be stirred. Michael Eigen is a soul whisperer.

Michael Eigen doesn't just write: He paints a verbal picture of the soul. He infuses his artistry with the richness and texture that arises from a palette of raw honesty, the primary colours that emerge before the variants that provide nuance and shading are added to the mix. He creates a canvas for his readers, an opportunity to consider the brushstrokes of their own lives, to gaze upon themselves and acknowledge truths, with perhaps just a little less judgement and murderousness.

Eigen is also a man obsessed with the authentic language of truth, and the truth of authentic language. His search is ever to go deeper, to unclothe every thought or idea, to find poetry in every phrase, to turn every word on its head, to extract meaning out of every inch of everything. Just when you think you've read something profound that he has written, you read the next sentence. Just when you think you've gotten to the core or the kernel of his argument, he takes you to another plane ... or planet.

This chapter grew out of my love for Michael Eigen's essay, "I don't know" (2009b), and grew and grew and grew. I did not realize when I began that his notion of "not knowing" could not be – and indeed, *was not* – contained within the bounds of that single essay. Everywhere I turned in his work, it appeared: His entreaties to patients, interviewers, politicians, analysts, thinkers, feelers, to allow ourselves to not know; even to protect the universe by not pretending to know what we don't and can't possibly know.

Perusing Michael Eigen's bookshelf in the service of following a single theme like "not knowing" was also, I discovered, virtually impossible. Eigen relates everything to everything else. You might *think* you are following a thread, but before you know it, the thread has woven its way into a myriad of rich connections, a tapestry so compelling it defies any attempt at traditional organization. Not knowing opens infinite possibilities, makes for ultimate creativity. Eigen plays with synthesis within syntheses. He tries on ideas for size in varying shapes, forms, and combinations, layering one thought or idea now with this possibility, now with that. He links psychoanalysis with Kabbalah, with love of God, with political science, with omniscience. He weaves his way through by splitting infinities, by finding meaning in everything, by leaving no stone unturned, no idea unexamined. He plumbs the breadth and depth of not knowing not only by seeking out the perspectives of those who have not known before him, but the boundless, infinite intimacies of his own soul. Indeed, if things are unknowable, it is not because Michael Eigen hasn't tried to figure them out.

There is no way I could capture the flavour, the nuance, the spiritual, and the emotional connections contained within Michael Eigen's words in my own words – that would be like trying to hold a proverbial moonbeam in my hand. And so, I offer you Michael Eigen in *his* own words. The following is a narrative of quotations I have pieced together from various volumes and sources of Eigen's work. It is, of necessity, a *highly* redacted summary – and deciding what to include and what to leave out was *painful*. Nevertheless, I hope it provides some small insight into his notion – his "no-shun?" – of not knowing – what I believe to be not only his "psychoanalytic attitude," but his awe-inspiring gift to the world.

Beginnings

> Not knowing is an experience in its own right ... a gateway to possibilities of experiencing yet to come ... a powerful state that can open us in unimaginable ways.
>
> (Eigen, 2011a, p. 52)

One never recovers from being human.

(2016b, p. 137)

Whatever happens opens reality.

(2011a, Dedication page)

Eigen and Winnicott

Winnicott (1988) touches a moment when the infant is unaware that it is supported in life by the mother. Even a sense of being alone requires support one does not know is there.

(Eigen, 2011a, p. 18)

Aloneness has in its very core a sense of unknown infinite other ...
If you penetrate to the core of your aloneness you will not only find yourself, there will also be this unknown boundless presence ...

(2011b, p. 20)

If development proceeds well from the alone core, the background boundless other stretches; Its elasticity grows into new places ...

(2009a, p. 27)

If something goes wrong with the support one doesn't know is there, the growing personality is affected...the possibility of contact with oneself is at risk, pressured, injured. Reactive fear, rage, isolation, or addiction to others can help one get through but thwart fuller unfolding.

(2011a, pp. 18–19)

In my adaptation of Winnicott's variant, originary, emergent being is supported by invisible, unknown God given over to adaptive care of the newborn ... A forerunner, template ... an *anlage* of an unknown god: a god who cares, who helps ... I am positing a boundless aspect to the support that is not known, the unknown support of experience of being ... a boundless incommunicado core of ongoing being, supported by boundless unknown God ... [which] forms a basis for the feeling of being loved in one's core.

(2009a, pp. 22–3)

I, personally, experience something sacred in this core. I think Winnicott also did. Our lives tap into a sense of holiness connected with a background aura of infinite unknown support.

(2009a, p. 12)

It seems to me that something like a sense of a boundless unknown is part of the background sense of existence. It provides a basis for emergent trust and faith.

(2011a, p. 10)

Eigen and Bion

Bion calls faith the psychoanalytic attitude ... (2016b, p. 3) [and] describes the psychoanalytic attitude as being without memory, expectation, desire, or understanding. A radical openness ... a special kind of faith he expresses as F in O, where O is unknown, ultimate reality, in this context, an emphasis on psychic reality, ineffable, infinite ... The fundamental reality is 'infinity,' the unknown, the situation for which there is no language ...

(2011a, p. 41).

F in O [is] a kind of zero or radical openness, letting go of self and mind-operations ... freedom from self and mind ... K [Knowledge or knowing] formulations result and can prove important, but waiting on O, and not prematurely closing it off with K, can open transformational possibilities that may not happen without F[aith].

What goes on in O we do not know, but we sense impacts, hints, intimations, some kind of contact with the unknown, although we cannot say what it is or what it is not. As a physicist once said, perhaps Eddington, something unknown is doing we do not know what. Its impact affects us, and we work with what we can. We, too, are that unknown or part of it. We are the unknown responding to itself.

(2011a, p. 5)

[Bion] reaches deep in the well, calling the naked attitude he expresses faith. It is as if a certain kind of faith peels the skin off the psyche and opens a world of raw impact and transformation, a substratum of emotional experience seeking and seeking and undergoing transformations.

(2011a, p. 44)

If one catches on – deeply catches on – that things are in some ways changing, that transformational processes are always at work, for better or worse, one has more of a chance of experiencing areas of freedom or possible exploration ... One can, to a certain extent, transcend one's current situation or, better, dive into it, be with it, work with it.

(2014b, p. 100)

It was salutary to come upon a respected analyst who said the subject of analysis is unknown.

(2016b, p. 3)

Bion (1970, 1994) does not use the word mystery, but privileges the unknown as a basic category of experience. We act as if we know ourselves, take ourselves for granted, yet what we take to be our identities are parts of unfathomable depths ... Respect for the unknown and seemingly unsolvable difficulties of ourselves is a beginning.

(2016a, p. ix)

Bion urges us to return to more fragmented states, start from scratch, and lessen the hold of built-up narrative organisations of emotion that remain largely unfelt and unmet.

(2014b, p. 103)

By implication, Bion is reminding us to be cautious about what we think we know. We may think we know a lot about ourselves, but the emotions we can focus on are a small part of where they came from.

(2014b, p. 104)

Bion's work is an avenue of access and aid to cultivating the openness to experiencing he touches. To accept this challenge is a humbling act to respect and care for psychic reality that necessarily requires leaving room for the unknown in others and oneself.

(2018, p. 73)

Faith and God

Faith is rooted in the unknown, if it can be said to have roots. Whether it is an unknowable God or a state of affairs ever receding from the knowledge quest ... There is a state where K and O are not distinguishable, at once co-nourishing and coincident.

(2011a, p. 72)

I've used the term psychoanalytic faith. By that I don't mean faith in psychoanalysis. Any treatment may be better or worse, work sometimes in some ways and not in others ... Anything one says is not quite it. Even dissolution, helplessness, and loss of faith can be part of a growth process. Faith beyond faith. Faith in face of loss of faith. It is something more or else I can't pin down but very real in experience and consequence ... And yet the faith I mean persists in the face of obliteration, cancellation, nullification. I can't explain it. I've heard the term blind faith, natural faith. I can see it working in animals. I can feel it in my body. But that is not exactly it either. It is a felt faith that runs through the body, mind, psyche, spirit. It pervades existence, even in Holocausts, personal Holocausts. How is this possible? I don't know, but I feel it. It is.

(2016a, p. 13–14)

Ein Sof is one try to evoke the uncommunicable, the mystery of contact with what cannot be known.

(2014b, p. 92)

Thus God may be a name for the infinite unknowable, which is a name for whatever God is a name for, which is unnameable.

(1998, p. 82)

The philosophical notion that only God has the whole picture touches our condition, acknowledging that whatever our perspective, it must be partial. God may have the whole picture, but we have at best bits and pieces ...

(2011b, p. 61)

It is said that God creates many angels that come and go in an instant. They are present for a moment, then are gone. I wonder if this expresses something about certain moments that come and go – moments of beauty, terror, need, curiosity, wonder. A moment that bursts for an instant, giving all it has, then gone. We are left to wonder if we really felt and saw a shooting star flash through our beings or did we imagine it?

(2014c, p. viii)

To not know who we are or who God is – isn't that releasing? It makes room. What if God doesn't know either? In the Bible, when asked his name, God says, "Tell them *I am* sent you." Or perhaps, *I am what I am* or *I will be what I will be* or *I will be there*. I will be there for you. I am here for you ... When I was in my thirties and all alone, sometimes I would wake up in the middle of the night saying "I love you." Who was I speaking to? Where did these words come from? It is easy to guess and make up answers, but I do not know. They opened a deep place. Today I often feel an "I love you" presence while awake. The deep place in the night is spreading.

(2011a, p. 46–7)

Job ultimately says of God, "I know you in my flesh." What kind of knowing is this? In old age, as in my youth, I love planet earth, colours, sky, water, those close to me and many far away, trinkets, grass, and autumn leaves, sun, moon, music, art, depth psychology – you name it. But a love of the invisible has grown. A love I cannot pin down. I used to locate it in my chest. But now it is more elusive. It can be anywhere. A sense of the invisible keeps growing.

(2014c, p. ix)

The "Ethics of the Unknown"

If Socrates confessed ignorance in the face of problems related to thinking, we might begin by confessing ignorance when it comes to problems of feeling. Confession of ignorance is part of self-knowledge. Ideologies of regulation and control tend to jump the gun, since we aren't sure what it is we are trying to control and regulate or how to go about doing it. Understanding doesn't do the trick if we don't know what it is we are trying to understand. We are not sure what use to make of understanding or what to expect of it. We do not understand very much about understanding and often miscalculate what it can do.

(2005, p. 20)

We say God is omniscient, omnipotent, but these are capacities we wish for ourselves. More, we act as if we are omniscient and omnipotent in important ways. That is, we act as if we know everything, or more than we do, and that we have the power to do whatever we want, or are deluded to think so. Omniscience and omnipotence as powerful fantasies that permeate our behavior, often with disastrous results, sometimes with astonishing creative results. As analysts, we might say we project omniscience – omnipotence on to God, reflecting our own preoccupation with knowledge and power. Look at all the trouble we get into thinking we know more than we do and acting as if we are more powerful or should be ... It is best to acknowledge this dangerous, at times perverse quality we have, that we think we know more than we do.

(2012, p. 6)

There is an ethics of the unknown. An attitude of unknowing leaves things open, protects against false omniscience ... If we assimilate the fact that we do not know everything about ourselves and the other and that, like the universe, we are mostly unknown to ourselves, a sense of humility and openness may have a chance to grow. We may become more interested in learning more about who we are and readying for further development. This is an entirely different attitude than slamming the door with dogma.

(2016a, p. 19–20)

We try to water reality down to make it handleable. But some of us, some of the time, and some of us more of the time, develop a taste for the mystery itself and all that reality does without our knowing.

(2011a, p. 72)

Beginning never stops. If we take that seriously, deeply, we begin to undergo an ethical transformation as well as other changes. The unknown is felt as a partner in the creativity of our lives and meeting with others. A deeper respect for what we do not or cannot know underlies what we do and can know. Bion reaches for the term "Faith" to portray the growth of a psychoanalytic attitude, openness to the unknown emotion of moment. Rather than static, our approach to experience is ever in process, a humble, caring part of our beings.

(2018, p. xii)

On psychoanalysis

Not knowing is an important part of psychoanalytic methodology. Freud, informally, wrote that he did not know where a sentence would end up when he began it ... His advocacy of free association and free-floating attention add further dynamism to the role of not knowing in psychoanalytic work.

(2011a, p. 41)

"I don't know" in psychoanalysis was often taken as a sign that the patient was defensive about something, perhaps resistant to further unfolding or contacting difficult material. Fliess (1971) associated it with rips in the person's psyche, unspeakable, unknowable trauma. One does not know because one does not want to know or cannot know.

(2011a, p. 42)

Bion goes more deeply, associating the patient's fear with the fear of emotional experience generally. To an important extent, our emotional experience makes things feel real. The patient's "I don't know," in this instance, is an index of a freeze put on feelings ... that the patient may not yet be able to acknowledge, let alone bear, sustain, or digest.

(2011a, p. 43)

Part of the impetus for [the] work ["Kabbalah and Psychoanalysis," 2012] although I did not suspect it then, was a spontaneous interchange I had with Wilfred R. Bion in 1978, the year before he died. We were speaking, and out of the blue he asked, "Do you know the Kabbalah, the Zohar"? As far as I was aware, there was no preparation for this remark. He just said it. I was a bit taken aback and said, "Well, I know it, but don't really know it" ... He quickly said, "I don't either, really know it," modestly reassuring me. It was established that neither of us were scholars, experts, "knowers," but had awareness, acquaintance. There was a pause. Then he looked at me and said, "I use the Kabbalah as a frame-work for psychoanalysis."

(2012, pp. ix–x)

Here is a bit of applied 'Kabbalah'" in Bion's (1994, p. 214) approach to analytic sessions:

I am concerned in a session with what I don't know. The session is the only time when I can have contact with what I do not know; at any other time I can only have contact with, or think about, phenomena which I believe – rightly or wrongly – that I have already observed, or have observed only partially. It is an opportunity that is not to be missed, for if it is it can never be repeated.

Bion emphasizes linking up with the unknown of the session, the emotional "*Ein Sof*" of the moment.

(2016b, p. 2)

But no one psychic moment is the one and only moment, even if at the time it seems so. Soon enough, other eternal moments qualify it. Alternate and varied infinities modulate one another, excessive as each may be when centre stage (Eigen, 1986). It is, in part, growth of faith that enables us to wait.

(2016b, p. 3)

"I don't know" can be a huge suitcase hiding a lot of sins or a guiding point for the openness of analytic work. It is not unusual that a psychic state is multi-faced.

(2011a, p. 43)

How does psychoanalysis, which we are repeatedly told is a verbal therapy, touch the infinite unknown, wordless reality? All kinds of un-known emotional transmissions occur during therapy. You do not have to be talking for them to occur. Your supportive presence, background atmosphere, tone, and texture has an impact over time that might be more important than anything you say.

(2012, p. 26)

When I got to be an analyst and entered the psychoanalytic world, I realized so many analysts pretended to know something they didn't know. They knew this, and they knew that. They knew Oedipus, a big knowing in itself. They knew a lot in a real way. But with patients, they pretended to know what they didn't know. They pretended to know Something, but they were making it up. They made it up as they went along and pretended to know.

(2011b, p. 81)

Bion blasts the idea of the analyst as knower, since it is openness to unknowing (perhaps the unknowable) that grounds the analytic attitude.

(1998, p. 76).

When I was younger, I was afraid of letting patients know that I didn't know. They were used to a milieu in which analysts knew ... Over time patients got used to me not knowing. It was a relief to them too because then they didn't have to know. And we could begin to let feelings come and talk about them, talk with them like welcome or unwelcome visitors. Maybe understanding them, maybe not ... The capacity to make contact and communicate grows.

(2011b, p. 84)

In practice, I often reach a deep point of not knowing, a kind of creative waiting, that shifts the ambience of the room. As time goes on, a person with me begins to sense something further, perhaps a still point of her own that is a little freeing. It is less a matter of solving problems on their own terms as shifting the center of gravity, allowing something more to grow.

(2018, p. 73)

Openness to experiencing enables growth of openness to experiencing. It is thrilling when a fearful patient discovers faith enough to risk spontaneously going through mad moments, to risk the recovery of spontaneity. When one begins getting beneath words like sanity-madness to realities they mask, one grieves wasting so much time knowing what they meant.

(1998, pp. 93–4)

[H]ow uplifting it can be to be released to go to the darkest or unknown places. To be able to sit in emotional darkness and find patience, endurance, care, and love even in frustration, hate, impatience, and hopelessness stimulate possible growth of a new kind of capacity, partly involving creative waiting, intuitive sensing, letting psyche speak or grunt or weep or rip. Hidden ecstasy runs through psychic life, as does catastrophic destructiveness (Eigen, 2001). Too often, the two are fused and indistinguishable.

(2014a, p. 75)

Emotional storm is real and ought not to be obliterated because we don't know what to do with it. Emotional sensitivity is precious. It is important to stay with impacts or, at least, discover that one is unable to.

(2005, p. 21)

Often we cut off impending storms by creating other kinds of storms. Instead of sensitivity storms, we create insensitivity storms.

(2005, p. 22)

One thing that can happen when you stay with an emotional experience with no solution … in an intermittent way – you keep coming back to it: it might not get "solved" but you change, you grow in the process. The problem might or might not give way, but something happens to you. Batting your psyche against an unsolvable problem forces you to develop … The intensity of pouring yourself into an insoluble problem perforates the psyche, and you find yourself in another place, a place you might not have imagined before it happened. The unsolvable can promote growth of experience in unsuspected ways.

(2012, p. 78)

If you know you don't know, humility grows, and doors open to use yourself in exploratory ways. If we know we don't know what the ultimate reality of the session is, we are freer to use imagination, to hallucinate, feel, sense and share without putting out what we share as gospel.

(2011b, p. 59)

I'm not against knowing. How could anyone be? We wouldn't be here joined in this search without knowledge and the need to know. But I also want to make room for not knowing, for un-dogmatic psychoanalysis, un-dogmatic psychotherapy.

(2011b, p. 80)

Much therapy is imbued with an ethics of waiting, an ethics of the unknown. There is always more that can happen. Infinities keep opening in the here and now, between you and me and within oneself. In a life of mystery, one unknown meets another, unknown to unknown.

(2020, p. 194)

[Psychoanalysis is] two people in a room waiting on the emergence of unknown emotional reality, everything expressible.

(2018, p. 72)

I don't know

There is so much pressure in public life to act as if one knows more than one does, or even believe one knows what one thinks one knows. An enterprise like psychoanalysis, grounded in unknowing, seems an odd beast indeed.

(2011a, p. 71).

To state that the fundamental reality is unknown, although we can be nowhere else, provides protection against necessary and inevitable deceptions. If we really know we are an unknown bit of unknown reality, we leave something open for further experiencing, knowing and lying. This sounds sophomoric, but the consequences are very real. So many individuals on the public stage and in our office leave little room for unknowing. So much destructiveness follows in the wake of feeling right about what one knows. It is harder (not impossible) to pull a trigger while exercising curiosity, doubt, wonder.

(1998, p. 82)

In my book *Rage* (2001), I write that the sense of being "right" has done more harm in human history than any other attitude. It is even used to justify murder. Self-idolatry goes deep, and it is hard to break out of the right–wrong trap.

(2016a, p. 20)

In my first book, *The Psychotic Core* (1986), and again in *The Electrified Tightrope* (1993), I wrote chapters on omniscience, how much more devastating acting from a position of omniscience is than mere delusions of omnipotence, since miscalculation linked with unconscious omniscience – thinking one knows more than one actually does – can wreak multi-generational devastation.

(2016b, pp. 135–6)

When I see world leaders making destructive decisions in a shell of power, I wonder what gaps, deficits, ignorance they push away … Hallucinated strength, hallucinated right and might become more important than what reality can bear. What a relief when someone says "I don't know, wait. There's more to learn. Let's make opening for learning."

(2011b, p. 84)

There's a taboo against not knowing in our culture. On the one hand, you're told its OK not to know – you can learn. On the other, there's shame attached to not knowing. You have to pretend to know. There's a lot of make believe knowing. All groups are built on make believe knowing. It's scary not to know but make believe knowing is scarier. There's a lot of delusional clarity floating around … pretense of omniscience.

(2011b, pp. 82–3)

In our current day, political-economic-military grandiosity carries devastation in its wake. The two extremes play out across the field of humanity. Processes that wreak havoc in individuals are writ large in society and problems ravaging society are read in the mayhem of individual lives.

(2011a, p. 53)

Sometimes I think of what it would be like if the whole world, every single person, top to bottom, chanted in synchrony three words little used in high places: "I don't know." A worldwide wave of unknowing together. It takes so much effort to pretend to know and to act as if one were better than one is, more whole and knowing, and the cost to individuals and nations is high.

(2012, p. 78)

Endings

The taboo against not knowing – being phobic about not knowing – is universal.

(2011b, p. 85)

In my own life, it took many years for the taboo against not knowing who I am to diminish. At certain junctures, it seemed sinful not to know. "You don't know who you are?" Then comes a list of ways to know and things to do … As I got older, not knowing who I am became a friend, welcome, freeing, serene. Blissful time of no-self or, at least, the possibility of taking myself less seriously. Such relief to be free of self, if only for moments. Moments spread.

(2011a, pp. 38–9)

Too often, we presume we know who the other is, we know all about him or her, and we become reactive. Our partial knowledge becomes totalized, and we saturate the space where another might be. I say "imaginary" because acting on partial knowledge as if it is total or more than it is to create a more or less make-believe other, partly real, but also partly imaginary. Often, we may not be able to distinguish our make-believe other from the being who confronts us, and our imagination fuels inflammatory reactivity.

(2011a, p. 52)

Bion emphasizes the dread of not knowing, but it is also a relief not to have to know. Is there a God, or is there not? Is there life after death, or is this it? Who am I? Am I this or am I that? Who are you? Are you who I think you are? How confining would that be? When I think I do not have to know the answer to these questions, I feel relief. I can breathe more easily. To not have to know what cannot be known. To be as open as one can or dares, intermittently, if not moment to moment. To sample openness throughout a lifetime, as part of the paradoxical mix of capacities we have and are. What a relief not only not having to know, but not pretending to know.

(2011a, p. 54)

I suggest saying and feeling I don't know as a practice. Not your only practice. We need analytic thinking and intuitive thinking, left and right brain. But make I don't know part of your practice, an important part. Try it as an exercise. Who am I? I don't know. Who are you? I don't know. Practice I don't knowing.

(2011b, p. 80)

There is no end to my "I don't know," no bottom. I sit in not knowing with an intimate presence, a close friend, amazing stranger, dreaded power, closer to me than I am. Some say that intimate presence is yourself, your own mind, part of inner dialogue, the broca area, your parents. I do not say no. But something eggs me on, not quite this, not quite that. Nothing I learn about it is quite satisfactory. An amazing presence is embedded in the heart's centre, an infinite, intimate presence. "Who are you" I ask. Who or what is it? I do not know. Yet the intimacy of Infinite Intimate Presence is better than "knowing."

If I am pinned to say so, I can be forced to call this a kind of knowing, a special knowing of its own often called a secret knowing. Can I pin this knowing down, know this knowing? To an extent, but in the attempt the deep knowing evades knowing … [F]or me there is no substitute for experiencing the deep unknown of this "known." With relief I set aside "knowing" and irritable reaching after facts and reasons, to taste the thing itself. I no longer want to pin it down. I just want to be with it, some might say to be it, although for me it is a presence inexhaustible by myself. I would rather jump in, stay in. The taste is miraculous. It includes the taste of our lives and the indefinable.

(2011a, p. 51)

It's a grace to be able to finally say out loud, "I don't know" and write about it, talk about it, a place for I don't know. To validate I don't knowing as an important state, activity, ability in psychoanalysis or therapy. I'm thankful that the child self who has been befuddled by my life so many years finally gets the chance to breathe freely and openly and honestly and fully say, "What's going on here? I don't know." It's a relief not to have to pretend you know.

(2011b, p. 82)

From deep not knowing, no one is excluded. We are partners in not knowing and the waiting, caring, sharing it fosters, the patience and sensing needed to live well together, to be intimate with ourselves. How is it possible to be intimate yet unknown, the deeper the unknown, the deeper the intimacy? To enter fields of unknown intimacies opens planes of existence where nothing is required other than to marvel and say thank you. More work comes afterward.

(2011a, p. 55)

References

Bion, WR. (1970). *Attention and interpretation*. Karnac.

Bion, WR. (1994). *Cogitations* (F Bion, Ed.). Karnac.

Eigen, M. (1986). *The psychotic core*. Jason Aronson.

Eigen, M. (1998). *The psychoanalytic mystic*. Free Association Books.

Eigen, M. (2001). *Ecstasy*. Wesleyan University Press.

Eigen, M. (2002). *Rage*. Wesleyan University Press.

Eigen, M. (2005). *Emotional storm*. Wesleyan University Press.

Eigen, M. (2009a). *Flames from the unconscious: Trauma, madness, and faith*. Karnac.

Eigen, M. (2009b). "I don't know." Seminar on Buddhism and Psychoanalysis, American Psychoanalytic Association. In M Eigen, *Contact with the depths* (2011a). Karnac.

Eigen, M. (2011a). *Contact with the depths*. Karnac.

Eigen, M. (2011b). *Eigen in Seoul: Volume two – Faith and transformation*. Karnac.

Eigen, M. (2012). *Kabbalah and psychoanalysis*. Karnac.

Eigen, M. (2014a). *Faith*. Karnac.

Eigen, M. (2014b). *A felt sense: More explorations of psychoanalysis and Kabbalah*. Karnac.

Eigen, M. (2014c). *The birth of experience*. Karnac.

Eigen, M. (2016a). *Under the totem: In search of a path*. Karnac.

Eigen, M. (2016b). *Image, sense, infinities, and everyday life*. Karnac.

Eigen, M. (2018). *The challenge of being human*. Routledge.

Eigen, M. (2020). *Dialogue with Michael Eigen: Psyche singing*. Routledge.

Fliess, R. (1971). *Symbols, dreams and psychosis*. International Universities Press.

Winnicott, DW. (1988). *Human nature*. Shocken Books.

Chapter 10

Canvassing *Illusion* and *Faith* in fragmentation

An Indian perspective

Ashis Roy

Contemporary psychoanalysis has been informed by the work of reverie, dreaming, and counter dreaming, which has changed the ways in which analysts know their patients. These powerful forms of unconscious communication have expanded the analyst's subjectivity. In this chapter, we will witness unconscious communication as it gathers the self-states (Bromberg, 1998) in women that exist before the formation of internal objects. These self-states remain unformulated, and they exist in a disintegrated psychic space (Phillips, 2007). We will witness how unconscious communication receives the infant-like states in a patient and how it absorbs the alienation in another patient. In both cases, unconscious communication intuits mental life that has been exiled and enables the therapist in sensing the illusion that has been missing in the lives of these individuals.

One of Winnicott's central contributions to psychoanalysis was his emphasis on *illusion*. Green (2019) writes, "Freud showed the importance of illusion, but, in his mind, one had to fight illusion and accept disillusionment." Analysis was supposed to free the individual from his illusions, in favour of the dictatorship of reason and rationality. Winnicott says, "'You are wrong. Illusion is absolutely necessary for healthy development, you can only accept being disillusioned, if you have been illusioned.' Those who have not had the chance of being illusioned can only fail" (Kohon, 2008, p. 29).

Bass, Black, and Dimen beautifully capture the theme of illusion and transitional experience in their paper "Reflections on Flat Mountain – a Tribute to Emmanuel Ghent." The paper draws us to a moment between Ghent, and his daughter Nadia, that captures the *route to the truth is through the intensity of illusion* (Ghent). Ghent enacts something as a father that unfolds in his daughter's life years later. They write,

> Nadia noted that it took many years to figure out that Flat Mountain "wasn't a real place at all, that it was only a stop made necessary by a hot, tired, cranky and whining four-year-old." The stop had indeed been necessary, and it was just Mannie's recognition of that necessity, and his lovingly playful and attuned response to Nadia's need, that made the day one that she would carry with her forever. And now we can all hold it as a

perfect reflection of something that we knew about Mannie, but perhaps had not thought in so many words. Flat Mountain was, after all (at least in one sense), "just a small patch of grass" along the parkway. But Mannie and Nadia had found in it a route to an alternate and sustaining reality.

(Bass, Black, and Dimen, 2005, p. 160)

The following vignette describes the creation of illusion in the reveries of the therapist as being the background for the beginnings of analytic work.

Roshni, a creative designer, came to therapy for the treatment of cyclical depression. On days that she was anxious, she would wake up and puke. In her depressive phases, Roshni would experience a state of paralysis within her. She would be unable to move and would describe herself as *marinating* in this state. At the beginning of her therapy, as 30-year-old Roshni lay on the couch, she would find it hard to find words. I would feel that the formation of her words needed support. I would imagine extending my fingers to her and that she needed to hold my fingers as she lay down. In those moments I felt like I was with someone who was much younger. My dream-like reverie was organic, and without my having any knowledge of her past. In Bion's words, it was without memory or desire (Bion, 1967).

A dream of hers will tell us how she would puke and evacuate her mental states – *I dreamt I am in Bombay, I go to the trial room to wear a jacket, but I throw up my intestines.* Our subsequent effort to find associations and give meaning to this *dream* failed. This terrifying dream was of an internal space where her insides could suddenly erupt. It had to be remembered by me as an unmentalized terror before terror could be given words. Many dreams remained unmentalized, and they would represent parts of her that she would run away from. Roshni needed a ground or a surface where preconceptions could become conceptions (Bion, 1993).

Not fully knowing what brought her to therapy since the description of cyclical depression was abstract, my reverie of extending my fingers made me rely on an organic process between us. Roshni lacked the words to describe her internal states and this experience became the ground for our alliance.

After a year of once a week therapy, she had stopped puking in her state of anxiety. She brought a dream into the session which communicated an unformed in-utero part of her internal life

> In this dream I am not a human. My body is like an egg and I am trying to move. In the dream I am panicking and trying to move. There is this tension and I am trying to stay within the shell. Something grows out. The form of the body. It's like me and the drawing that I have done in the first year of college. Visually it's somewhere. But there is a need to change. Every time I move the form changes.

Roshni's dream carried the paralysis within her internal world. She felt that if she moves her world may crack, if she stays still, she would not have had to come out. If she comes out, she will have to come to the school of life, which is a vast space, and there is no one to hold onto. She was terrorized by the world. Her dream contained her paradoxical mental state in which a part of her connected and a part of her withdrew from life. Something in her life had remained unhatched. Birth was scary for her.

In retrospect, I could connect with my reverie of extending my fingers to her, which was my way of sensing a wordless internal fragility. Her dream represents a caesura between her history and her terrors (Bion, 1993). Roshni's unmentalized experiences needed a maternal container.

I now turn to my brief therapeutic work with Sarah and my experience of being caught in a spell. We will witness the unfolding of a life that has been dominated by sensations and actions, and doesn't know where the sensations belong – inside or outside?

Five years ago, 30-year-old Sarah came to me for psychotherapy. Thin, tall, and attractive, there was something about her demeanour which was pleasant and charming. These weren't my first impressions. My first impression was a hallucination over the telephone, which made me feel when I saw her that she should have been more attractive than she was. Her thin outline, arms without flesh, and her bony structure made me wonder if she was a man or a woman. Sarah introduced herself by saying, *I should have come here ten years ago*. It's a rare thing that has come my way, and perhaps it's only Sarah who has ever said this. It is so rare that it can be missed and forgotten, and my supervisor, Professor Nagpal, helped me see it's rarity. The rare quality was in seeing a potential in psychoanalysis and in me as something that was waiting to be found for ten years. Perhaps a possible end to a search that was lifelong – the need to find a consciousness that could absorb the impact that life has had on her, and transmit a new spirit. I could have forgotten it, had it not been emphasized. There was something in Sarah that was waiting to meet me.

Her saying that she wanted to come here ten years earlier was the first impression of an impersonal element that she brought to me. Something within her could vaguely see ten as a signifier but not necessarily locate or find a need to explain why she was saying this. The faith with which this was mentioned needed me to find faith in others who could help me see this. Her mind was organizing a sense of time which could be understood only retrospectively.

Three years ago, rage had taken over her life. She had been in a relationship for six years, and her partner betrayed her. Sarah believed that cheating was the worst thing that could have happened. As I listened to her over many sessions, I felt the mind imagines more and more, and feels propelled to imagine the worst. Sarah had met the person that her partner had slept with. Her relationship with her boyfriend, Matthew, who was a foreigner was full of turmoil after this incident. She would discharge her hatred and anger at him, and he would apologize unconditionally. She couldn't move away from him, since he was more accepting of his faults. In her life there had been other relationships, but she wouldn't miss them. With Matthew, a sense of belonging and mourning had been born in her.

When Sarah was 22 years old, she ran away from her home and married her Hindu-Christian boyfriend. She loved him a lot, but after three years, one day it just ended. Neither did he try hard to understand, nor could she recover what went wrong. Her community exiled her for being with a Hindu. Then, she was in a relationship with a spiritually inclined older man. Even with him, the intensity faded. Sarah always felt inferior to him because he tried to put her on a good path. She would say, *he was too good for me.*

Sarah was born in a town in Kerala and grew up in a traditional Muslim family. She was a non-practicing Muslim. Her parents migrated to Dubai for a few years and then came back to India. Her father worked as a financial controller, and her mother was a homemaker.

One of the first sensations that she brought into the clinic was a raw childhood memory. *I didn't get along with my brother. My mother loved him and hated me. I bit him once.* This was the first juice of infidelity for her that she tried to attack, which made its appearance later in her life. Her brother's existence drove her to a rage which made her bite him. Orality drives us to possess or destroy, and Sarah was showing how urges and instincts can dominate the body so much that there is no way of personalizing them. There was no container for her raw instinctual sensations. Sarah felt, *when my parents go to my brother they are living out infidelity towards me.* Sibling relationships are defined by death, the presence of one sibling signifies the death of the other one (Mitchell, 2008).

Since childhood, Sarah was the hated one and was constantly controlled in her house. Although in her descriptions, she wasn't doing anything unconventional, but she did have an interest in boys that troubled her parents. Her mother would hit her, and once an exorcist was called to take the demon out of her. *I remember my grandmother telling me that there is a devil in you and that there were black threads tied around me and I was hit.* I said you must be very scared. *She shrugged and said, yes, possibly.* She only shrugged when I shared that I sense a lot of fear in her. These traumatic experiences were described in an affect-less way.

One of her recurrent dreams contained her scatter, fragmentation, and a significant relationship that had been internalized.

> *My grandfather is taking me out of this house onto a beach, and it's dark, and he asks me to look at the sky and the only thing I see in the sky is my own reflection Except that I am all in pieces – my limbs are somewhere, my head is somewhere, and then he is smiling at me.*

As I wrote to Eigen about her, he suggested to ask her, "When you fall apart, do you think you will ever get back together again? Do you feel that falling apart is final or sometimes you are more in pieces and sometimes not?" (Ei-gen, June 2015, personal conversation).

For Sarah, her grandfather was humble, and he loved her. I was unfamiliar with this level of fragmentation. Later, I could imagine that her grandfather extending her gaze to the sky with his smile may have stood for a *limitlessness* that could attend to her fragmented self.

When Sarah ran away with her Hindu husband, her father didn't talk to her for three years. Her relationship with her father oscillated between in-tense adulation and periods of non-communication. When they were staying together, they would not talk to each other for months, and for years when they were staying apart. In spite of this, she could recount in her sessions *that she was the one he loved the most.* I wondered, *what happens in a father–daughter relationship that it becomes completely wordless? Is this a communication of intense hatred or a way of preserving what is there? Or is it a desire to not know at all about parts of your daughter's life?*

Sarah intensely idealized men. Matthew felt that he had to cheat on her be-cause she would idealize him so much that he would feel unreal. Idealization can be a strong destructive force. You can feel so stuck in the idealization that you have to be cruel to free yourself. Boundaries can be fused, and separation from idealized relationships is fused with violence. As a teenager, she had been obsessively in love with her six-year-older cousin. She bared her soul open to her cousin, and he exposed her to the community when he wanted to distance himself from her. He maligned her by saying that she was a nym-phomaniac and by disclosing her abuse. He probably did this to get rid of her.

Sarah had been abused since she was 9 years old. It first happened in Dubai during weekends when she was made to sleep in the same bedroom with her cousins. Her mother's cousin would put his hand inside her panties. *I would never scream. At times he made me put my hand on his crotch – my hand would be like a robot, maybe he thought I was a baby doll.* She would tell her mother that she didn't want to sleep in the same room, but her mother wouldn't get the hint. When Sarah was older, a servant forced himself on her, threw her on the bed. She threatened to tell her parents, and he stopped. Her father's cousin would feel parts of her when the lights would go out. He told her *you kiss really well.*

After her family found out about her abuse from her cousin, her mother said to her, *Sorry I let it happen, I should have protected you. Her mother was crying. Sarah hugged her and said it wasn't your fault. That was the end of it.* Her mother shared with Sarah that she too had been abused. Neither Sarah nor her family had developed a language around abuse. Sarah responded to abuse by becom-ing counter-phobic. It made her more curious about sexuality.

Her narration about abuse provided a sense of waiting for the abuse to happen. When she was young, there was a non-reactiveness to her abuse, and slowly through other events in her life she became more responsive. Her response was, *why did they abuse me if I wasn't pretty?* and not that she shouldn't have been abused. Members of her family were living out desires in her and in her mother, which perhaps they could not express elsewhere. *It is very tough to imagine what makes an 11-year-old go silent and not scream. Why can't she bite?*

Sarah's memories of abuse evoked in me scenes from the Japanese film, directed by Wakamatsu, *Go, Go, Second Time Virgin*. In the film, a gang of young men rape a woman, and she lies there for long time with blood flowing out of her. One of the rapists falls in love with her. The camera shows her body being devoured and touched for excitement, and it focuses only on her breasts or her face, segregating them as pieces of flesh, much like Sarah's limbs in the sky. The film captures the deadness and blankness of these moments and induces an affect which is un-liveable so you can never think that you have imagined it enough or gone beyond it. In one scene, the victim's eyes blink, and you can see she has turned into something else. She is no longer protesting but has entered another space. Sarah's descriptions of abuse were similar.

A rageful and angry girl carried in herself events that were obliquely silent and wordless. These episodes needed to draw more from the internal recesses of others rather than speak for themselves. She could not cry about it, and as she said herself she was only disturbed. This was like a stir in her psyche, like a zephyr brushing her wound.

The wordlessness in the film helped me stay with Sarah's frozen trauma. *I wonder if in moments of abuse, can the body and the psyche be paired? The abuser is also someone who can't emerge out of the darkness. At that moment is it more prominent that this is my uncle or uncle's hand – or is it that as a growing child I have a relationship with this part which is getting excited. Here lies an intimate relationship with a part of the self becoming impersonal as an impulse, and the object animating it. For the abused, the experience can also be of an orgasm which cannot be enjoyed. This excitement cannot find any community around it and can't even find a person to own it. Sarah was an embodiment of a person who was screaming out the fact that older people in her family and community had been doing this for so long.*

Maybe she needed a lover, like the woman in the film, who could love her where several other men were forcibly present.

On a rare occasion, after one of the sessions in which we had spoken about her abuse, she said that she was affected. I said did you feel sad? She said no *I felt disturbed, I think I have dis-associated it.* This rare moment and surprise is akin to what Erikson calls the numinous. *Numinous is the rare thing that will emerge – like the mother waiting for the child to come out of his stuporous state to recognize her.*

Sarah felt more guilty and ashamed of being an abuser. She shared, with a lot of uneasiness and shock, that she would kiss her brother when they were young. She felt that he must hate her for it. She wished to take it to her grave.

Sexuality was introduced as an instinct to Sarah by those who could not protect her from their own desires. In moments of abuse, generations collapse (Ogden, 2014), since the abuser imagines the abused to be of the same age, mental state, wanting the same thing as he does. In Sarah's mind, the boundaries between sexuality and abuse had collapsed. With her brother, she felt a clear sense of guilt. My work with other female patients of the same age group who have experienced abuse has shown, when abuse is deposited in you and in your body, you need to discharge it into someone else before seeing what it did to you. This is another kind of exorcism.

Sarah's life was filled with shame. Shame obliterates parts of the self. It doesn't allow memories to get formed. *How does one hold shame in a session?* For her to talk in our sessions, meant to recover something that was not there. Links with the past, with anything historical, were ephemeral and fragmented. One event, especially, was telling of how she had met shame in her life. When Sarah was 23 years old, she went home for the wedding of her mother's cousin's daughter, who was only 15 years old. Her mother's cousin was the head of the Tabligh committee. He wanted her to apologize to the entire community because she had run away from home with a Hindu-Christian boy. The rumours were that she was pregnant. He announced to all that she will apologize. She had to hold everyone's hand and ask for forgiveness. As she was telling me this, she said,

I just froze. I asked her why didn't you say no? *She said he looked like Osama, the terrorist, and there was something very serious about him. After that, I went up and cried. I had to apologize to my cousin's mother, who was also there, and I looked away as I did. There were rumours that I was pregnant, and that's why I had run away.* Maybe she apologized on behalf of the weaker and scared parts of her parents who had not been as religious as their community. Not knowing what to say, I felt the need to support her. I said you must be feeling very alienated from your community. *She said yes.* She said yes in a good way. *I can't be around people who like Sidney Sheldon as an author.* I asked whom do you like? *She said Murakami and Ishiguro. I see you have Murakami on your shelf. There is something about the emotions present that I really like. I can feel it.*

It is touching, in retrospect to see that Sarah and I could sense goodness amidst so much humiliation. By touching each person's hand she was forced to disclose so much about herself. At that moment, she was at her uncle's mercy. The rumour of her pregnancy meant for her community that a part of her had gone into the *other* community. Humiliation was their way of getting her back. For Sarah, this was another moment which made her feel convinced that she had no desire or need to go back. She could also carry in her the sense that there was *something* good which could withstand all this and still exist within her to carry her forward. This something being good is my subjective sense of herself that could be retained in her after this humiliation. My mind did not get swamped by what happened or other such questions, but it received the part of her that survived all this. It felt like everyone around and had walked all over her, and I needed to hold onto what was left. My initial imagination and illusion that there should be something more attractive in her, a hallucinatory expectation, preserved something in my efforts at showing what was new in her life – *what was life*. As I think about it, my valuing her alienation maybe meant that she could leave things behind and not mourn about them. Her mind went onto the books on my shelf, to Japanese authors whose writings can make identities look fluid and limitless. She could move towards selfhood defined by modernity rather than feeling constrained by traditional signifiers. There was no space for Sarah to think of repairing her relationships although I was left with the question of what had happened in her relationships?

When she was forced to ask for forgiveness, amidst the humiliation, *Sarah froze*. Perhaps, her frozen state was her quiet rebellion that could withstand her community's hostility which demanded an apology. She had run away and married a Hindu, and the elders in her community wanted to possess her once again. If she had only apologized, her past traumas would have been a delusion – like the ghost that had to be exorcized. Exorcism was her community's way of protecting her mind. Sarah stood on the fringes of finite resignation of her past life which would have been silenced had she not frozen. The memory of this ephemeral state captured a sense of resolve which she deposited in me. *She hadn't fainted. Maybe she wanted all the values and ethics to make sense of that state. Apology in good circumstances would have washed away her shame. Apology would have been a re-conversion. It was her community's way of saying – you can come back through this from being a Hindu. She couldn't say no because her father was a part of the same community. Her impersonal frozen state was a deep defence which manifested in a resolve to find creativity.*

Much of Sarah's experience resonated with these lines by Emily Dickinson (1993),

> Pain has an element of blank,
> It cannot recollect,
> When it began, or if there were,
> A day when it was not
> It has no future but itself
> It's infinite realms contain
> It's past, enlightened to perceive,
> New periods of pain.

Piecing herself together was a huge task. In various moments in her life, the core of herself had been trampled upon. Her cousin exposing her, the humiliation she faced in her community – she had lived out something that no one could identify with. There was an intensity, an unquestioning idea of love, amorous salvation that she would look for, which her lovers would fail to understand.

In his essay "On being too much for ourselves," Adam Phillips writes about the nature of excess, prohibitions, and the excesses and excitements that prohibitions are made for. According to him, each child grows up feeling that he or she was too much for their parents and that simultaneously shapes their experience of themselves (Phillips, 2010). Excesses are dealt with punishment which is meant to silence them. *It is hard to evoke curiosity in the one who is caught in the throes of excess.* People around have to deal with the impact and consequences. For Phillips, to work out our excesses we need help from others (Phillips, 2010).

Maybe what Sarah needed of me was to retain moments of her life – crying with her mother, a figure like her grandfather waiting to greet her. Unfortunately, like many episodes in her life, she stopped therapy suddenly, and my efforts to communicate with her failed. In the last session that we had I experienced something which was not a complete experience. While sitting in front of her, I felt that my head was bleeding. At that moment, I could not move away from this and what was happening was very unsettling. It felt like a film in which I had seen a coin split through someone's head and come out from the other side. One of her communications was that there is no room for feelings here. As I tried to make sense of this experience, I wrote to Eigen. He said *maybe she is trying to stuff something in your head. Try and stay with it.* This made it thinkable.

In the book, *The Logic of Madness*, Resnik, describes the psychotic response to feeling through his work with a psychotic patient Renata, who would cut off her feelings. His writing describes how psychotic patients project themselves into the analyst (projective identification) in order to test or to feel protected inside the analyst's mental space and/or body ego (Resnik, 2018). As Sarah left, she taught me something about her mind's incapacity to tolerate certain mental states which needed to be projected into others because they were unbearable.

As I am left with Sarah's extremely fragmented dream, her undigested impersonal instinctiveness, with impressions of her annihilated self (Eigen, 2007), fragmentation, and shame, her grandfather's smile stays. Perhaps she was in search of someone who smiled at her, and my attraction to her was one way of restoring that. The need on my part to bless her was a way of joining the smile that her grandfather extended to her. I think this is what Eigen calls Bion's F in O – Faith in the midst of Catastrophe (Eigen, 2011). Amidst her traumatic experiences, her grandfather was an uncontaminated figure whose gaze could preserve the blessings that she was in search of. Her scattered limbs in the dream, abuse which carried animations of a hand had not found an intersubjective space. Working with her made me aware of being Hindu differently. As she left, I wondered in retrospect whether I, as a Hindu therapist, was giving her ongoing support *around* her sexuality and her broken self that had not arisen in her community. Evacuation was all that her community could give her. The dream gave Sarah a span of limitlessness. Maybe Limitlessness was her container.

References

Bass, A, Black, M, and Dimen, M. (2005). Reflections on flat mountain. *Psychoanalytic Dialogues*, 15 (2), 159–68. doi:10.1080/10481881509348824.

Bion, WR. (1967). Notes on memory and desire. *The Psychoanalytic Forum*, 2, 272–3, 279–80.

Bion, WR. (1993). *Attention and interpretation.* Maresfield Library (originally published 1970).

Bromberg, P M. (1998). *Standing in the spaces – essays on clinical process trauma and dissociation.* The Analytic Press.

Brown, LJ. (2018). "Notes on memory and desire": Implications for working through*. *The W. R. Bion Tradition,* 333–43. doi:10.4324/9780429483738-36.

Dickinson, E. (1993). *The collected poems of Emily Dickinson.* Barnes & Noble Books.

Eigen, M. (2007). *Feeling matters.* Routledge.

Eigen, M. (2011). *Contact with the depths.* Routledge.

Kohon, G. (2002). *The dead mother: The work of Andre Green.* Routledge.

Mitchell, J. (2008). *Siblings: Sex and violence.* Polity.

Ogden, TH. (2014). *Rediscovering psychoanalysis: Thinking and dreaming, learning and forgetting.* Routledge.

Phillips, A. (2007). *Winnicott.* Penguin Books.

Phillips, A. (2010). *On balance.* Picador.

Resnik, S. (2018). *The logics of madness.* Routledge.

Chapter 11

More than a word

Reverberations between Eigen's notions of deadness/aliveness and Bion's grid

Adam Shechter

Introduction

What type of written words stay with a psychoanalytic reader long after the book has been put down? In particular, what is the quality and nature of a text that excites and influences the reader with what is beyond words – words that go further than the sole purpose of being written in order to be read on the world of a page? Categories for such words could fall under headings that include scripts for dramatic plays, manuals for home appliances, and haikus that inspire meditation; yet these listed genres of word use, in all their instruction to the imagination to go into action, can still be motionless in terms of the words' living influence of one psyche upon another. Wordless words (Eigen, 2011) or words that clear the way of their own page-shackled utterance inspires a specific kind of excitement; call it developmental for the moment. A recent passage that awoke me along such lines is in or *is happening in* Bion's paper, *The Grid* (1989). The words are:

> C elements are used to provide anchorage for the relationship – mouth is one anchor, breast is the other. Both of these terms have been treated as if they were the essential features of the analogy. It is exactly this point that marks the divergence of the path of growth from the path of decay. The breast and the mouth are only important insofar as they serve to define the bridge between the two. When the "anchors" usurp the importance which belongs to the qualities which they should be imparting to the bridge, growth is impaired.
>
> (p. 26)

A meditation into this plucked-out group of sentences brings what is helpfully nurturing about psychoanalysis to the surface, as though a colouring agent applied to the outline of an invisible picture, one that deepens clearness with each next application to the psyche. Bion's criteria generalizes about words spoken in a session, sifting the space for what is said as either producing growth or decay. This task of workable aliveness and language underscores and shows that *the fixed image of what is therapeutically correct* can easily contract and wither before the boundless possibility of the therapeutic moment. How then to stave off the pressure toward immediate interventive action that extinguishes the transmutative spark? How to elicit a moment of calm before rote analogies take over as beasts of the status quo? It is important to note that the imagistic analogy of the breast and the mouth that are biologically native to the original relation of the mother feeding the infant is equally susceptible to stagnation and decay. Precious movement and growth are found across styles of analogizing that go beyond any one organ-system that represent the therapist–patient dyad as a living, growing organic relation.

I find myself repeatedly drawn to such lines as Bion's, ones that do what they can to cross over into another form, state, realm, as if the cartoon magical image of the words shape-shift off the page embodying the content of the text for the reader in the present moment of reading. I say all this to highlight the importance of finding what is therapeutically transformative in terms of how psychoanalytic writing meets the controversial borders of its own practice – the therapeutic drama that is also the narrative struggle of the writing itself.

Drawing from the sample pool of clinicians that surround me, including those who do and don't write, two strong feeling trends emerge about clinical writing: There are those who don't write or write in a specific emotionally technical way who put forth the critical argument of emotional aliveness and assert that the abstractly writing clinician gets lost in intellectualization and thereby cuts off the therapeutic value of writing as it is limited to a theoretically tentative map of the author's psyche's defences. Others, particularly those who do write, and deeply so, throw the argument the other way, and conceptualize the perceived defence of intellectualization as a way of life inherent to their psychoanalytic cure. My experience is that writing is much more than just an isolating fortress of words, but in fact a required container for my practice, especially in terms of how words are kept in a constant state of bubbling aliveness within the cauldron of their transformative potential – regardless of the final destination of the words.

Usurping of the bridge

I will now turn to Michael Eigen's writing as he fulfils Bion's criteria for words that nurture the path of growth by the bridge usurping the static anchors of breast and mouth. I will place a passage of Eigen's writing from his book *Psychic Deadness* (2004) inside of Bion's analogy and see what sprouts and unfurls between. Eigen writes:

> Writing is longing. One writes with a voice more intimate than one's own. Writing is fulfillment, plenitude: lack and overflow. In writing one is closer to the Other (as inner presence) than one ever will be in real life. One hopes to draw the inner presence to one through veils of exteriority (the work), a real dream Other.

> (Loc, 4002 of 4951)

Eigen's words open the mouth of Bion's anchor, in that the action of writing is restated by Eigen as longing. This inhabiting of the inside-out vulnerable state of words enlivens the connection between writer and reader, touching both anchors of mouth and breast as they uphold a living bridge through words that quietly draw from the matrix of inferred psychoanalytic complexity. To touch on the biological origin in words is the historical cornerstone of the psychoanalytic verbal act, so I will nudge out an image from the word "longing" and emphasize, writing as in "longing" elongates the lips. An opening of the lips that returns to Bion's anchor of mouth in need of usurping through the living explosivity of the therapeutic connection. *What happens to the voice of the writing?* Eigen calls the voice more intimate than his own, or in this case the human writing voice that he is speaking for. As writers and readers, we share an intimacy that furthers the feeling that actual contact is being prioritized over inert words isolated on the page. While the actual little printed word symbols are totally still, this intimacy leans towards a hope that is more. Writing takes on a unifying quality of intimacy that is an expanding oneness as the author is more-than-one in his writing through this hope of leaving-ascending the breast-scape of the page. The idea and experience of oneness becomes fluid through faith and in so doing permits the interpretations of surrender to be many. The position of reality is held through the author acknowledging his impregnation by the potential for his internal objects to be more alive and pronounced inside of him and so realer beside him as within the written down words that the reader, in turn, can identify with. As the reader is outside, so he may come in. By theoretical association the described sensuousness of language-making as an intimate longing gives rise to the implicitly psychosexual or the intimate antecedent to words that is the primal history of the apparatus that creates them, therefore the mouth that longs through the initial feeding purpose, now a cultivator of text infusing the exigent-desirous relation to the breast.

The breast is challenged by the fact of the breast being itself, and for the fact of those who never nursed at one, or only did so minimally. The fundamental unit of structure surrenders to the initial latticework of the primal taking-in of nourishment and accompanying psychic mosaic of sensory impressions, textured expectations, patterned attitudes, sensations, and feelings. The breast-relation as an original psychic fabric spans and collapses the bridge of mouth and breast into a malleable theory of feeding manifestations. The breast starts with itself and quickly opposes in the form of absence, the presence of an absent-present, and the deeper feeding of a qualitative relationship, a total emotional-body environment that delivers nourishment through a specific scope of sound, smell, vibration, rhythm of psyche, and senses at the time that the living metaphor of breast is being developmentally linked to life and experience formation. Freud's hallucinatory return of the breast under the flooding conditions of its absence (1900; Eigen, 2005), further outlined by Klein's (1946) good–bad split/psyche war waged by the infant over the

stimulated unbearable aggression, fills out the original characters and background materials that come to be a creative set of relations. Good and bad are
mixed in a formula of toxic nourishment (Eigen, 2010), an ambivalent sustenance of personality as indigenous to the life–internal–interpersonal matrix
of the patient; a nutrient–toxin unity of original development that roots the
patient to the projective soil of the therapist's office. This environmental sustenance, in turn, absorbs the therapist within its projective terrarium as the
patient is mutually pulled into the therapist's diet of feelings – each are archi-
tects/gardeners/cooks creating the materials of an overdetermined bridge as
they cross from primal breast to mouth and back again.

Before further unpacking Bion's analogy through Eigen's passage, I will
gaze at the community of primates encompassing the infant, or the pre-
human use of the now human mouth. Eric Gans (1981) posits what he calls
an originary event, not dissimilar to that of Freud's band of brothers who
unite to overthrow, murder, and consume their more powerful primal father,
and then proceed to share the resources that he had been greedily hoarding.
In Gans' case, the mythical event of origins has a less flowery backdrop and
cast of characters and involves a key group of hominids competing over what
he calls a central object. At the evolutionary time of this event, language and
communication limits to grunt and gestural signals. Gans locates the competing hominids around a central object as the birthplace of language. Instead of
attacking and fighting each other for possession of the object such as a food
resource (e.g. a single hunted animal) that is their centre, language emerges
as a mitigating medium of communication. By being able to put the coveted
centre into words, each member of the group shares in a symbolic division
of the actual object on a linguistic basis of possession or as Gans writes, "the
individual language user has internalized the context of the originary event
in a scene of representation, a private imaginary space independent of the
community" (1993). The "private imaginary space" of language as internally
recreated in psyche separate from and replacing of an original desired object
echoes Freud's infant who hallucinates the breast at the frustration threshold
of hunger for and absence of a similarly urgent object; the collective/indi-
vidual mirror reflecting fractals of attention and growth. Both events share
an ongoing status of perpetual new beginnings, building and elaborating
up to this day – including this moment and these words. Micro-stages of
language evolution inaugurated from the renunciation of an original object
that transcends the thing of its origin as a unit of sub-structure embedded
in both group and breast as mutually creating symbolic verbal sustenance.
A trans-developmental process that goes backwards and forwards/across the
timelessness of new zones of psyche-food, usurping body and brain in the
loosely regulated ecosystem of the breast-forest.

The patient's freedom to say anything or almost anything alludes to this indefinable unit of sub-structure that usurps the public shape of the personal –
the freedom of anything-speech in the consulting room trading in the

currencies of the evolutionary-breast feeding interstice. The mitigation of the developmental fight symbolically housed in the controlled analytic consultation. In other words, the patient can say whatever he wants so long as the therapist can bear and metabolize the maturational *as well as evolutionary* implications.

Returning to Eigen's quote, writing/longing re-views in the long-range mirror of the collective, as a longing that reflects the first experience of separateness from the mother-breast. The frustration of a premature separation, one that is self-referential and flooded with loss, rage, and sadness, simultaneously inspiring a desire for and acquisition of her in representational form. Writers write to make contact with the mother as well as possess the central resource of the group, one that, according to Gans, is a source and site of divinity. And for Eigen writing being one that fulfils but also lacks and overflows. The bi-directional sensation of overflow against lack emotionally paints a picture of inner sensitivity and contact, the infant's lips touching the breast, as though the point of the quill that begins to dip into the oily black ink of a well. This writerly well collapses the two image anchors of Bion's analogy, and so has an inside and outside location across baby and mother, writer, and reader. The milk flows into the baby's mouth from the breast as the writer's words flow out from his pen to the page. The milk comes in, and the milk goes out at the same time in order for both to become the bridge in an organic analogy of writing relation.

While writing is the mouth making contact with the nipple and breast, writing is not warm bodily milk. Alimentary reality limits writing to its production of mediating developmental symbols. Writing lacks by necessity and thereby places one in the reality principle and on an object field of competitive resources that include its creative production process and landscape. Writing makes primal contact up to the point of actual flow. Yet, writing also overflows, the breast bursting and spurting forth with the streams of its own representation. Psychically, writing frees the memory of oneness with the abundant breast, allowing one's thoughts to pour uninterrupted into the mouth of the page, a blissful harmony with an infinite containing space of the word-milk inside that is aching to come outside from the engorged breast of loneliness. A closeness with the most intimate other; the other being the object, or the part-object as in the breast, and also the part-object in all future forms, hybrids, manifestations, everyone and no one who cannot be physically inside the writer at the time of the psychic genesis of the text. As the words come out, contact is made with the body-memories of the loss that belies the origin of language, or the wish-yearnings of the infant to be close to what abandons and is abandoned, pushing the instinctual cry of hunger into a dissatisfaction with its own animalistic response and into a need for a new relational zone of transformation. These cries cross the synaptic sea of development through the emotionally magnetic draw of word formation, a process of development that is reaffirmed and reinforced in the collective renunciation for the central object. In the moment of writing, the fantasy of the other is as real as the tactile contact produced by the scribble of the pen on paper, the cascading dance of the fingers across the laptop's keys; all the music of vibration that notates the limits of surfaces that is the body of the untouchable primal mother. The dream of the inner presence is the feeling to be closer to what no longer exists, and that which metabolizes its absence through this work of inner-breast seeking, the scribble and tap of the infant's fingers upon the nipple. The writer orchestrates and plays back the fantasy of the blissful suckle coming true, the baby-dreamer waking up into the actuality of a mothering dream as being what he always knew to be true. The longing is met. The bridge crossed as its anchors surrender their definitions to the unknown form of new meanings being made, *the path of growth* beginning on a bridge that digests its own infrastructure in the ephemeral clarity of a myth called writing.

Towards the vulnerable map of unknown contact and investigating an Eigenic epistemology

I will now begin drawing a map that is both like and unlike the one in Borges (1975) story, "On exactitude in science"; that story's map being one that expands into such specific geographic detail, that the physical map sprawls across the land, "point for point," occupying the empire's entirety. Representation enshrouding reality by covering over what is represented with the representation supplies the basis for an invisible variation of such a depiction, one composed of emotional line drawings of the psychotherapy session, an under-map for sensing-into psychic contours, and organizing what is there but cannot be tangibly seen or touched. The map I am proposing unfocuses the lens on the map's details sifting out sensed patterns across Eigen's work on psychic taste buds (2006), and traces the path of the unknowable session – a diagrammatic style of drawing through interoceptive feelings and the compass of the gut, surveying the interpersonal territory that is just beyond. A drawing that covers over what is known in order to restart its sketch inside the conclusion of an implied feeling of what is left unsaid and absent, yet throbs the needlepoint north of what has always been intuitively known through the trail left in-between the lines: The way that leads to the edge parallel with emotional reality.

Key land features of this map-less-map are the theoretical formations below the surface that are as subtly perceptible as ancient mountains that have been slowly eroded over thousands and thousands of years and now barely show the superficial head of their original idea's structure. The structure being there nonetheless, yet now only in fluid represented form, but still just as integral to the articulation and flow of the creative formulation that comes to make up the surroundings of contact. Subjective poetic description contemplatively distils through submerging the technical construct in the warm developmental pulp that emits from the intent mixing of two hearts. This implied depth of clinical knowledge and experience runs the terrain of Eigen's books with ever-disintegrating and emerging essences of a theory that speak out as signs on the continuously moving trail of the transformative process.

A key to the coordinates of the map-less map

i. Closeness is distance. Just as reifying the theoretical construct to the level of emotional reality is a covering over of what is actually there, exalting the emotional aliveness of the therapist similarly erases the reality of the patient's isolated feelings that lack direct links to sensation. Emotional aliveness is a distancing agent when making contact with emotions in psychic graves. To speculate on resurrecting states from the emotionally dead point, the therapist circles the locations of such deadness within the self; and paradoxically, makes living contact with the enlivening point of what is emotionally dead in the patient.

ii. Intellect is a living terrain of deadness. The isolated psychic geography of emotional deadness can be expressed in many physical ways. This chapter primarily concerns writing and books. These intellectualized forms are accessed as hallucinatory maps of what-is-not-there for contact yet leave a compelling cartography of presence before absence that is there-as-can-be. Hence, the writing in a book is a real space of contactless contact and comprises a place that is also a guide for what is so alive about the dead-seeming session.

iii. Total absence is complete contact. The pain of the non-being–being paradox cannot be reconciled in the emotional appreciation of its experience; only divided by survival, and is the infinite wisdom point where absence as being present may begin to tell us something of which way to go. To be able to be with the metaphor that is and is not there feels equivalent to a death wish, a psychic one that feels so real, and yet, in so psychically dying, the beginning of new states of being occur.

The Grid's hyper-linear form is a reducible structure of psychic space in which two elements can meet and become understandable to each other through the unifying structure that underlies their connection; a mirroring that is already evident in psychotherapy, and yet always discovering new vistas for the capacity of mirroring that occurs structurally in deep-psyche. The component headings of each column and row in the grid seem to call out to each other over a lined body of water, pre-existing guides that mark the place for building a bridge or pathway that directs each to a meeting point. Before row C we find beta and alpha elements, rows A and B, respectively. From the agonizing pre-verbal frustration of A and the drifting metabolizing maternal reverie of B emerges the humble voice of omniscience or *dream thoughts*, *dreams*, and *myths*. The mythical voice that knows because it has known, not because the speaker knows everything, but because he is performing as an interlocuter of rebirth and feels the alpha-function-birth-pangs of a psychic place that opens up in the unknown, that is also the burgeoning of new growth in the patient's being.

Eigen's text, *Psychic Deadness* contains bridges that traverse the time of when a book is written and when it is read, occupying columns 3 and 4 of the grid, *attention and notation*, or where in the early development of the ego a special function of *attention* arises that searches the world and whose "activity meets the sense-impressions half-way, instead of awaiting their appearance" and the system of *notation* "whose task it was to lay down the results of this periodical activity of consciousness – a part of what we call *memory*" (Freud, 1911). An author in id-dialogue with the original replacing function of the object accesses a regenerative field of Freud's attention and notation. A creative inner space that is fertile with psychic elements and able to give rise to the symbol before total contact with sensory stimulus – creative access to the collectively personal memory of the infinite absence of the breast. The need for language is an original site of loss that rises to contact contactless-ness. Writing and reading being synonymous with the psychic materials born from the maternal-infantile merge in the instant before relating seals a conversation to the symbiotic reality of the other conversationalist's physicality. By attending to the absent and unknown reader as though as precious as the collective baby abandoned, the unconscious communal baby is empathically gone towards by the author. The reader is greeted and held half-way in anticipation of the author's desire for holding and remembering the forgotten in-between field of growth potential that the reader aches for when he sits down to read a book. Beta elements call out for attention, alpha function embraces notation, and so does the inquiry of the dream begin on a sea of text.

An inert book is a stranded one, a body helpless and alone on an emotional island that cannot make contact beyond the boundaries of an imposed isolation. In *Psychic Deadness*, Eigen delineates territories of psychic aliveness and deadness that locate and charter the zones of cut-off union fundamental to emotional life. I will set down three coordinates in the form of quotes from Eigen's book that culminates in the text's crossing into another form of contact by the aesthetic nature of its finishing and so coming to total life as a read/consumed object, one internalized as a relationship that then exits the inanimate boundaries of the book in relation to the psychic reality of the text.

The question of how the therapist can bridge to the patient's island and make helpful contact repeats throughout *Psychic Deadness*. A theme emerging from the therapist who blocks or inhibits contact with their patient through denial of what is their pathological likeness to that patient. In particular, Eigen visits the utility of aliveness in the immediate moment of the therapist seeking to make a therapeutic impact on the patient as questionable insofar as such emotional aliveness is only helpful to the patient if the patient can make use of let alone tolerate such emotionally alive intensity. He writes an addendum to his chapter on supervising, "Being too good." More than the relationship Eigen has with his supervisee and the relationship between the supervised therapist and patient, I am interested in how the matrix of these relationships are emotionally housed in his authorial voice as it informs the relation between himself and his readers in terms of the reader being incorporated as a clinical character; regarding Bion's bridge, how anchors of breast and mouth are usurped by this active reorientation of the reader's passive position. Eigen (2004) writes:

> I can see Jackie opening to what happens between her and Tina. How much can she and Tina take? They are discovering that there is the direct transmission of feeling between them. How will the discovery of this kind of openness transform or fail to transform them? The flow between us is real. What will we do with it, it with us? It spreads in waves between Jackie, Tina, and me and now, also, you.
>
> (Loc, 3502 of 4951)

What will the reader do now? Just keep chugging along in the hum of consuming text, or pause/reflect on the wave? Inculcating the reader with the narrative struggle to metabolize new points of clinical contact awaken the wish for the book to be the milk that literally flows. Eigen, the author who is also a practicing therapist recasts the passively remote eyes of the reader as alive and engaged in the drama of the patient's emotional and psychic development. We are with Tina's therapist, that is Jackie, who also grows as she sensitizes to what is real about her patient's suffering within herself. This quote marks *coordinate one* on a psychically climbable mountain that reaches towards contact with the author. One whom lives at the border of a page that is both inanimate and also suggesting of a transmission of direct contact, an emotional touching of the breast and the central object, the source divine as attainable, if not by anything more than the aliveness of the psyche, and all that can be done through the therapeutic passion of words.

Increasing height on this map-less map, the faint dotted line of psychic tracing paper is placed over or is it under Eigen's text, bringing us next to Mara and Sandy. A similar dynamic between this clinical two being that the therapist distances herself from her patient through the disowning of mental states that isolate emotional reality from the interpersonal present. Eigen (2004) writes:

> When Mara tells me that Sandy is an avid reader of psychological writings I am taken aback. I ask her more about this and encourage her to tell me as much about his readings as she can. She reluctantly paints a picture of Sandy's passion for psychoanalytic literature. She disparages

it, distrusts it. She feels it is escapist, an intellectualization, part of his avoidance of emotional contact with people. I have no doubt she is right, yet something quickens in me. It is a passion I share with Sandy, a passion Mara lacks. Mara is a down-to-earth, common-sensical person. For the first time I begin to wonder if I am more like Sandy than Mara, although I feel I share something with each. I feel my walled-off, secret self, like Sandy. Yet I am emotionally permeable, like Mara. Mara mentions that Sandy reads my writings, is moved by them, is critical of them. I feel Sandy, light years away, tuned in to me. We are plugged into a common current.

(Loc, 3976 out of 4951)

Coordinate two on the map of psychic deadness to aliveness is embedded in this psycho-geographic entity of secluded closeness that Eigen inhabits by identifying with a patient who emotionally isolates himself into psychoanalytic text. A therapist prioritizing this intellectualized location of writing in contrast with direct emotional contact infuses the dissociated site with its opposite, the potential for all emotional oneness to be reborn as it never was from the trauma that drove Sandy from what she needed to get from original contact. Eigen's jumps over Mara, yet both Eigen and Sandy remain isolated from each other. A calling out over the chasm of being as non-being that may never get fully healed through the original nourishment, but is honoured by identifying it as a place that can therapeutically exist in book form. A book being a thing that can be shared at the moment that language goes beyond itself as mere words and returns to its originary event, when hominids deferred violent action over competitive gain and compromised on sharing the central object through its representation; so many thousands of years later the psychoanalytic text that is read in the privacy of intellectual division, a division that is alone from direct emotional connection and yet still makes contact by drawing from this site of divinity that repeatedly becomes the acquisition of the breast-that-was-never-there. The words are read, and the words make ecstatic union as the snake path unwinds at the limit of the clouds, perhaps the same one that the Tower of Babel sought to reach and what its builders understood as a language of architectural God-form. Inevitably the tower of contact crumbles at the summit point, the tip that touches but cannot sustain as the actual milk, the word that is the animal renounced and replaced by a represented portion, a share, a word of the beast that can be privately spoken by all.

Eigen concludes *Psychic Deadness* through his work over the course of a single and abridged session with a patient he calls Janice, a patient who is raised to the level of clinical archetype in her feeling-experience of having been destroyed by a former psychoanalytic treatment. Janice reports she is unable to find a therapist who can sustain giving her the parental nourishment she so very much needs. Eigen wades this turbulent and concentric

reverberation of making contact with a beautified and mystified past en-
shrouded by the series of failed therapists before him. During the consultation, an uncertain "no" arises in him against her request for him to be sure
that he can give her the parenting she needs. *Coordinate three* on the map-less
map that crosses from book to psyche is a natural world of colliding ab-
sences, one that Janice marks by leaving flowers in Eigen's office following
the consultation that did not result in further treatment. A meeting point
that reduces the therapist to the common denominator of considering all
that could have been said and yet could not have been thought of until after
the session. What of Eigen's words then survives the destruction? Where
does the therapeutic influence of his thoughts go regarding her treatment?
Eigen (2004) ends this final chapter with:

> Please, Janice, let us agree to fail for as long as it takes. I believe the
> force can be outflanked. There is something deeper, something more.
> You sense it, or you would not be here at all. It is afraid to breathe now,
> but perhaps it will wait for us. It will feel "our" breathing. I understand
> that it is buried under the collapse of the entire earth, that all existence
> has become the killer. You see, I know the force well; I am part of that
> constriction. I write too, like you. I am writing you this testimony. For
> I too slip away when we speak. I am telling you, from my aloneness to
> yours, writer to writer, that I believe you. I believe in the flowers you
> gave me. We are those flowers, the missing links. I believe in writing,
> the writings you never gave me. I am writing to you, Janice, any Janice,
> who may read this testimony and respond with the next-to-last breath.
> I have breathed my last breath many times and want to go with you to
> that place. Between the words, breathing starts up again.
>
> (Loc, 4834–8 out of 4951)

Language is a myth born from the psyche metabolizing the original frustration of losing the object; writing continuing to reach out through a developmental mouth, the ongoing drama of language's manifestations seeking
return and contact with the breast/centre point of the group. As in a sensuous
tone of voice that is the alpha elements being produced from the caring function of soothing sound, not only containing but empathically gnawing at,
savouring, crunching, holding, staying with the anxiety and overwhelm of
the hysterically helpless infant-as-patient entering the unknown. Psychoanalysis enfolds oral and written knowledge as the locus of the clinical encounter
inextricably intertwines the two, the heart to heart, psyche to psyche, the
everything-ness of the words and wordlessness that flow between recorded
text and unbound conversation dissipating into interpersonal growth. The
session is written in the lost moment; the tip of the pen tapping upon the
uncannily present body.

A found map delineates the gradations of psychic altitude that permeate an ascending trail throughout Eigen's *Psychic Deadness*, word by word, little ancient stone steps that start out in a theory of what deadens the psyche and culminate in a unifying plea as having reached the edge of the psychically deadened sky so alive with that deadness that inanimate words fully bloom to life with their potential for wordless connection. Resurrection of the killed-off cry can be heard in an inside that travels silently through the nightly heavens between book and reading eyes, an emotional leap off the page and into the life of the reader. *Whose cry?* The author has taken his last breath in the same way as the patient who cannot endure his office, an echo of the reader who breathes on the other side of his words. The breath contracts and expands with the topography of the text, as if to touch psyches that are soma on the plane of the humble omniscient. The surface of the page softens to an organic pulp-like material, permeable with a free space of air and permission to feel tears of life not-only-known-to be-there. A psychic area creates in the interpersonal-less session, extending as an instruction sheet for the meditation that brings about a single feeling-image, one that opens the developmental possibilities of an original loss – a text in-between healing.

References

Bion, W.F. (1989). *Two papers: The grid and caesura*. Karnac.

Borges, JL. (1975). *On exactitude in science: A universal history of infamy* (NT Giovanni, Trans.). Penguin Books.

Eigen, M. (2004). *Psychic deadness*. Karnac.

Eigen, M. (2005). *The psychotic core*. Karnac.

Eigen, M. (2006). *Feelings matter*. Karnac.

Eigen, M. (2010). *Toxic nourishment*. Karnac.

Eigen, M. (2011). *Contact with the depths*. Karnac.

Freud, S. (1900). The interpretation of dreams. In J Strachey (Ed. and Trans.), *The standard edition of the complete psychological works of Sigmund Freud* (Vol. IV). Hogarth Press, pp. ix–627.

Freud, S. (1911). Formulations on the two principles of mental functioning. In J Strachey (Ed. and Trans.), *The standard edition of the complete psychological works of Sigmund Freud* (Vol. XII). Hogarth Press, pp. 218–60.

Gans, E. (1981). *The origin of language: A formal theory of representation*. University of California Press.

Gans, E. (1993). *Originary thinking: Elements of generative anthropology*. Stanford University Press.

Klein, M. (1946). Notes on some schizoid mechanisms. *International Journal of Psychoanalysis*, 27, 99–110.

Chapter 12

Psychoanalysis a prayer

The construction and breakdown of faith in dissociative states

Neetu Sarin

> I'd woken up early, and I took a long time getting ready to exist.
> Pessoa and Zenith, *The Book of Disquiet* (2003)

Winnicott (1971) wrote towards the end of his days, "Oh God may I be alive when I die." In this chapter, I discuss how psychoanalysis works like a prayer for dissociative states where a complete breakdown of faith occurs in relationships due to trauma, absence, or neglect. Eigen's works maintain the precariousness of aliveness in everyday living. His work illustrates whether Winnicott's prayer is for death or to create a going-on-being. "May a part of me be alive while another dies." Is prayer a resonance of faith or creation of it?

This chapter is an illustration of how sometimes our patients need faith that creates a bearability of their psyche. Eigen's works, for me, create faith when breakdowns occur. I begin with this quote that I often return to in my work with *Ananya*,[1] a 21-year-old, her name meaning "like no other." A bundle of contradictions, life and death force twinned, someone who hadn't really been born. Eigen's work remained an invisible background prayer, a silent communion with an "other," providing musicality in an otherwise deadening psychotherapeutic relationship.

Ananya came to me four years ago after having consulted a variety of mental health professionals, and having received a myriad of diagnoses such as autism, social anxiety, and childhood psychosis. My first impression of her was someone who was just floating and hadn't yet found a psychic home. In our first session she told me, "I feel trapped in my body." She was dysfunctional, wouldn't bathe for days, dropped out of college and spent her time couped up in her room listening to podcasts.

Early history

Consultations with her parents revealed that she didn't speak until she was five. Bullying, isolation, and alienation started early, and her mother would rush to school to make her teachers understand her "special needs." Her parents were well-educated, upper-middle-class professionals, who afforded the best privileges for their daughter. On being asked how they conceived her, they looked stumped and exclaimed, "we've never thought about it." Her father confessed, "I was disappointed in her. I wanted a child who was more articulate and alive and functional." At the same time, he empathized with her difficulty in speaking and attributed it to the sophisticated language and "big words" that were prevalent in her grandmother's home, owing to their caste and class superiority.

Ananya: Am I real?

Ananya is hard to remember and harder to forget. She was overweight, unkempt, wore black, and looked like a grown-up, but with a babyface. The first few months of our work were indescribable, something akin to when I spoke with her parents: *There was blankness.* There were no associations, no history, no events. She would arrive at the designated time, largely mute, but in a sense she never arrived because she did not offer anything to be taken up by me. Distance, silence, monosyllables, and drudgery marked our early work. It was like talking to a *"present absence"* (Gerson, 2009). Emily Dickinson's words haunted me,

> One need not be a chamber to be haunted,
> one need not be a house.
>
> (1927, p. 333).

After a few months, a few utterances emerged:

SHE: I feel trapped in my body.

I: Do you feel like you were not meant to be in this body?

SHE: Yes … not a gender confusion, it is not that I would like to be a man, I am just trapped in my body.

I: [struck by her clarity] Sometimes we cannot associate ourselves with the body we have.

SHE: [makes eye contact]) ya … hmmm.

I: Do you sometimes float outside your body and see yourself from the outside?

SHE: [Looked astonished, as if someone had read her close secret] ya … why does that happen?

I: These are often states of depersonalization, sometimes some parts of us behave out of sync with other parts of ourselves.

SHE: [Looking relieved] I have never heard that, why do I do that?

I: I don't know right now, but we will need to work together to find out.

She nodded, and that seemed like our first authentic exchange. I experienced myself explaining many things to her like a mother indicates to her child, "*this is your nose, these are eyes*" etc. In the first few months of our meeting, I discovered her multiple problems: Psychosomatic distress such as insomnia, bingeing, pains, addictive behaviours such as chain-smoking, an unrelenting constipation, perversions such as taking off her clothes in front of unsuspecting strangers and voyeuristic indulgence on social media and dissociative fugues.

It seemed that different self-states were operating independently in the absence of an organizing ego. Her silence felt like an implicit challenge to me, "*you cannot do anything to know me.*" A repeated narrative was that her father was intrusive and controlling, and her mother was passive and subservient. Since turning 15, her father took it upon himself to "bring her life on track." Horrified by her gaining large amounts of weight, he laid down a strictly regimented schedule for her which made her retreat even further.

Secretly bingeing, she fooled her father by signing into the gym but not exercising. "He can ensure he doesn't give me junk food or that I have to sign. But how can he ensure I will listen to him?" I commented that she was feisty and that her black clothes were a sign of her protest. She felt surprised that I wasn't angry at knowing her secret, or unlike her previous therapists I wasn't goading her to be functional. Mostly, she felt surprised that I could see meaning in her behaviour.

Her internal world seemed like a secret, and I didn't have the passcode. It wasn't hidden. It simply had not formed yet. As Bion (1984) would say, it had not gained a tolerance for the intensity of experience. Eigen (1999), in illustrating Winnicott's central clinical preoccupation, suggests that one of the biggest struggles patients bring into the clinic is feeling unreal to oneself, and Ananya's un-mantled self-suffered this derealization. Her psyche was a colourless canvas that would be visible in brief vignettes:

I: Maybe you are not sure if you said something you'd be heard.
SHE: Everyone just knows what I mean even before I say it. Most people don't understand. I don't either.
Or,
SHE: I don't really know what I want. It seems not wanting and not being understood is the most authentic me. I am different from others. People don't understand that.

"Everyone" reflected her undifferentiated inner world. They all are *one*. A mass psyche. Implicit in this impersonalness (Eigen, 2004) was the narcissism inherited from the parents where the child-Ananya ends up asking, "Who was I for my parents? Am I a product of love and imagination?"

Primitive withdrawal: Negotiating life and death

Eigen (1999) writes in *Toxic Nourishment*, "to be alive is amazing, but it is also disturbing." Ananya negotiated this disturbance by withdrawing, and numbing her inner creativity. She appeared to me like an artist; a troubled artist who had not made her art yet. Often, her honesty and a sense of inherent goodness struck me. Like most artists, she was deeply perceptive and sensitive to her environment, however, lacked the usual neurotic filters, and felt everything in its acute vividness without the equipment of adequate defences.

SHE: I feel things for a few seconds and then they just go away. It is like they were never there.
I: You feel like you have no skin ... nothing to protect you from the onslaught of feelings.
SHE: No skin ... never felt it ... I or anyone can enter me through my skin.

For our sessions, she would carry a safety pin and press it into the uppermost layer of her skin. She seemed to feel no pain, no wincing, no crying. Did my presence feel like the needle entering her skin, making her feel defenceless? Sometimes even mere presences feel like impingements. She binged to escape from this sensorial tyranny while smoking turned her feelings into ash. The heavier the junk, the more potent it was in burying down her affect. Bingeing and smoking became companions in moments of desolation and isolation. *She did not need anyone because she had her loneliness.* Bingeing also provided a much yearned-for-surrender to her affective impulses and moods, something that she militated against. But it happened in a *not-me* dissociated state, unlinked with other states of her mind.

I: What did you eat?
SHE: Junk ... I ate a whole pig.
I: [In spite of myself, I laughed]

The absurdity of her eating a pig made me laugh. She eased up. Letting myself be taken up by absurdity, she felt I could cohabit her "alien" inner world. And said, "and if that was not enough, I ate a cow too." We both laughed. "Don't tell the government," she said. "I swear," I replied. Laughter suddenly and momentarily reduced the shame of being a hog. She moved from the site of shame to observing the shame with me. Eigen (1999) writes how therapy can allow a dip into the original madness in manageable doses. This laughter was a manageable dose of thinking about her madness. "Don't tell the government": It brought to light her extreme internal rage projected onto authority (government/paternal introject) who seemed persecutory and may punish. Through this little speck of laughter, we began working through her destructiveness. This was a moment when "destructiveness did not need to be controlled, but could breathe, enter into feeling communion, and further creation/discovery" (Eigen, 1999, p. 26).

Faith as a transitional space

It began dawning on me that I needed to shift my therapeutic stance from interpretive to clarificatory: Analysis of *content* to analysis of *form* (Grotstein, 1995). There was no articulable "past" or traumatic memories available, and I could only turn to *my enactments, my dreams, and somatic responses.* There was no symbolized material, which, when brought to consciousness, would create insight. All I had was faith, yet I did not know what this faith was. It seemed to be allied with "intuition" (Eigen quoting Bion, 2014). Our dyad was becoming like Winnicott's "transitional space," creating an interiority.

Frequently, she expressed a deep lack of faith in our work. She demanded to be put on stronger medication. She dismissed me, calling all therapists "unskilled and amateurs." Among the many ways I have understood her arrogance is by not focusing on the death drive but the way life force creates enough havoc (Eigen, 1999). She was watching me closely not so much for what *content* I had in my response to her arrogance, but a nonverbal response to her attack: My facial expressions and my bodily stance. She would get upset if my face showed hurt or agitation or if I raised my voice, as if it was a premature reminder of my separateness. She seemed to need us to be one, fused and together.

My usual analytic interpretations often fell flat. She simply did not have sufficient ego strength. Interpretations demanded *secondary relatedness* (shared play such as mother and baby playing with a toy); however, the focus was needed on primary relatedness (looking at me). Eigen (2004) in *Psychic deadness* writes that primary processes need long-term support. A "primary aloneness" (Winnicott, 1958) eluded her. I wondered if she ever babbled playfully? Did her little young mind take it upon herself to create adult coherent mature sentences ("big words")?

Slowly, she began playing with sounds in the session. Initially, these sounded like mistakes, but I began to see something else:

Fem-I-NIS---TTTT (Feminist)
  Cap-city (Capacity)
  Labe-err (labour)
  Partinparceee (Part and Parcel)
  Alliance (Alien)
  Farreeee (Far reaching)
  Shuttlecock (shuttle)
  Pagal[2] (pardon)

She played around with sounds, pronunciations, interchanged nouns ("I" was replaced for you and vice versa). I dabbled in mirroring her. Should I say "cap-city" or "capacity" like I usually do? In short, should I babble back? I had to stay close to these mental dilemmas and learnt to keep them as questions without answers.

In one session, when I suggested to her that she try taking public transport to the session instead of being driven, she stared at me and froze. "I cannot do it," she said flatly. She criticized me for assuming she could do something that she in fact *could not*. It became a tussle between "I cannot vs I will not" (Alvarez, 2006). I became like her internal objects which were constantly expecting her to be alive and functional. Aliveness was seen as a demand, pushing her further and further into a psychic cocoon. I wondered if by expecting her to be independent, I was countertransferentially "pushing her out quickly out of my womb"? Through my countertransferential demand that she became independent, I was identifying with her "incomprehensibility of twoness" (Bion, 1959; Alvarez, 2006), inability to look at *two objects at once*. This enactment was a powerful grease in the therapeutic impasse. Could we think of *absence and presence together?*

Disappearing and appearing: The work of "representation"

Work with her demanded of me the work of "representation." Freud, in speaking of repression, thought of only a mature, well-functioning ego, whereas unintegrated states may have a weak or an immature ego which require a representation.

In the absence of representation, enactments and somatic discharges became Ananya's "psychic retreats" (Steiner, 1993). She started disappearing for multiple sessions, leaving me guessing and waiting. "Ghosting" is the word that came to me as I talked with peers and supervisors. Loewald (1960) writes that the work of the psychoanalyst is to lay the ghost to rest so that they can turn into ancestors and watch over us. Waiting for her, I would be haunted by her ghostly presence, often becoming sleepless and bingeing myself. It is as if her unmetabolized injuries made a home in me. Filled with inchoate sensations of deadness and self-hatred, my body mimicked her symptoms, and I plummeted into states of dysfunctionality, unable to feel alive. One night I had the following dream:

> I was in space familiar but strange. I could see some light … stuck between two walls, coloured light grey. The space between the two walls was like a long canal, enough to hold me but not allowing movement. I felt stuck and unable to get out.

I woke up terrified and disoriented, feeling paralyzed. The next day I met Ananya.

SHE: I have been feeling trapped in my body ... so ya [looks at me if I understand. Going on, perhaps I have passed her test]. It's a strange feeling ... no one understands ... like someone has caged you and you cannot get out ... it is not so dark so you don't feel ...

[Unable to make sense of these utterances, my mind gradually floated to my dream from the other night ... my feelings of being stuck in the two walls came back to me]

I: It feels like there is room for your body ... has enough space but you cannot get out ... is that how you feel in your room all day ...? It is a familiar place but perhaps strange, because it does not give you the home you need.

[Her eyes welled up ... this was happening the first time]

SHE: It is my safe haven. I cannot go outside, but I also feel trapped inside.

It felt uncanny. Eigen's panoramic work suggests that fragmented states such as those in psychosis and dissociation are not available to us for healing through words. Even though we were not talking, she and I seemed to be communicating unconsciously. It seemed that I got access to her internal world through an *unconscious attunement*, a dissociated state of dreaming. Dreaming of stuckness, being in a strange but familiar space created comprehension of her entrapment. Dreaming is the space where representations can begin before words, where psychic digestion can happen (Eigen, 1999). This understanding of dreaming received from Bion and Eigen looks at dreams as portals that open gateways to further experiencing. Without focusing too much on the content, the process of dreaming brought with it new avenues of psychic health.

The "Disclosure Project": Self as an alien

The "Disclosure Project" was her code word for her interest in aliens and extraterrestrial beings. Obsessed with aliens, she listened to podcasts about the "conspiracy theory," a research led by American scientists on the existence of aliens and the conspiracy of the developed countries to hide it. Elaborating in great detail on the spiritual, intellectual, and civil superiority that aliens possessed over humans, she enchanted me with mystical details, such as the five dimensionalities of the alien world. Perhaps, she was in search of an intersubjective, nonlinear, multidimensional construction of herself and the others? She would say,

Many people ask, why don't they just come help us? Why are there UFO sightings and why do they stand at the horizon, watching from far?

Because we humans are cruel. They see what humans do to each other: we have killed billions of people in wars, and we don't stop. They could hurt us in a second and the world's superpowers wouldn't be able to do anything!

I offered several interpretations such as a) her identification with these spiritual aliens watching the mortal humans b) her ambivalence at being in contact with (her) human parts, and c) a dissociation and projection of her rage onto these aliens. Year after year, as she recounted stories of these aliens, my interpretations made little headway.

One day, after I shifted my office space temporarily, she said, "It is okay, spaces do not affect me that much," although she woke up with panic and several mutating pains in her body. She then described *The Shape of Water* (2017), a film about a "strange creature which has healing powers," who was brought in during the World War but discarded once its use was over. I ventured that perhaps coming to a new clinic had disoriented her and created panic? However, since her rational mind had already committed to the numbing of any affect, she had discarded these *strange* feelings of panic and mutating pains like aliens. Like a dream, this further created more material wherein she brought in a mute girl who fell in love with this strange creature in the film. She saw him for what he was, and definitely did not see him with only deficits.

I: Your feelings of being affected by the newness of the office feel strange and alien, perhaps, which become trapped in your human body. Perhaps, taking off in your dissociative fugues is a hope to be accepted naked with your strange feelings?

SHE: [Nods ... begins weeping]

[Quiet]

I: Maybe you are surprised that I can comprehend your panic. Like the mute girl in the film who does not find you strange?

SHE: My parents always say "we are here for you." I don't believe it. You have to make sense of me. Otherwise, you are just a blank presence.

I: Perhaps at this moment, as I comprehended your feelings without you explicitly saying them, you experienced me as "being there for you."

She simply nodded and said "yes." Towards the end of the session,

SHE: I scratched myself rigorously in sleep, and when I woke up in the morning, I was alarmed at how much. The scratches were becoming scabs.

I: Maybe in your sleep, you may have experienced your inchoate feelings getting under your skin, which needed scratching, like one does after one feels itchy. Perhaps you have to scratch me out as well, lest I get under your skin ...

As we struggled with her inability to receive care, my own mind went to an early memory of my grandmother gently scratching my head as I lay in her lap, gradually falling asleep. This "soft" memory was a crucial "affective hologram" (Ferro, 2009) for me as working with her created danger and madness within me.

I: When you feel attacked by your feelings such as in a World War scenario, maybe you need someone to mutely love and touch you, scratch the itchiness of the horrible feelings away.

SHE: [almost whispering] You are like a back rub.

We smiled gingerly, letting this moment envelop us like my grandmother's soft mul-mul saree. Navigating this madness within me, I only had these soft memories or my own dreaming – like *prayer states*, where I could be alive to my own states of inchoateness. Like Winnicott's prayer, life and death appeared to be *linked* rather than contradictory.

After this session, I felt hopeful after a long time. In my becoming an object for her, our work together was becoming a *representation* of her inner life. *My image of her was that of an extraterrestrial being: Someone who did not belong to this world, who retreated and watched from the horizon, where words were unnecessary.* I thought to myself, "she must really feel so out of place all the time"! It's like going to a party you are not invited to every minute of your life.

The Disclosure Project became the personal label of her psychotherapeutic work. She had spent her growing up years witnessing the incomprehension and the horror in her parents' eyes as they groped for clarity about her. "Everyone wanted to give me one diagnosis." I said, "maybe you were metamorphosing, from one stage of life to another, from one self-state to another. Maybe you were defying the laws of this planet, the laws of diagnoses like the ET beings!"

The metamorphoses: From being a creature to creating

A recurring reverie for me was Kafka's story "The metamorphosis" (1996), the story of the transformation of Gregor Samsa. Gregor wakes up one day, only to realize that he has turned into a grotesque cockroach-like figure. His family worries about their finances as he was the only earning member, and they hire an unclean cleaning lady who gave him rotten scraps of food to eat. Gregor occupied himself by climbing the walls of his home, much to the shock and disgust of his family when he appeared in front of them. One day, Gregor dies and his family is relieved.

Thinking of this story was the alpha function (Bion, 1962) in our work: The carnival of amazement and horror standing side by side. Had I become the cleaning lady from the novel, the only one who could stand her sight? And had I also fallen from grace precisely because I was in touch with her?

As her "cleaning lady," she allowed me to see her with the same hazy focus that Gregor sees himself. The mutating pains in her body, like "the little many legs" symbolized her life had gotten out of hand, scattered, too much of everything. The missed sessions were like the metamorphosing into an alien bug whose presence could only be felt in a ghostly orbiting way. Experiencing the trauma at her own pace, her withdrawal from the world like Gregor was a refuge from unmanageable proto-emotions.

In one session, she brought in a dream:

> There was a large bug. It kept getting bigger and bigger. It had things coming out of it and there was another creature-like thing or things growing inside of it. It was quite ugly, but in the dream I was fascinated by its belly: Sometimes I could see through the belly and sometimes it would be opaque.

The first Gestalt that strikes us is her experience of being a creature, a bug, not a person. What did the creature refer to here? Did it yet have a meaning? Eigen (1999) in his essay "A bug-free universe" writes that to wish for a universe free of bugs is to display unbearability of the buzz, bite, and itch of life. To dream of creatures (bugs) was perhaps to find the first symbol of her pain. Her unsymbolized alive parts were ginger-like obtrusions emerging haphazardly from her like a young sapling. Eigen writes,

> A loose equation tends to hold in dreams: bugs = babies = madness = destruction … babies are born into a world that does not know what to do with them. The very aliveness of a baby stresses adult caretaking capacities.

(p. 68)

Ananya was this coming-to-life baby whose very aliveness needed to be tolerated. And like her parents, I too carried a confusion whether she was being destructive or simply alive. Eigen (2014) in his essay "Beauty and destruction" guides us that "it is important to note that Bion does not limit catastrophe to psychosis. It can be part of creativity as well" (p. 42). This reminder that perhaps pressures from unmetabolized beta elements are transformed into a bug (dream) that Ananya begins to bear as a growth and an obtrusion. For a work like this, Eigen's reminder that "dreams might be attempts to call attention to catastrophic realities" are nothing short of reveries themselves, that provide the alpha-dance through producing an image.

The aliens, constipation, childhood asthma, mutating pains, dizziness seemed to be characters which could be thought of as *beta element aggregates* which have been expelled by her at some point but returned to invade her.

As I developed a capacity to tolerate her aliveness, these beta elements also began doing the alpha-dance gradually, creating in her tolerance for her aliveness.

Gradually, she started taking charge of her life. She picked up a job in a news agency, her job being to decode "one-minute news clips." Her job became symbolic of our work together: Creating a narrative of little tiny beta elements orbiting in space, which could gradually be made into short stories or "news" about herself. Work mediated contact with others. Using her newly found internal regulator, it provided her with brief, yet meaningful interactions with others. She said, "this work chose me," perhaps speaking of a gratitude for the avenue to channel her intellectual and aesthetic parts. This "alphabetization" (Ferro, 2009; Bion, 1978) opened suffering as she could no longer avoid contact with the outside world. Work began becoming a slow marker of identity, and for the first time she began realizing her adolescent life-stage. Becoming a good internal parent to her own baby self, new images of patience and fatigue began developing: all markers of real, authentic, albeit brief contact with others. She started drawing parallels between her therapy and job: Both were slow and arduous. The slowness was a necessary requisite of the alpha function, where preconceptions could be turned into thinking, a gestation of this yet-to-be born baby.

Eigen and the work of Faith

What allows us therapists the continuing psychic strength to work with patients like Ananya? Patients who require not an analysis, but a construction of self, a building up of the psyche. "Just as a baby is supported in an alone presence by a not cognized presence" (Eigen, 2009, p. 11), my presence and liking for Ananya remained an invisible background for our work. Her "primary aloneness" was paradoxically supported by a non-cognized dependence on me by her. Eigen writes,

> The mother is there helping the baby, but the baby might not take in the fact that another being distinct from him is keeping him in life ... Our lives tap into a sense of holiness connected with a background aura of infinite unknown *support*.
>
> (p. 12)

Sometimes, I wondered if this quiet sitting in with my patient was it not like a prayer, a deep communion with an unknown, invisible other? It often felt like a meditation: Where words were simply hypotheses, a "living one's way into a dream" (Eigen, 2014, p. 69). Eigen further writes,

> our ideas and feelings about dreams share the same limitations as all mediated productions. They are particular slants at particular moments,

relative generalizations, perspectives on reality that could also mean something else.

(p. 69)

In hindsight, what seems to have impacted me most about Eigen's thinking was the possibility of an emotional experience being *both* real and temporary. This paradox requires staying content with the unintegrated parts of the patient, which may be experienced by us as a primordial continuity of being. When meaning and identity are not cast in stone (indicated through her babbling in sessions), an authentic self-experience can appear. Moving from well-constructed narratives ("big words") to babbling created a freedom from a predetermined, superimposed reality of the over-present internal parents. Perhaps, this is one way we could define faith in clinical work! Touching these mystical states of a deep connection was only possible with Eigen's work as a background support. In states of deep distress and faithlessness, I would pick up his book(s), that uncannily allowed a birth of experience in me.

I will end with the following lines by Eigen (1999) that seem ostensibly simple. However, in the face of dissociative trauma lines in patients like Ananya, they work like a prayer.

Feeling normal is somewhat like free-floating. What feels normal changes. Some people need solitude to feel normal. Feeling off-on or right-wrong changes too. What feels right now may feel wrong later. To try to live only by what feels on or off now can be quite maddening, and possibly destructive.

(p. 104)

Notes

1 Name has been changed to protect confidentiality.
2 A colloquial term in Hindi, used to denote craziness.

References

Alvarez, A. (2006). Some questions concerning states of fragmentation: Unintegration, under-integration, disintegration, and the nature of early integrations. *Journal of Child Psychotherapy*, 32 (2), 158–80. doi: 10.1080/00754170600780331.
Bion, W.R. (1959). Attacks on linking. *International Journal of Psychoanalysis*, 40, 308–315
Bion, W.R. (1962). *Second thoughts*. Butterworth-Heinemann.
Bion, W.R. (1978). *Four discussions with W. R. Bion, in clinical settings and other works.* Karnac.
Bion, W.R. (1984). *Learning from experience*. Karnac.
Bromberg, P.M. (2001). *Standing in the spaces: Essays on clinical process, trauma, and dissociation*. Analytic Press.

Dickinson, E. (1927). *The complete poems of Emily Dickinson: With an introduction.* Little, Brown and Company.

Eigen, M. (1999). *Toxic nourishment.* Routledge.

Eigen, M. (2004). *Psychic deadness.* Karnac.

Eigen, M. (2007). *Feeling matters: From the Yosemite God to the annihilated self.* Karnac.

Eigen, M. (2009). *Flames from the unconscious: Trauma, madness, and faith.* Routledge.

Eigen, M. (2011). *Faith and transformation.* Karnac.

Eigen, M. (2014). *The birth of experience.* Routledge.

Eigen, M. (2018). *Eigen in Seoul: Faith and transformation.* Routledge.

Fairbairn, WRD. (1994). The nature of hysterical states. *From instinct to self: Selected papers of W. R. D. Fairbairn,* Vol 1 (D Scharff and E Birtles, Ed.). Jason Aronson, pp. 13–40 (original work published 1954).

Ferro, A. (2009). *Mind works: Technique and creativity in psychoanalysis.* Routledge.

Grotstein, JS. (1995). A reassessment of the couch in psychoanalysis. *Psychoanalytic Inquiry,* 15 (3), 396–405. doi: 10.1080/07351699509534045.

Kafka, F. (1996). *The Metamorphosis and other stories* (D Freed, Trans.). Barnes & Noble Books.

Loewald, H. (1960). On the therapeutic action in psychoanalysis. *International Journal of Psychoanalysis,* 41, 16–33.

Pessoa, F and Zenith, R. (2003). *The book of disquiet.* Penguin Books.

Steiner, J. (1993). *Psychic retreats: Pathological organizations in psychotic, neurotic, and borderline patients.* Routledge.

Winnicott, DW. (1958). The capacity to be alone. *The International Journal of Psychoanalysis,* 39, 416–20.

Winnicott, DW. (1971). *Playing and reality.* Basic Books.

Part IV

Spirituality and becoming

Chapter 13

Difficulties of faith

Rachel Berghash and Katherine Jillson

Faith in the unknown is not easily summarized, nor is it easily practiced. How many of us can apply Martin Luther King's idea that "faith is taking the first step even when you don't see the whole staircase."

Having faith involves accepting and enduring mystery – the mystery of the unknown and also of the unseen. It includes a mystery about what will transpire.

We cannot talk about the unknown and ignore the greatest unknown: God. The poet Rabindranath Tagore, among other thinkers, appreciates science for its uses and great practical advancements, but he recognizes its limits. While science divests God of reality, Tagore asks us to consider a person's experience of God as a legitimate force. In fact there is converge of evidence to this statement in that saints in several religions knew God and experienced intimacy with Him.

The way to know God, according to Saint John of the Cross, is by unknowing:

> My mind has found a surer way:
> a knowledge by unknowing,
> rising beyond all science.
>
> (St. John, 1990, p. 59)

Faith in the unknown is the basic path of psychoanalysis for the psychoanalysts Wilfred Bion and Michael Eigen. Bion calls faith the attitude of psychoanalytic practice. It signifies tolerating not knowing. It requires attention and endurance. Intuition is the equipment the psychoanalyst needs, according to Bion, to be receptive to the patient, which requires being without memory, desire, understanding, and expectation. When these states of mind are absent, the psychoanalyst is more likely to be absorbed in what the patient is saying. Unburdened by anything that might interfere, the psychoanalyst is left open to the patient's emotional reality, or truth. The analyst beginning each session that way reflects faith in the unknown. (It is interesting that this skill is akin to the capacity of the Jewish prophets to hear God's message through an ego-free channel.)

It is crucial to distinguish between faith and belief. The confusion between the two tends to reduce faith to one that can be easily summarized. According to Eigen, belief is about a system that organizes experiences of faith around something we can hold onto. It can include rationality, structure, words, and thoughts passed down by believers who follow their authorities. Eigen says that belief may be a necessary part of the human condition, but it tends to prematurely structure processes that remain unknown. Faith supports experimental exploration, imaginative conjecture, experiential probes, and poetic wordplay (Eigen, n.d., MEigenworkshop Yahoo group, private). Belief, according to the psychoanalyst Preston McLean, is about presenting evidence of what we believe in. Faith, on the other hand, is experienced without evidence. It is about the unseen.

The unknown quality of faith allows for openness and, according to Eigen, protects against "false omniscience," which indicates the assumption of always knowing, always being right. Accepting that we do not know opens us up to something new and unexpected and releases the need to know. So often our arguments are encased in a strong feeling that we are right and the other must be wrong. However, it is freeing to concede that we do not know everything about the topic of discussion at hand, and we are ignorant about ourselves and the other. It paves a path for personal development and a path for growth in humility.

Paradoxically, faith in the unknown involves nothing to hold onto and, at the same time, unknown background support. Faith in the unknown is, according to Eigen, supported by another that one doesn't know is there. The psychoanalyst DW Winnicott stresses that the possibility of the baby's growth depends on this unknown boundless support of the mother.

William Wordsworth says in his poem "It is a beauteous evening":

> Dear Child! dear Girl! that walkest with me here,
> If thou appear untouched by solemn thought,
> Thy nature is not therefore less divine:
> Thou liest in Abraham's bosom all the year,
> And worship's at the Temple's inner shrine,
> God being with thee when we know it not.
> (Wordsworth, 1959, p. 95)

Poets and the religious write about their experience of not knowing God and staying in the dark as a way of achieving the soul's expansion. Saint John of the Cross writes:

> the higher he ascends
> the darker is the woods.
> (St. John, 1990, p. 159)

The poet Rainer Maria Rilke, in a letter to Ilse Jahr, has a similar sentiment: "But this very abyss is full of the darkness of God; and where someone experiences it, let him climb down and howl away inside it (that is more necessary than crossing it.)" (Rilke, 1982, p. 332).

And in his "Tenth elegy," Rilke writes:

> How dear you will be to me then, you nights
> of anguish. Why didn't I kneel more deeply to accept you,
> inconsolable sisters, and surrendering, lose myself
> in your loosened hair. How we squander our hours of pain.
> How we gaze beyond them into the bitter duration
> to see if they have an end.
>
> (Rilke, 1982e, p. 205)

To kneel, to go inside our dark depths, to surrender and lose ourselves, not to flee pain, or darkness, or unknowing, but tolerate them, stay steady with them, is what these authors find necessary for spiritual growth.

To tolerate pain and darkness, we need support. As mentioned before we may not know the support is there. Psychoanalysis may provide a sense of a primary support. Emphasizing the significance of support, Eigen proposes that one reason Freud used the couch is for the patient to feel support from below, an experience that mitigates a traumatized aloneness. Prayer too brings forth a sense of being alone with and supported by another – whomever one prays to.

An example that strengthens Eigen's view of faith and aloneness supported by another that one doesn't know is there, is indicated by the monk Thomas Merton. Writing about the doctor in Camus' *The Plague*, Merton says he could not have done what he did "without the Gospel or without some cryptic compassion that is more than simply humanistic" (Merton, 1991, p. 71). Merton seems to think that the source of the compassion the doctor feels, which embraces his "nobility," is some kind of mysterious background support.

Such mystery occurs in the natural world. For instance, there are plants that when attacked are known to communicate with other plants and leaves, quickly transferring information about impending danger. In *The Hidden Life of Trees*, Peter Wohlleben tells how underground forest fungi connect tree roots and "transmit signals from one tree to the next, helping the trees exchange news about insects, drought, and other dangers" (Wohlleben, 2017, p. 10).

Robin Bagai writes that Eigen emphasizes unknown possibility, which in its essence is supportive of life. He says that Buddhists sometimes call it "emptiness that is not nothingness," and that the psychoanalyst Marion Milner called it a "pregnant void." The idea of a pregnant void hints at the formless and empty world pregnant with creation, before God's command, "Let there be light" (Bagai, n.d., MEigenworkshop, Yahoo group, private).

Possibility, exploration, patience, and waiting are supportive of faith. Possibility is intertwined with faith as it enables openness. It stands out as a beacon of light. It sheds light on thoughts, feelings, and aspirations. It opens up gates of heaven – ultimate reality.

The philosopher AN Whitehead puts weight on the idea of possibility by characterizing it as a survey of possibilities. God, in Whitehead's view, enables the possibilities to become real. "He confronts what is actual in the world with what is possible for it" (Whitehead, 2005, p. 159). God exhibits in the actual world as a creativity of infinite freedom and infinite possibilities, which opens us up to envision a better life and to be stirred to make a possibility into a new instance.

According to religious thought, faith may facilitate contact with possibility, which becomes fact. This phenomenon has emerged in different religions. We are told that Jesus healed the paralytic in Capernaum through the faith of the sufferer, and the prayer of Moses healed Miriam of her leprosy.

Art and literature put forth products of imagination, where anything is possible. In his "Sonnets to Orpheus," Rilke expresses the possibility of being:

> O, this is the animal that never was …
> It had not been. But for them, it appeared
> in all its purity. They left space enough
> And in the space hollowed out by their love
> it stood up all at once and didn't need
> existence. They nourished it, not with grain,
> but with the mere possibility of being.
> And finally this gave it so much power
> that from its forehead a horn grew …
> (Rilke, 1982d, p. 241)

Rilke's sensibility is so expansive that he embraces possibility as actually existing, and he gives it equal power to reality.

One way we reduce or eliminate possibility is by labelling ourselves and others, including things, and stamping them with conclusive identities. The philosopher Cornelis Verhoeven challenges this tendency. In his "Philosophy of wonder" he embarks on the astonishing idea that philosophy like life is "a movement within the same nonidentity"; a movement in which identity is deferred, and in which everything is becoming (Verhoeven, 1972, p. 130). Verhoeven says that when we live our lives we need to settle in a space of possibilities – completely different from the ones we are attached to – in which we might be this or that, and the thing under discussion can be this or that.

Philosophy, as Verhoeven tells it, is "obstinate ignorance" in which we make a leap from knowing to unknowing, and not from unknowing to knowing, as one would expect. Deferring identity requires endurance. Deferring identity also does away with force. God is deformed into an idol if He is used to eliminate wonder by determining His identity as a matter of fact (Verhoeven, 1972, p. 165). If we defer His identity, we wonder who or what God is – we have faith in God, but still wonder.

The poet Rumi has an unusual viewpoint on ignorance:

> Whatever you say about mysteries:
> I know or I don't know, both are close
> to being true. Neither is quite a lie.
>   (Rumi, 2005a, p. 88)

> Changes do happen. I do not know how,
> or what remains of what into the absolute.
> I hear so many stories
> and explanations but I keep quiet
> because I don't know anything,
> and because something I swallowed
> in the ocean
> has made me completely content
> with ignorance.
>   (Rumi, 2005b, pp. 171–2)

Faith in the unknown may be a trigger for exploration. The drive to explore propels us to be where we have not travelled before, virginal territories that add to our knowledge and stir our emotions. Poets such as TS Eliot perceive exploration as a lifelong task. Eliot says:

> We shall not cease from exploration
> And the end of all our exploring
> Will be to arrive where we started
> And know the place for the first time
>   (Eliot, 1971a, p. 145)

Rilke probes human nature and wants to know what is behind our experiences. He talks of the Open as the realm of freedom. He berates us and most likely himself for tuning to objects instead of to the Open, in his "Eighth elegy":

> Forever turned toward objects, we see in them
> the mere reflection of the realm of freedom,
> which we have dimmed.
>   (Rilke, 1982a, p. 193)

In his "Tenth elegy" Rilke asks to "sing out jubilation" after "emerging at last from the violent insight" (Rilke, 1982e, p. 205). Exploration, albeit difficult, has been worthwhile. He has survived, as he wrote to his friend Lou Andreas-Salomé: "Imagine! I have been allowed to survive until this. Through everything. Miracle. Grace" (Rilke, 1982b, p. 332).

Rilke's "Open" reverberates in the work of Bion and Eigen. Bion uses O as a sign for the unknown. It is a baffling notion that is hard to pinpoint. It is constantly evolving. Bion refers to O by different terms – "Absolute Truth," "Ultimate Reality," "reverence and awe." For Eigen, Bion's O includes the unknowable emotional reality of the moment. The moment in itself is unknowable, but the analyst who aims at the emotional truth of a session opens himself with faith that he will meet it.

Religious saints relate to "Absolute Truth," which requires growth in virtues, such as humility. The way that leads to truth, according to St. Bernard of Clairvaux, is humility. Bernard envisions a ladder of virtues, where every step one climbs, from virtue to virtue, is ascension towards truth. When one admits not knowing oneself, humility grows. The top of the ladder signifies the achievement of the virtue of humility, from where you see the truth.

> What else is signified to us by the fact that the Lord was seen standing above the ladder which appeared to Jacob as a symbol of humility, but the fact that knowledge of truth is established at the summit of humility?
> (Bernard, 1963, p. 127)

Eigen has a psychoanalytical viewpoint concerning humility. In *Under the Totem* he says that if we accept the fact that we have very little knowledge about ourselves, we may have more humility and be more open. "If we assimilate the fact that we do not know everything about ourselves and the other and that, like the universe, we are mostly unknown to ourselves, a sense of humility and openness may have a chance to grow. We may become more interested in learning more about who we are and readying for further development. This is an entirely different attitude than slamming the door with dogma" (Eigen, 2016, pp. 19–20).

Eigen explores Faith in O. With faith, the unknown can be seen as a trigger, or a challenge, to see things in myriad ways, to see them one way and another, "chew them, and turn them around," open to the other's point of view. In addition to Faith in O, Eigen explores Bion's Transformations in O, which although unknown, may have an impact on us. "We may have hints, inklings, intuitions, but we can't be sure" (Eigen, 2011b, p. 59). Though this reality is unknown, it works on us; it is not passive, or powerless, but rather an active doer who is unknown. Not knowing is not a dead end. On the contrary, it encourages us to continue to explore, keep an open mind, underscoring the existence of something that is worth exploring. Robin Bagai says that more than being a trigger, Faith in O fertilizes Transformations in O (Bagai, n. d. MEigenworkshop Yahoo group, private).

Faith in O requires the capacity to wait. It also can serve as background support for the growth of that capacity. In his best moments, Tagore sings about enduring waiting for God: "If thou speakest not I will fill my heart with thy silence and endure it. I will keep still and wait like the night with starry vigil and its head bent low with patience" (Tagore, 1973, p. 8). In a number of poems, God is the one who is patient and waits for the poet's love.

While waiting, Tagore vacillates between great sadness and deep hope. The waiting, at times, brings shame and humiliation. Misunderstood and ignored by others he waits with offerings for God, often in vain: "And only I who would wait and weep and wear out my heart in vain longing?" (Tagore, 1973, p. 16). At other times he delights in waiting. Waiting is associated with hope, and the mood is happiness: "From dawn till dusk I sit here before my door, and I know that of a sudden the happy moment will arrive when I shall see" (ibid.). This waiting is also accompanied by an excited proclamation, "Have you not heard his silent steps? He comes, comes, ever comes" (Tagore, 1973, p. 17). But later he is back to despairing: "The night is nearly spent waiting for him in vain" (ibid.).

Contrary to the tender, compassionate tone of Tagore, the piercing tone of Eliot invites his soul to wait without hope and without love. He seems to experience the dread of facing the frustrations and disappointments of reality:

> I said to my soul, be still, and wait without hope
> For hope would be hope for the wrong thing;
> … there is yet faith
> But the faith and the love and the hope are all in the waiting.
> So the darkness shall be the light, and the stillness the dancing.
> (Eliot, 1971b, p. 138)

The last line shows a sudden shift in the poet's attitude, startling in its grasp of what may issue out of faith.

The importance of waiting is emphasized in religious writings. Saint Paul, in Letters to the Church in Rome, says to rejoice in hope and be patient in tribulation. Sometimes the Psalmist is hedged in by hesitation, or more likely by impatience. He cannot tolerate not knowing what God is going to do with him, a state of mind contrary to faith. This is made clear in the Christian theologian Gale D Webbe's "The night and nothing," where the author quotes the saying, "God is slow pay" – in his responses to our quests (Webbe, 1983, pp. 23–4). We can cultivate faith, practice faith, waiting to receive God's answer in his good time. Eigen gives the Talmudic example of the Biblical Cain. Hurt by God's preference for Abel's sacrifice, Cain acts without hesitation, failing to have the faith to wait and give room for something deeper to happen, to let further processes develop (Eigen, 2014, p. xiv). Eigen says that you can teach yourself to create more distance between yourself and your first reaction by beginning to sense signals inside you that tell you to step back, not to do anything but wait.

Keri Cohen, writing about Eigen, says:

> Even at nearly 82, he continues to amaze me in his ability to wait, be humbled by time and space. It's as if time and space are two areas he deeply respects along with the human figure in the office, the tangible being floating in time and space. By space I mean universal space, the galactic space of the universe and all the unknown forces that shape us in ways we cannot ever understand. Eigen seems humbled by the universe and in awe of its energy that affects all living creatures.
>
>   (Cohen, n.d., MEigenworkshop Yahoo group, private)

The value of experience is pivotal to Eigen's thinking; it cannot be overestimated. In his mind, one's own experience and that of the other must not be violated; it is sacred. Openness to experience indicates faith. This kind of faith embodies "caring, devotion, sincerity, respect, an imaginative loving objectivity, a drive to do life justice, a need to do right by experience" (Eigen, 2004, p. 9). A possible result in an increased sensitivity to the other; an ability to "wait on each other, wait for each other … Waiting, patience, certain passivity are important" (Eigen, 2004, pp. 9–10). Respect and caring are shown in accommodating the other, which McLean characterizes as the highest conduct. Accommodating the other may include waiting on and for the other.

On the same topic, Burton N Seitler says,

> Waiting is love; it is forbearance, and it is patience. To be patient with someone is to wait for the proper time to say or do something – or even to do nothing, but 'simply' wait. Waiting is also anticipating, or awaiting, and thus, it is related to hope (that something will happen). Waiting implies a passivity, and one is inclined to assume that it means powerlessness, but in fact, it is extremely powerful, simply because of its faith, faithfulness, and ultimate hope.
>
>   (Seitler, n.d., MEigenworkshop Yahoo group, private)

Having faith in the unknown does not mean that things will turn out to be fine. Eigen describes Bion's faith as a response to catastrophe, which means that we remain open to whatever transpires, including catastrophe. We need the patience to be able to continue to explore and be aware that to digest emotional life takes time, care, and development.

The theologian Paul Tillich construes faith as a state of mind that consists of the courage to accept doubt and despair, much like Bion facing catastrophe with faith. Tillich says, "We embrace doubt as being alive in the act of faith." He states that every existential truth contains an element of insecurity, and to accept this insecurity is an act of courage. According to Tillich, "The courage to be is an expression of faith and 'faith' must be understood through the courage to be" (Tillich, 1957, p. 12).

To illustrate facing catastrophe with faith, Eigen uses the Job story. "Everything is stripped away, family, wealth, health, and honour." Friends tell Job that his plight must be a punishment for sins. Job rejects their rationalizations. And "God offers no justification. He simply shows Himself. He cows Job with the display of creation … Suffering and loss bring Job to immediate God-contact. There is nothing left but God. Job and God. You and God" (Eigen, 2011a, pp. 33–4).

According to Eigen, Job discovers in himself a new faith, which begins to grow. He sees God in his own flesh.

Bion says that faith is allied with the growth of intuition, and he allies intuition with attention. Eigen adds that faith is an inherent support for attention and concentration (Eigen, 2014, p. xiii). The Jewish story of Honi the Circle Maker tells about Honi, who asks God for rain in a time of drought, makes a circle around him in the sand, and says I will not move until God sends rain down. He seems to be so concentrated on the request and to have such faith in God that rain does come. Saint Teresa of Avila prays for a man who sinned, and the man does change. The faith of these two that God will respond to them, shown in their determination to persist, is so strong that it changes the direction of Nature and the conduct of people.

Bob Dylan's "Tangled up in blue" touches on faith's persistence in his beautiful quirky way:

> The only thing I knew how to do
> Was to keep on keepin' on like a bird that flew
> Tangled up in blue …
> Slowly, slowly, slowly, learning, learning learning, stumbling here and
> there, a knife in the back, another in the ribs … Oy, O and thanks …
> (Dylan, 2016, p. 331)

This chapter demonstrates a convergence of ideas from psychoanalysts, poets, philosophers, and religious figures, each shedding a different light on the demands that faith entails. The confluence of ideas enlarges their scope, opening us to further exploration of what faith is, and what it is not.

References

Bagai, R. (n.d.). MEigenworkshop Yahoo group, private.

Bernard, Abbot of Clairvaux. (1963). *The steps of humility* (G Bosworth Burch, Trans.). University of Notre Dame Press.

Cohen, Keri. (n.d.). MEigenworkshop Yahoo group, private.

Dylan, B. (2016). *Bob Dylan: The lyrics 1961–2012*. Simon & Schuster.

Eigen, M. (2004). *The sensitive self*. Wesleyan University Press.

Eigen, M. (2011a). *Contact with the depths*. Karnac.

Eigen, M. (2011b). *Faith and transformation*. Karnac.

Eigen, M. (2014). *Faith*. Karnac.

Eigen, M. (2016). *Under the totem: In search of a path*. Karnac.

Eigen, M. (n.d.). MEigenworkshop Yahoo group, private.

Eliot, TS. (1971a). "East Coker." *Four quartets. The complete poems and plays, 1909–1050*. Harcourt, Brace, & World.

Eliot, TS. (1971b). "Little Gidding." *Four quartets. The complete poems and plays, 1909–1050*. Harcourt, Brace, & World.

Merton, T. (1991). *A vow of conversation*. Farrar, Straus and Giroux.

Rilke, RM. (1982a). "The eighth elegy." *The selected poetry of Rainer Maria Rilke* (S Mitchell, Ed. and Trans.). Random House.

Rilke, RM. (1982b). Letter to Ilse Jahr, February 11, 1922. *The selected poetry of Rainer Maria Rilke* (S Mitchell, Ed. and Trans.). Random House.

Rilke, RM. (1982c). Letter to Ilse Jahr, February 22, 1922. *The selected poetry of Rainer Maria Rilke* (S Mitchell, Ed. and Trans.). Random House.

Rilke, RM. (1982d). "Sonnets to Orpheus." *The selected poetry of Rainer Maria Rilke* (S Mitchell, Ed. and Trans.). Random House.

Rilke, RM. (1982e). "The tenth elegy." *The selected poetry of Rainer Maria Rilke* (S Mitchell, Ed. and Trans.). Random House.

Rumi, J. (2005a). "Close to being true." *Rumi the book of love* (C Bates, Trans.). HarperCollins.

Rumi, J. (2005b). "Ignorance." *Rumi the book of love* (C Bates, Trans.). HarperCollins.

Seitler, B. (n.d.). MEigenworkshop Yahoo group, private.

St. John of the Cross. (1972). "I came into the unknown." *The poems of St. John of the Cross* (W Barnstone, Trans.). New Directions, p. 2a.

St. John of the Cross. (1990). *Dark night of the soul* (A Peers, Ed. and Trans.), from the edition of P. Silverio de Santa Teresa. CD Image, Doubleday, p. 4b.

Tagore, R. (1973). "Gitanjali." *Collected poems and plays of Rabindranath Tagore*. Macmillan.

Tillich, P. (1957). *Systematic theology, Vol. 2*. University of Chicago Press.

Verhoeven, C. (1972). *The philosophy of wonder* (M Foran, Trans.). Macmillan.

Webbe, GD. (1983). *The night and nothing*. HarperCollins.

Whitehead, AN. (2005). *Religion in the making*. Fordham University Press.

Wohlleben, P. (2017). *The hidden life of trees*. HarperCollins.

Wordsworth, W. (1959). *Wordsworth* (R Wilbur Ed.). Dell.

Chapter 14

"Unity of opposites"

Hope in psychodrama group psychotherapy based on the Jewish Hassidic spiritual approach and Michael Eigen's psycho-spiritual relational approach

Ziva Bracha-Gidron

Introduction

Hope is a dialectical experience that expresses opposites such as fragmentation and inspiration. It reflects the role of our psychological structure together with our knowledge of the human spirit. The loss of hope is one of the main reasons that most of us will ask for help and turn to psychotherapy. The dialectical experience of hope as it is expressed in psychodynamic theories appears to be an emotional movement between opposites. One side contains fragility, breakdown, and despair. The other side contains fearlessness, authenticity, and creativity that can appear unexpectedly. Therefore, one who yearns for hope encompasses both sides of this longing. This approach that integrates spiritual knowledge with psychological aspects can help psychotherapists and their patients create space for hope as they broaden their perspective on the human-experience. Hope, in group psychotherapy, has a significant effect on the group participants (Yalom and Molyn, 2005) and also affects the mental structure of the group's sense of affiliation (Foulkes, 1986); it resonates within the members of the group as a "collective virtue" (Hopper and Weinberg, 2011). Stephen Mitchell (1946–2000), one of the founders of the Relational Psychoanalysis approach, emphasizes that hope is the most constructive essential attribute that awakens vitality (Mitchell, 1993/2003). Yet, for the most part, there are no significant references in psychodynamic theory to the spiritual dimension of human-existence. However, the experience of hope as a psychological and spiritual phenomenon that can be created from within opposites is rooted in Jewish history and in Jewish spirituality, i.e. Kabbala and Hassidut. According to Rabbi Yisrael Baal Shem Tov, the founder of the Jewish Hassidic movement, hope is the source of inner growth and the drive for redemption, in both personal and interpersonal relationships (Rabbi Yisrael

H'Baal Shem Tov, 1793/1998). Michael Eigen's psychoanalytic approach acknowledges the spiritual side of psychotherapy as it appears in Jewish spirituality by describing the sense of being "finite and the infinite," as being "broken to pieces," as well as having the "sense of whole" (Eigen, 2012a, 2014). Eigen's conception that "psychoanalysis recognizes the opposites such as body, soul and spirit" (Eigen, 2004/2014, p. 68) emphasizes the patient's capacity to generate an image that consists of all the parts of his/her self: to realize that she/he is a whole consisting of opposites that represent multiplicity.

This idea leads to the Jewish spiritual notion that hope is a dialogical experience (Rotenberg, 1983/1990) between all parts of the "multiplied self" that are structured as opposites (Rabbi Shneur Zalman of Liadi, 1772/1953). It is based on the belief that paradoxical situations are an integral part of human existence that consists of fragmentation and reparation (Scholem, 1967). In the first part of this chapter, we will try to understand how this experience of hope as a psychological and spiritual phenomenon can be created from within opposites. We will begin this journey by explaining the way in which hope is rooted in the Hebrew language, in Jewish philosophy, and in Jewish history throughout the centuries.

Hope in the Hebrew language and in Jewish philosophy

Hope in the Hebrew language – Hope has been a fundamental component of Jewish theology and within Jewish history throughout the centuries since Biblical times. The Hebrew root KVH (קוה) appears more than 414 times in the Bible (Even Shoshan, 2000). It reflects hope as a central aspect in Jewish theological literature, specifically in the halakha (conduct of living according to Jewish law) as it appears in the Talmud (2nd century CE), and in Jewish mysticism, as it appears in Kabbalah (13th century CE), and in Hassidism (18th century CE).

Hope in Jewish philosophy – Hope is expressed through yearning, expecting salvation and redemption, and having faith that they will indeed take place (Rotenberg, 1983/1990). Hope for redemption is part of the process of acknowledging the effort one can make to understand and reduce the gap between reality as it seems on the outside and the "spark of life" that is hidden inside, beyond, and above reality (Rabbi Yisrael Baal Shem Tov, 1774). This conception is manifested in the following Talmudic expression: "Even if a sharp sword is hanging over one's neck, one should not prevent oneself from praying for mercy" (Talmud, tractate Berakhot 10a). It is also expressed in *The Zohar* (Jewish book of mysticism dating back to the 13th century CE) as quoted in 1772 in *The Tanya*, one of the main Hassidic books, written by Rabbi Shneur Zalman of Liadi: "We all need to carry opposites in daily life, for there are tears embedded in one side of the heart, and joy embedded in the other side" (*Tanya*, Chapter 34, based on *The Zohar*, Chapter 3, p. 5a).

Rabbi Yitzchak Luria ("Ha'ari," 1534–72), the significant Kabbalist of his time, explains that in order to be able to contain this inner light one must make an emotional and cognitive effort to create a "vessel" for her/his "hiddenlight." This "vessel" is, in fact, the practice of Jewish law (halakha), but it is also the ability to listen to one's inner authentic voice, the gift of one's uniqueness that is "hidden" underneath every crisis (Kahana, 2010, pp. 40–5). This mental effort can be created by a mental movement of *reduction*. By reducing the negative effect, one can generate inner regulation that is the result of extreme emotional situations (Rotenberg, 1983/1990, pp. 45–58). In this way, one can "make a vessel," for both the crisis and its expressions including pain, fear and anger, but at the same time create a space for new meaning, change, and creativity. This demonstrates the experience of growth in Jewish mysticism as well as the ability to create hope. How is this approach expressed in Jewish history? In order to understand the development of these perceptions, we will discuss the historical background of Hassidism.

Hope and opposites in Jewish Hassidic history

The Hassidic revolution (1730) was initiated by the founder of the Hassidic movement, Rabbi Yisrael Baal Shem Tov (1700–60), who relates to the fragility of life through a psycho-spiritual approach that is based on five principles:

1. *Chaos, persecution, and social crisis.* Hassidism emerged as a social movement following the persecutions that befell the Jews of Poland in the first half of the 18th century, together with the crisis of Sabbateanism (17th century), a radical Jewish spiritual movement that threatened moral boundaries (Elior, 2014, pp. 170–255). The nature of such social and theological crises and the message of Hassidism are linked together (Etkes, 1998). In addition, the Hassidic historical documents indicate that the Baal Shem Tov was "courageous and gifted in his ability to find new meaning in tragic situations, in unexpected ways" (Elior, 2014, p. 253).

2. *The emotional realm is at the center.* In Hassidism, one's emotions, battles, dreams, and hopes are considered the essentials of one's life, and thus they are at the center of attention. According to the Baal Shem Tov, hope for salvation and redemption begins within one's private realm, and can be found in one's personal and interpersonal space, within human ethics (Rotenberg, 1983/1990, 1997) and in the relationship between man and God (Rosenzweig, 1921/2014). In order for a person to fulfil his potential one must, according to the Baal Shem Tov, "stay true to one's genuine/authentic intimate self. One cannot help others while denying himself" (Wiesel, 2010, pp. 37–8).

3. *In every crisis there is a spark of good.* Hassidism emphasizes man's capacity to believe and hope that in each and every personal and cosmic occurrence, there is a "spark of good" (Elior, 1992; Kahana, 2010;

Rotenberg, 1983/1990). Moreover, things have the potential to turn around and "upside down" for the good (Rabbi Yisrael Baal Shem Tov, 1794; Rabbi Shneur Zalman of Liadi, 1837/1974).

4. *"Unity of the multiplicity."* In Hassidism, the multiplicity that exists in creation, in God, and in man, is considered a component of God's unity, hence of the oneness of man himself (Elior, 2014, p. 253). The unity of opposites consists of elements such as male and female, materialism and spirituality – and regarding all of the above, it is claimed that "All contradictions are connected as one" (Lederberg, 2011, p. 12). What do we mean by the word "multiplicity" in Hassidism? It refers to the multiplicity of paths of faith as well as the multiplicity of parts that exists within man on the intra-psychic level. However, it also derives from the differences between human beings mostly represented as opposites. Jewish philosophers such as Martin Buber (1878–1965) indicate that this approach expresses the idea that there is not only one path to God, and "all the ways can be considered as a movement in the direction of God if it meant to exert an influence for good" (Buber, 1957, p. 17). The Hassidic movement affirms the ability to "create hope" in man's/woman's own subjectivity through human ethics (Rotenberg, 1983/1990). This path is the way hope can be developed on the inpersonal and interpersonal levels.

5. *Revolution in the status of being a Jewish believer.* The Baal Shem Tov's Hassidic revolution puts the "self–other" and "man–God" relationships at the center of Jewish religious practice along with personal prayer. Thus, he opposed the tradition of the critical analysis of sacred texts (*pilpul*). This determined that a new interaction should take place between Talmudic rationalism and Kabbalistic and Hassidic ecstasy and between the simple person (*am haaretz*) and the scholar (Etkes, 1998). The Hassid may indeed be learned, but, at one and the same time, he may also be the "underdog" due to the way he differs from the classic scholar, and due to his inherent flaws (Rotenberg, 1997).

The concept of "carrying of opposites" in Jewish theosophy

According to Rabbi Nachman of Breslev (a great-grandson of the Baal Shem Tov), "the disadvantage testifies to the advantage" (Nir, 2017). Later on, Rabbi Shneur Zalman of Liadi, known as the *Alter Rebbe*, included the two expressions "carrying of opposites" and "unity of opposites" in his book, *The Tanya*, the book of Jewish theosophy and the practice of Hassidic spirituality according to halakha, which was first published in 1772. The concepts "carrying of opposites" and "unity of opposites" reflect the two main contradictory experiences that characterize the human mind: a) the physical urges and instincts, and b) the divine side of the mind (1772/1953, *Tanya*, pp. 10–24). Spiritual practice can help us recognize each side of the mind and elevate the physical needs to spiritual ones. This mental process is accomplished without ignoring, repressing, or denying the existence of those needs.

Rabbi Shneur Zalman emphasizes the idea of "spiritual unity that is expressed in the divine infinite" (Elior, 1992, p. 30). In addition to the idea of continuity between opposites, this reflects the belief that any situation may end up turning around and "upside down" from bad to good. The *Alter Rebbe* claims that "in every situation of descent of 'breaking down' or despair there is a 'spot of elevation'; the higher spiritual level of a person the lower his fall" (Rabbi Shneur Zalman of Liadi, 1837/1974, p. 65).

This psycho-spiritual idea was expended by the last Chabad leader Rabbi Menachem Mendel Schneerson, the Rabbi of Lubavitch (1902–94), who explained that within every mental experience, it is possible for one to contain both a negative and a positive aspect alongside one another. The capacity of attaining hope is called "it'hapkha" – the turning around-and-upside-down of elements through intellectual effort, as opposed to "itkafya," which is hope that is "imposed" on a person through suffering and crisis. The Hassidic approach implies that man – while in an emotional, existential crisis in which one experiences sorrow, pain, and need – is capable of containing or carrying two opposite states, side by side, in a healthy way on the same continuum of life (Rabbi Menachem Mendel Shneerson, 1990). It can be implemented by internal, spiritual, theological, and transcendental observation (Elior, 1992). This notion preserves hope in two forms: a) as an inner light that needs to shine and as a vessel for the self-revelation of one's uniqueness, and b) by as an ability to influence others in order to create a better world (*TikunHa'Olam*). As Rabbi Yisrael Baal Shem Tov said: "So you should spread your wellsprings outwards" (1794).

Hope in psychodynamic approaches

Sigmund Freud (1856–1939) claimed, in the early days of psychoanalysis, that hope is an infantile and delusional gratification that represents pathological-defensive demanding (Freud, 1927). Later on, it was Freud who declared that the therapist's inspiration should take place through the development of a wise and realistic point of view (Freud, 1937). Unlike Freud, the psychoanalyst Erik Erikson was among the first who made space for hope as an expression of internal tension that is significant in the development of babies. He claimed that in babyhood (the first stage of childhood), as the conflict arises within the baby between basic trust and basic mistrust, the ideal completion of this stage involves the development of hope when the baby knows his mother is not beside him, yet hopes she will return (Erikson, 1955, in Mitchell, 1993/2003 p. 264). Erikson claims that hope is already present in early babyhood in the oral stage, in which the basic trust develops alongside fundamental mistrust. At this stage, initial hope is formed. It is considered an essential element because it awakens within the baby a vitality that is maintained in every stage of the continuum of the baby's life. Erikson considers hope to be constructive and growth-enhancing, and not restricted, as Freud argued, to infantile longing (Freud, 1937); it is not a thing that one must learn to let go of when one matures (Erikson, 1963).

Hope in D. W. Winnicott approach

Winnicott believed that hope brings about self-healing through the return to the moment in which growth became stagnant (Winnicott, 1955). According to Winnicott, it is necessary to awaken this longing in order for it to grow and transform from childish longing into mature longing (Winnicott, 1947/2009, pp. 65–75). Winnicott differentiates between a wish for hope that represents the "true self" versus an experience of hope that represents the actualization of the desired adjustment to society's demands, the "false self." Moreover, he observed hope within the anti-social tendencies of adolescents as well as the maturing teenager. He believed that the teenager would like something new to happen – not necessarily as an expression of her/his need for control and boundaries, but as a wish for healthy boundaries through which good hope can be formed (Winnicott, 1960/2009, pp. 74–84).

"The moment of hope," writes Winnicott, "gets wasted or withers due to poor management or intolerance … The remedy to an anti-social tendency is not found in psychoanalysis, but in management; in rising to greet the moment of hope, and in facing it" (Winnicott, 1947/2009, pp. 65–75). In Stephen Mitchell's relational approach the contradiction that exists in the therapeutic field is evident when one enters the therapist's room and claims hope, yet unconsciously does everything he/she can to "sabotage" it (Mitchell, 1993, p. 260). It is possible, then, to conclude that hope exists within the capacity of carrying the opposites on the continuum between a destructive experience and a yearning for change. In fact, those perceptions are the source of the relational approach (Greenebrg and Mitchell, 1983). However, neither Erikson nor Winnicott referred to the spiritual side of the self as a healing part. Michael Eigen's relational and spiritual approach continues to merge between this psychodynamic point of view and Jewish mysticism. What made him different and unique?

Hope in Michael Eigen's relational and spiritual approach

Michael Eigen, a leading psychoanalyst in relational psychodynamic theory, was one of the first to connect therapeutic concepts and the process of therapy with the concepts of mystical Judaism according to Kabbalah (Eigen, 1981). Eigen's perception reflects hope as an inpersonal and interpersonal "emotional movement" that can be developed within the relationship between the patient and the therapist, and even more so from within the human experience that is related to the tension that exists between the "whole" and the "broken parts" within the self (Eigen, 1996/2010, p. 23, 2012).

The concept of "wholeness" in the psychodynamic field can be referred to as the integration of the self (Klein, 1985) or the "unit core" of the self (Kohut, 1979). However, in Jewish mysticism, the reparation process is more than integration; it intimates the feeling of "wholeness." According to the psychodynamic conception, the "fragmented" self ("broken parts") refers to parts of self objects that are a reflection of an inner split (Klein, 1946, 1985). Eigen, however, claims that every mental action involves a continuous breaking into parts (Eigen, 1996/2010).

Eigen also agrees with Klein and Bion, who perceive one's emotional life as "categories of particles as opposed to the whole," and the split is a result of the will to conserve the good object. True, this conservation takes place via denial, idealization, and manic defense, and this is reflected in the way through which some part of the self attempts to maintain the positive feeling over the negative feeling by splitting the parts, so that "the right hand isn't aware of what the left hand is doing" (Eigen, 1996/2010, p. 22), which causes an unstable stiffness. However, through a careful and creative process, it can also support the experience of idealization that is needed in order to create "the area of faith" (Eigen, 2004/2014). Moreover, "The area of faith is part of the unconscious sense of rebirth ... the feeling that we can breathe freely as well as the inner sensation that something different can happen" (Eigen, 2014, pp. 64–5).

Michael Eigen and the Kabbalistic-Hassidic approach

Eigen's approach is compatible with the Kabbalistic-Hassidic approach in the following ways: a) as an expression of man's creation of his own life from within the fertilizing tension between body, spirit, and soul; b) as a recognition that man is "fractured and whole at once" (Eigen, 2012a). One travels along the continuum of fragmentation and repair as two elements that do not exist at the expense of one another, and not only as a manic bi-polar defence, but as complementary opposites (Mitchell, 1993/2003, p. 68); c) as a recognition that hope emerges out of the flexibility of one's thinking, i.e. an expression of mental movement (Eigen, 1996/2010); and d) the concept of mental movement as inner creative freedom, "Freedom is a state of motion, that finds and loses, comes and gets lost, takes on different shapes and forms" (Eigen, 1996/2010, p. 68). The essence of freedom is that it motivates man, in Bion's words, "from one form to another, from acquiring a shape to being shapeless, again and again" (Eigen, 1996/2010). The emotional movement, according to Eigen, pendulates between opposites: Between the sense of the death of the self and the experience of freedom and vitality (and vice versa).

This way the inner tension is not only considered destructive, but it can be transformed from a destructive force into a creative one by way of therapeutic relationships. Eigen mentions that "psychoanalysis recognizes the opposites" (Eigen, 2004/2014, p. 68), such as body and soul/spirit, as well as the sense of internal death and vitality the finite and the infinite (Eigen, 2012b). One can conclude from Eigen's approach that the capacity to "carry opposites" requires us, first and foremost, to pause and linger in the experience of the "death of the self" (Eigen, 1996/2010, p. 96) that exists in situations of crisis. The therapist's capacity to contain the collapse of the patient and the catastrophes of her/his life is an essential component of the patient's capacity to generate an image that consists of all the parts of the self and to realize that she/he is a whole that consists of multiplicity. When the therapist is capable of carrying the rich experience of the patient's sincerity, generosity, courage, and authenticity, the completion of one dimension with its opposite can take place – a completion that the patient may also internalize throughout his/her life. Eigen educates therapists to acknowledge their own opposites and to develop the capacity to "carry opposites," not only as contradictions – and not only as a destructive experience – but also as an experience within one's ongoing continuity. He encourages therapists to search for hope not as a "fake hope" that will satisfy family, society, or governments, but as a true hope: A subjective, inpersonal, and interpersonal one. It requires us, first and foremost, to pause and linger in the experience of fragmentation that occurs in situations of crisis or any kind of stress that reduces our sense of vitality. In Eigen's perception the therapist's capacity to contain the patient's collapses and the catastrophes of her/his life, as well as the ability to remind her/him of the spiritual aspects of life, mainly the "hidden light" that wishes to be explored, is an essential component of the patient's capacity to generate an image which consists of all parts of the self.

When the therapist is capable of carrying the rich experience of his/her patient's opposites alongside his sincerity and humor, generosity and authenticity, fear and courage, then he or she can help the patient and her/himself as well to have faith that hope is not lost. If these theories can be put into practice in a therapeutic session, what are the therapeutic ways to reach this continuity and transformation between fragmentation and reparation in order to create space for hope? Can it be created not only by verbal ways but also by experiential ways? Psychodrama group psychotherapy has the capacity to manifest the idea of "unity of opposites" as an integration of the psychodynamic relational approach and the Hassidic approach in creative methods.

The "drama of hope" – psychodrama group therapy: A new approach

Psychodrama group therapy was created by a Jewish psychiatrist, Jacob Levi Moreno (1889–1925), who believed in creating a theatrical stage platform for the self to play out (Moreno, 1932, 1934, 1985). It is considered the theory of a therapeutic culture (Artzi, 1991). He claimed that psychodrama is an integration of body, mind, and soul that can be played out in every therapeutic session. In psychodrama group therapy, conflicts and contradictions are part of the intrapersonal and interpersonal drama. Psychodramatic methods can be used in order to help patients discover the roots of one's "drama of pain and loss" and drama of disappointment as authentic feelings, but also to present moments that can be part of the "drama of hope" (Bracha-Gidron, 2019). In order to generate integration between these approaches, a new qualitative study was carried out in Jerusalem between 2015–19 (Bracha-Gidron, 2019) which will be described below.

"True hope" – Michael Eigen's contribution to the concept of hope in psychodrama

The Hassidic idea of the "unity of opposites" has its counterpart in the psychotherapeutic insight that in order to create hope, one must recognize one's own subjective opposites as mental parts of the "unit self" (Kohut, 1979). It can be compared to the integration capacity of the self that can be comprehended instead of the "split" mental disintegrated self (Klein, 1946). However, Michael Eigen's contribution to the concept of hope as it is manifested in psychodrama is that hope can be developed in the therapeutic space, which can be referred to as the "area of faith" (Eigen, 1981). Eigen points to Bion's last declaration about the idea that "the basic reality is the infinite ... it is terminology that is not borrowed from religion, but it connects to Buber's 'I-thou' to all ways of relationship" (Eigen, 2004/2014, p. 76). This area is a mutual space that invites both the therapist and the patient to stay in present time in the feelings of collapse as well as moments of elevation. And as Eigen declares, the therapist must be suspicious, responsible, and careful in the face of the patient's hope, as it might be a defense mechanism (over-idealization). The psychodrama psychotherapist can enable his/her patient's brokenness and vitality as she/he dwells with them in the "area of faith." This way "holding the end of the thread of hope" is no longer a Sisyphean experience.

How hope within opposites is expressed in a recent study

The research was conducted in two groups of 24 women who participated in psychodrama. The purpose was to examine the capacity to create a space for hope which evolves from within opposites, and to examine the ability of the participants to express an experience of hope from within opposites, within inpersonal and interpersonal relationships. The research resulted in the following three discoveries:

a) When there is an acknowledgement of two opposite mental situations such as "feeling broken" as well as a sense of "being one whole person," it allows for mental flexibility and internal regulation.
b) Creating a sense of inpersonal and interpersonal continuity indicates that any and every contradiction is an integral part of the sense of unity and

not only the feeling of being "torn apart" which can present the feeling of the capacity for "unity of opposites." Using the term "carrying opposites" becomes a fundamental expression for creating hope. The term *neshamah* (soul) as well as "finding the point of the *neshamah* (soul)" (Eigen, 1981, 1996/2010, 1998, 2019) becomes an expression that helps in understanding the idea of opposites.

c)   Playing on a psychodramatic stage allows transitions between opposites and can regulate between extreme emotions.

Summary

The concept of hope, from the psychodynamic point of view, is a dialectic experience, but in Jewish spirituality hope is a dialogical experience (Rotenberg, 1990). Nevertheless we, as therapists, can integrate psychodynamic aspects and Jewish spiritual knowledge to try to touch "the end of the thread of hope." Hope in Jewish is expressed tradition through yearning, expecting salvation, and redemption. The hope for redemption is part of the process of acknowledging the effort one can make to understand and reduce the gap between reality as it seems on the outside and the "spark of life" that is hidden inside, beyond, and above reality (Rabbi Yisrael Baal Shem Tov, 1793/1978). In Jewish history hope is a fundamental phenomenon that expresses the ability to transform from fragmentation to reparation. In new research that took place in psychodrama groups, the therapist used Jewish Hassidic mysticism as part of the therapeutic session. The results of this research expressed hope by the ability of the participants to "carry opposites" and create a "unity of opposites" (Rabbi Shneur Zalman of Liadi) in a theatrical therapeutic method (Bracha Gidron, 2019). In Michael Eigen's psycho-spiritual approach, searching for hope is like an "ancient game" that one plays, an "elusive game of hide-and-seek with divinity" (Eigen, 2012b).

References

Note

★ All quotations are from the Hebrew editions of the English publications.
★★Books written in Hebrew (some also have an English translation).
★★★ Jewish religious scriptures.

*Atzi, E. (1991). *Psychodrama*. Dvir.
Babylonian Talmud (2 CE). tractate Berakhot 10a; Adin Steinsaltz interpretation (1989) published by Steinsaltz institution Jerusalem.
★★Buber, M. (1957). *The path of man according to Hassidim*. Bialik Institute.
Bracha-Gidron, Z. (2019). "Unity of opposites": Hope in psychodrama group psychotherapy based on the Jewish Hassidic spiritual approach (PsyD diss.). The Professional School of Psychology.
Eigen, M. (1981). "The area of faith in Winnicott, Lacan and Bion." *International Journal of Psychoanalysis*, 62 (4), 413–33.

Eigen, M. (1996/2010). *Psychic deadness*. Karnac. Hebrew edition.

**Eigen, M. (2004/2014). *The sensitive self*. Wesleyan University Press. Hebrew edition.

Eigen, M. (2012). *Kabbalah and psychoanalysis*. Karnac.

**Eigen, M. (2012b). Interview in the Israeli newspaper *Makor Rishon*.

Eigen, M. (2014). *Faith*. Karnac.

Eigen, M. (2019). "Rebirth: It's been around a long time." International Psychohistorical Association Conference, New York University.

*Etkes, I. (1998). *The beginning of the Hassidic movement*. Broadcasted University. Ministry of Defense. Second edition. Hebrew edition.

*Elior, R. (1992). *Unity of opposites: The mysticism of Chabad*. Bialik Institute.

*Elior, R. (2014). *Israel Baal Shem Tov and his contemporaries. Kabbalists, Sabbatians, Hassidim and Mitnaggedim*. Vol. 1. Carmel.

*Even Shoshan, A. (2000). *New Bible concordance*. The New Dictionary Publisher.

Foulkes, SH. (1986). *Group analytic psychotherapy: Methods and principles*. Karnac.

Freud, S. (1927). The future of an illusion. *The standard edition of the complete psychological works* (Vol 1). Hogarth Press, 3–56.

Freud, S. (1937). Analysis terminable and interminable. *The standard edition of the complete psychological works* (Vol 23). Hogarth Press, 211–53.

Greenberg, J and Mitchell, SA (1983). *Object relational in psychoanalytic theory*. Harvard University Press.

Hopper, E and Weinberg, H (Eds.). (2011). *The social unconscious in persons, groups, and societies* (Vol 1: Mainly theory). Karnac.

**Kahana, B. (2010). *Breaking and mending: A Hassidic model for clinical psychology*. Rubin Mass Ltd Publishers & Booksellers.

Klein, M. (1946). Notes on some schizoid mechanisms. *International Journal of Psychoanalysis*, 27, 99–110.

Kohut, H. (1979). *The search for the self* (Vol. 4). (PH Orenstein Ed.). International University Press.

*Lederberg, N. (2007). *Sod HaDat-Rabbi Israel Baal Shem Tov, his spiritual character and social leadership*. Reuven Mas Publishing House.

Mitchell, SA. (1993). *Hope and dread in psychoanalysis*. Basic Books & Prescuse Books LLC.

Moreno, JL. (1932). *First book on group psychotherapy*. Beacon House.

Moreno, JL. (1965). "Therapeutic vehicles and the concept of surplus reality." *Group Psychotherapy*, 18 (4), 211–6.

Moreno, JL. (1985). *Psychodrama* (Vol 1). Beacon House (original work published in 1946.)

**Nir, E. (2017). *A Jew at night: A journey, followed by Rabbi Nahman's Dreams*. Yediot Aharonot. Hebrew edition.

Rosenzweig, F. (2014. orig. 1921). *Star of redemption* (B Pollock, Trans.). Indiana University Press.

**Rotenberg, M. (1983/1990). *Dialogue with deviance: The Hassidic Ethic and the theory of social contraction*. Institute for the Study of Human Issues.

*Rotenberg, M. (1997). *Jewish psychology and Hassidism*. Broadcasted University. Israeli Ministry of Defense. Second Edition. Hebrew edition.

Scholem, G. (1967). *Major trends in Jewish mysticism* – Enlarged version of *Nine lectures* (G Lichtheim, Trans.). Schocken Books.

Wiesel, E. (2010). *Hassidic soul: Portraits and legends of Hassidic masters*. Yediot Aharonot.

Winnicott, DW. (1955). Metapsychological and clinical aspects of regression within the psycho – analytical set-up. *International Journal of Psycho-Analysis*, 36, 16–26

Winnicott, DW. (1947/2009). Hate in the countertransference. In *The maturational processes and the facilitating environment*. Basic Books.

Winnicott, DW. (1965). The maturational processes and the facilitating environment: Studies in the theory of emotional development. In *The maturational processes and the facilitating environment*. Basic Books.

*Yalom, ID and Molyn, L. (2005). *The theory and practice of group psychotherapy*. Basic Books.

**Rabbi Yisrael Baal Shem Tov (1793, 1998). *Tzava'at Harivash: Testament of Rabbi Israel H'baal Shem Tov*. (JI Schochet, Trans. and annotated). Kehot Publication Society.

***Rabbi Yisrael Baal Shem Tov (1794/1975). *Keter Shem Tov – The crown of the good name*. Chabad Kehot.

***Rabbi Shneur Zalman Shneurson (1772/1953). *The tanya*. English Translation. Chabad Kehot.

***Rabbi Shneur Zalman of Liadi (1837/1974). *Tora or*. English Translation, Chabad Kehot.

***Rabbi Menachem Mendel Shneurson, Rabbi of Lubavitch (1990). *DvarMalchut*. Chapter 12. Chabad Kehot. Hebrew edition.

Chapter 15

The influence of Kabbalah's conception of Eros on the psychoanalytic Eros, according to Michael Eigen

Ruth Golan

Some time ago, I published a book [in Hebrew] which was the fruit of several years of research, on the connection or influence of *Kabbalah* and *Hassidut* on Freud's formulation of psychoanalysis. The book is called *The Unconscious Spirit* (Golan, 2017).

This exploration was a result of extensive research, which, among other sources, looked deeply into the teachings of Mike Eigen – not only his books written specifically about Kabbalah, but the entire process of his work. In his books I found a wellspring of knowledge and experience that contributed immensely to, and even revolutionized my conceptions of this influence – conscious and unconscious.

This chapter deals with the question of whether and in what ways we can conceive a connection between Kabbalah, which is the archaic cosmological teaching that I refer to as *Jewish mythology*, and psychoanalysis, which is the revolutionary product of modernity and science.

Kabbalah, and later Hassidut, are ancient teachings that deal with the cosmic and human break with creation and the process of mending – *Tikkun*.

Kabbalah is considered to be the underlying mystic interpretation of Jewish wisdom, the esoteric and even paganic teaching that was revealed to the general public only relatively recently. Its principal work is the book titled *The Zohar* (splendour), which is traditionally attributed to Rabbi Shimon Bar Yochai, who lived at the time of the Romans. Modern researchers, however, attribute it to Rabbi Moshe Di Leon and other 13th century contemporaries (Scholem, 1941).

There are various different schools of Kabbalah, but all of them see the main purpose of the human as Tikkun Olam, which means mending or repairing the catastrophic fracture in creation, which occurred as a result of the light projected by the creator to create the world being too great for vessels to bear it.

The innovation of Hassidut is that it reviewed Kabbalistic cosmic discourse with the emphasis mainly on the *tikkun* of the human soul and psyche. In light of that, it can be seen as a precursor of psychoanalysis, on condition that we relate to the mystical concepts in a metaphoric sense, relating to the concepts as metaphors for the various levels of the psyche.

I based my research on the assumption that knowledge is continuous, which means that every new knowledge rests on the foundations of the knowledge that preceded it, is influenced by it, and takes the preceding knowledge to a new place. This is true for science as well as for the study of the psyche. The evolution of knowledge is a spiral – what was exterior to us was displaced and reappeared from within.

The animistic beliefs of our forefathers in which gods and demons are represented by natural phenomenon and objects – this animistic knowledge didn't just disappear but was displaced into split and conflictual psychic dynamics.

But with another half turn of the spiral one could claim that what we experience as interior – our consciousness, our unconscious, our drives – are not necessarily merely interior and subjective but also exist in the inter-space between people. We tend to refer to "my consciousness" like "my body" or "my psyche." Such statements are not falsities, but at the same time it would not be too farfetched to look at consciousness as an inter-subjective field that we're all part of – a field that we share with others, others like us, and others unlike us, such as animals, plants, and even the entire cosmos. Did Freud invent psychoanalysis, or discover it? Didn't he rather discover the different layers of the human psyche, which formulated and organized this new knowledge in a new way that shed a new light on the psyche and the psychic causality? I tend to hold the second assumption, and there is nothing in it to detract from Freud's greatness.

Like in the Hassidic story about the angel who teaches the baby in its mother's womb the entire Torah and at the moment of birth slaps the newborn, causing it to forget everything, our own knowledge of ourselves is a revelation of something we already knew and have repressed.

Mike Eigen, who was influenced mainly by Bion but also by Melanie Klein, Winnicott, and Lacan, uses Kabbalistic terms, as well as psychoanalytic concepts in a free-way, in an attempt to create a more holistic way of understanding the psyche – a way that emphasizes the experience dimension. His writings are both poetic and erotic. He doesn't formulate his thoughts like a rigorous academic but like a person who is attentive to his psyche, as well as to the psyche of the other. He uses concepts in a very elastic way. He is present in the experience and not just an onlooker. Out of the tumultuous abundance of his writings a human pearl is rising, which reminds one the writings of the Baal Shem Tov (the founder of the Hassidut, who lived in the 18th century), Rabbi Nahman of Breslow (a Hassidic and mystic Rabbi who lived at the end of the 18th century and founded his own school), and the Jesuit Christian mystic Teilhard de Chardin (a French palaeontologist and founder of the spiritual school of evolution, who died in 1955). To these experiences and insights Eigen applies his psychoanalytic understanding.

Sometimes in an organic and deep way, and sometimes in a way that raises questions or looks (in my opinion) too emotional. One can mainly say that he touches the heart, expands its compass, and gives new meaning to the Biblical phrase: "With all your heart, with all your soul and with all your might" (Book of Deuteronomy: 6, 5).

Eigen points to the fact that the main characteristic that connects Kabbalah to psychoanalysis is the concept of mystery.

You might be aware of the fact that Freud, early on in the creation of psychoanalysis, established a "secret" group similar to the Kabbalistic groups. Beginning from the year 1912, he gave each of his loyal psychoanalysts a signet ring (Grosskurth, 1991). One can call it "the group of the ring," similar to what is described in Tolkien's *The Lord of the Rings*. In psychoanalysis, Freud saw a discipline that deals with a secret realm in the human psyche, and in this respect it has, in his opinion, much in common with the ancient mystery groups that emphasized rebirth.

In his book *Psychic Deadness* Eigen writes:

> I think of Freud's remark to Fliess about psychoanalysis being like ancient mystery cults, with secret rites of transformation. Psychoanalysis lives off a sense of the secret. Its concepts are concerned with ways that human beings keep secrets from themselves. Its methods are ways of opening the secret self. Early psychoanalysis doubted that human beings can keep a secret and gambled on the ability to decipher secrets that words and behavior indirectly betray.
>
> (Eigen, 1996, p. 182)

Eigen relates to two modes that characterize Freud's relating to the mystical:

1. A primal I sense, a limitless I sense, where one experiences a limitless inclusion, or as he called it – after the writer Romain Roland – an "oceanic feeling." In this concept Roland meant the feeling of union with God. Freud related this experience to the feeling of the baby after breast feeding (Freud, 1930, pp. 72–3). If you look at a baby's face after it is fed, you can see it glowing and calm with no desire and no lack. It might be similar to the way one experiences the Buddhist Nirvana. Perhaps this is the reason why in all the statues of Buddha his face is glowing and smiling.
2. The perception of the id. Freud defines the mystic experience as the vague self-perception of the reality that is outside the I, the perception of the id (Freud, 1941).

Note that Freud relates to the id as being outside the I and in that, he connects the mystical experience to the perception of the id. Now I would like to make a short mention of another central concept that is part of the mystery – Eros, or the erotic.

Eros is one of the central concepts on which Freud established psychoanalysis. We can find a wonderful description of Eros in Plato's *Symposium*, from which Freud took his description of Eros – as desire that cannot be satisfied, as indestructible life energy. This is how Eros is described in *The Symposium* by Socrates, who was quoting Diotima:

> And as his parentage is [the son of poverty and plenty], so also are his fortunes. In the first place he is always poor, and anything but tender and fair, as the many imagine him; and he is rough and squalid, and has no shoes, nor a house to dwell in; on the bare earth exposed he lies under the open heaven, in the streets, or at the doors of houses, taking his rest; and like his mother, he is always in distress. Like his father too, whom he also partly resembles, he is always plotting against the fair and good; he is bold, enterprising, strong, a mighty hunter, always weaving some intrigue or other, keen in the pursuit of wisdom, fertile in resources; a philosopher at all times, terrible as an enchanter, sorcerer, sophist. He is by nature, neither mortal nor immortal, but alive and flourishing at one moment when he is in plenty, and dead at another moment, and again alive by reason of his father's nature. But that which is always flowing in is always flowing out, and so he is never in want and never in wealth; and, further, he is in a mean between ignorance and knowledge.
>
> (Plato, 360 BCE)

Eros is the core drive responsible both for the motivation of the human being and their psychical structure. According to Freud, Eros or libido resembles in many respects the life force or universal energy, and this definition resembles in my opinion the way Eros is considered in Kabbalah. On the background of the moral values of the Western world of the 20th century, Freud's ideas on sexuality and its significance were received with suspicion and resistance. It is astonishing to discover the resemblance between his ideas and Kabbalistic notions. Kabbalah scholars based their cosmic and mystic teachings on the fight between good and evil, breaking of the vessels and repairing them – Tikkun, or as was later formulated by the Greeks and Freud – Eros versus Thanatos, the death drive. Freud encountered much resistance and hostility towards his theories of Eros and Thanatos, not very different to what Aboulafia, one of the important Kabbalists from the 13th century, had to go through. The Rabbis, especially those from the orthodox Lithuanian sect saw the drive as an obstacle to a life of righteousness and as a force that explains the origin of evil in the world. They measured the moral value of a person as something that emanates from his/her ability to resist his/her urges and channel them towards holiness. In this sense, the Kabbalists in *The zohar* and later the Hassidic Rabbis like the Baal Shem Tov or Nahman of Braslow included the libido in the worship of God, and talked openly on the holiness of sexual relations as helping the unification of God and the Shechina (Idel, 2010).

In a similar way, Freud emphasized the necessity of limiting the urges in order for culture to be able to develop (Freud, 1930). Freud, and Lacan after him, did not think that there is a possibility to overcome the drive, rather to sublimate parts of it, as the drive is also the source of creativity. In Hebrew, even the letters are the same – *Yetser/yetsira*. So, one needs to dominate the drive rather than to suppress it.

In Kabbalah and Hassidut, the relationship between a man and a woman was perceived as parallel to the relationship between God and the Shechina (the feminine aspect of God), as well as the relationship between the human being and God and between God and the people of Israel, which functions as his wife. (Recently I learned that the Kabbalistic attitude to Shechina developed in Europe around the same time of the rise in importance of Maria, mother of Jesus.) From this assertion arises a discussion of the place of woman in Kabbalah and the place of love, which is conceived as a cosmic force that binds reality in its entirety into one unity (Idel, 2010, p. 21).

The way many Kabbalists describe God, it seems to me, is very similar to what Eros is. God's relations with human beings are erotic (Idel, 2010). One can say that the conception of Eros in Kabbalah is its stormy dynamic core. That is probably why the religious authorities tried to keep this aspect of Judaism secret, up until this generation. According to Kabbalah, creation is possible only by combining together the masculine and feminine forces. The Kabbalistic Eros is one aspect of the love of the person to his god, and not just a way of contemplating the love of god to the human being. The spiritual aspect of Eros attracted the mystic to identify with it but also to imitate in his erotic behaviour god's eroticism.

According to the Kabbalah of The Ar' i -Rabbi Izhak Luria – who was one of the major Kabbalists teaching in Zefat in the 16th century, the aim of creation is the marriage/matching between two opposite forces that existing in reality, carrying symbols of divine femininity and masculinity. (This matching reflects eternal unification with the mortal vehicle.)

Matching was presented in Kabbalah in the way that The Ari saw it – as the relation between the individual self, which is the feminine aspect in the human being and the void, the eternal abstract being, which represents the masculine aspect. Creation is viewed as a long historical process of construction, becoming, and developing, through which the eternal is fused in mortals, the masculine in the feminine and the void in the self. This process also includes separation, destruction, lack, and longing.

Sexual relations are used in order to help solve the tension between the psychic/spiritual attraction and the physical one, as students of Kabbalah are ordered to have sexual intercourse with their wives on Friday evenings (Idel, 2010).

Friday evening is the central erotic time. The main function of the divine phallus is to raise the power of the feminine goddess, which is represented by the Shechina or royalty, at the special time that is suited especially to it – the eve of the Sabbath. Sexual intercourse in this context actually becomes a ceremony, a ritual of union with the divine.

Like in psychoanalysis, one finds in Kabbalah concepts like sublimation, replacement, satisfaction, and lack of completeness as a solution to the problem of sexual frustration. One can also find in both domains mentions of incest and its relation to grace. Eigen shows this in very appealing ways throughout his writings.

One of Freud's important insights is related to sexual curiosity at the period of the developing of the child's self-consciousness in connection to the origin of things and his own place, and the relation between this curiosity and sexuality (Freud, 1905, pp. 194–5). The realization that the origin of being is erotic, and that the erotic is one with the metaphysic and the theological, is central to Kabbalah (Idel, 2010, p. 21). In a similar way, one can relate to the mystery of the Oedipus complex as the story about origin, about birth. So according to Freud, the secret of the origin of things is the secret of the creation of the individual.

Among other reasons, Freud wrote *The Interpretation of Dreams* in reaction to the death of his father (Freud, 1900, p. xxvi). According to him, it was only then that he could eat of the fruit from the tree of knowledge and recognize his desire to the mother and his rivalry with the father, which in a similar way to Kabbalah can be interpreted as acquiring knowledge through the unconscious and dreams. Freud had been able to penetrate the unconscious and reveal the inner lining of the psyche, and in that way to lower it from its ideal position. *The Zohar* too describes the fall of Adam from paradise. It emphasizes the function of knowledge in the primal sin. In Kabbalah, the masculine and the feminine are two poles of essential unity and disruption of the balance between them leads to sin and flaws.

Eigen adheres to this definition in his book, *Kabbalah and Psychoanalysis*, in which he relates to the libido as an erotic flowing energy, like electricity and water, which changes into various forms. He claims that imagination and even hallucination play an important role in the creation of erotic desire.

In his book *Feeling Matters*, Eigen already unites sex with God. He believes that God exists everywhere, and the divine eternal is characterized by eternal vibrations. Eigen claims that Freud refined this kind of experience in the energetic model of the libido, and that this energy is presented with fluidic and electric images, as well as changing intensities that are constantly transferred from place to place. Eigen sees in it a cosmic sexual vision. In this book he relates to sexuality as an act of deliverance (Eigen, 2007, p. 18).

In his book *Lust*, Eigen gives as an example the story of Adam and Eve:

> Adam, Eve/Pandora, the serpent, the fruit, the bite, the taste. Sweet and bitter fruit, juicy, succulent. Lust for life and knowledge slide up and down sensory-feeling-mental scales. Past barriers and prohibitions, whirls of meaning, Faustian moments. The one thing you mustn't do. Even God you don't listen to, especially God. A course of history is set: rulers want obedience: living breaks the seams. But who are the rulers? The same who break the seams.
>
> Command givers-obeyers-breakers. Clash of personality, clash within personality. Serpent mind: eat and be like gods, immortal, know what's good and bad. A promise that turns into its opposite: eat and know death, you are going to die. Eat life, eat death. Rise, fall. Fallible, gullible mortality, hungry for everything.
>
> (Eigen, 2006, p. 10)

I will conclude with another reference to *The Symposium*, where Socrates in the name of Diotima shows a spiral of development of Eros:

The lover who desires eternal beauty is at first only attracted to the reflection of it, in the physical beauty of the beloved. This physical passion is only the first step on the ladder. This is erotic love or the realm of sexuality.

The second step is Agape, the sublimation of Eros. It is the phase of creating the new.

The third step is Philia, the phase of identification with the creator, or as described by Plato – The love of wisdom or erotic knowledge. The impulse is towards creating a new awareness in the world (Idel, 2010).

In this respect, the evolving Eros expands the limits of the self and goes beyond it. It moves from passion and desire to the product of desire and in the end, becomes the desirous one – which gives birth to the creator.

The entire process of Michael Eigen's teachings and works – not only his books written specifically about Kabbalah, but the entire process of his work contains a wellspring of knowledge and experience. It can assist in a connection between Kabbalah and psychoanalysis, which is the revolutionary product of modernity and science.

References

Bible. Book of Deuteronomy: 6, 5.
Eigen, M. (1996). *Psychic deadness*. Routledge.
Eigen, M. (2006). *Lust*. Wesleyan University Press.
Eigen, M. (2007). *Feeling matters: From the Yosemite God to the annihilated self*. Karnac.
Freud, S. (1900). *The interpretation of dreams*. SE 4–5. The Hogarth Press.

Freud, S. (1905). *Three essays on the theory of sexuality*. SE, 7: 125–234. The Hogarth Press.

Freud, S. (1930). *Civilization and its discontent*. SE 21: 59. The Hogarth Press.

Freud, S. (1941). *Findings, Ideas, Problems*. SE 23: 300, 22/8. The Hogarth Press.

Golan, R. (2017). *The unconscious spirit: The influence of Kabbalah on psychoanalysis according to M. Eigen* (Hebrew). Resling.

Grosskurth, P. (1991). *The secret ring: Freud's inner circle and the politics of psychoanalysis*. Addison-Wesley Pub. Co.

Idel, M. (2010). *Kabbalah and Eros* (Hebrew). Schocken.

Plato (360 BCE). *The symposium* (B Jowett, Trans.). Retrieved from http://classics.mit.edu/Plato/symposium.html.

Scholem, G. (1941). *Major trends in Jewish mysticism*. Schocken.

Chapter 16

"My kingdom for a widdler"
Michael Eigen – A beta-watcher's midwife

Stefanie Teitelbaum

I was Mike Eigen's student in 2000. His talks about "his" Bion started the labour of bringing "my" Bion to life. An element of Mike's Bion thinking that consistently holds my attention is the beta element, especially Mike's assertion that beta elements are not objects of interpretation. When I asked, "What then do we do with them?" – he answered, "Just watch them; see them float around in the room, see where they land, or maybe watch them fly out the window." I was hooked. Eigen (2014, p. 27) said that Bion (1971/2018, Vol X, pp. 1–32) stated he had never seen a beta element, but had some idea of what it might be, and left a few spaces for it on his grid so that, just in case he ever saw it, he would know where to put it. Sounds like a function of Elijah's cup on a Seder table. Bion (1963/2018, Vol V, p. 12) used a table as an example of faith in the thing in and of itself.

I turn to *The Birth of Experience* (Eigen, 2014, pp. 1–64), Chapter 1, "Beauty and Destruction," to think about beta elements. It is the most concentrated collection of Eigen's own beta visions I have found in his body of work. Eigen (2014) called on – among others – Freud, Shakespeare, Kabbalah, and comic books to help me see without sight those elusive bits of psychic life that Bion (1963/2018) called "objects compounded of thing-in-themselves, feelings of depression-persecution and guilt and therefore aspects of personality linked by catastrophe" (p. 37). By the publication of *Birth of Experience*, my attention in reading Eigen and perhaps Eigen's own attention shifted from beta elements to beta experience. I use Eigen's (2018, pp. 1–10) concepts of a "distinction–union structure" and "alternate infinities" to organize flights of fancy in this chapter.

The shock of distinction may have a beta quality. Eigen (2014) speaks of his life-long passion in treatment: "what can we do with those who do not get better, with those we cannot seem to help, can we help some of the unhelpables?" (p. 31). The language of beta, saturated, congealed, clotted, seem to go back to the unhelpables. I have a hunch that cogitating on beta experience might help me with at least one unhelpable.

Margot (Teitelbaum, 2008) calculated a recent session as our 25th anniversary. I wondered if the 25th was the silver anniversary, she looked at her silver sandals, laughed, and said she wore them in honour of the occasion. She cannot bear the "work" of psychoanalysis as it keeps taking her to her self-hatred (Eigen, 2014, p. 27). The "work" unleashes her own attacking beta forces, what Eigen (1996b/1991, p. 93), after Bion (1963/2018, p. 51), called the Pac Man figure that keeps destroying after all has been destroyed. She is angry that I have not helped make daily life happier, but then feels greedy about wanting more, and guilty about not taking steps to help herself. When she can no longer bear a "session," we talk about politics, TV, movies, our cats, the Brooklyn Botanical Gardens ... The song from *The Sound of Music* (Rodgers and Hammerstein, 1959) plays in my head; these are a few of my (our) favourite things. I read aloud some notes of this chapter. Her comments helped me. Her curiosity and fine intellect overpower the beta attacks for a while as she uses the inanimate pages' thoughts for self-analysis. The novel thoughts are less noxious on the page than from my mouth. She could digest ideas more easily from the pages, and we found a way to talk to each other that was not excruciating for her.

> Bion is saying be grateful for a headache/heartache or a nightmare that scares you half to death ... It might be a beta element trying to say hello, or an alpha ache trying to get your attention.
>
> (Eigen, 2014, p. 37)

Margot suffers both the hello and the heartache. The beta hello of our silver anniversary was seemingly tolerable. The alpha call for attention in psychoanalytic self-exploration becomes agonizing; I wonder if we are in the session when we are not on Row 3 of the Grid (Bion, 1971/2018, Vol X), the row of dream, dream thought, and myth. In my mind's eye, Dr Bion is bemused and Dr Eigen is amused over the anniversary session (bemused for beta, amused for alpha?). A personal if self-serving Eigen–Bion distinction. When I heard James Grotstein speak at the 2012 Bion Los Angeles Conference, he mentioned Bion's bemused notice that American analysts seem to talk to their patients. I've heard Mike Eigen speak about psychoanalytic hanging out, and interesting things that happen off the grid. Maybe all the elements of our favourite things have potential to be Freudian (1900a/2001, p. 27) royal roads.

Eigen (2014) says, "Let's make believe the body is animate" (p. 27). Freud's (1909b/2001) Little Hans case lays out the complexities of such pretending:

> When he [Hans] was at the station once (aged three and three-quarters) he saw some water being let out of an engine. "Oh, look," he said, "the engine's wildling. Where's it got its widdler?" ... he added in reflective tones: "A dog and a horse have widdler; a table and a chair haven't." He had thus got hold of an essential characteristic for differentiating between animate and inanimate objects.
>
> (p. 9)

"POW!, BANG!!" says Eigen (2014, p. 34), pointing us to comic book language expressing beta states of catastrophic impact in onomatopoeic words that impact with material force. Eigen (1973/2018, pp. 21–4) titled an early version of distinction–union structure as "The Recoil on Having Another Person." The word recoil invokes my cartoon visual of Elmer Fudd (from Warner Brothers *Looney Tunes*) being blown backwards out of the screen frame shooting a shotgun. This recoil image drove the first paper I wrote about Margot (Teitelbaum, 2008). I called her recoil a people allergy. Her childhood Crohn's disease blew her out of her body frame. She is flooded by Eigen's (1986, pp. 215–50) infinite reversals of material/immaterial, animate/inanimate, psyche/soma. I re-read Hans' phobias and terrors as beta impact co-existing with and recoiling from the vicissitudes of Freud's (1915c/2001) instincts.

Eigen (2014) said:

> A beta moment might embody and transmit an impact translated as flooding (one of Freud's terms for primal trauma) or nameless dread... Bion does not limit catastrophe to psychosis. It can be part of creativity as well.
>
> (p. 42)

My mind's eye saw drawings of the table without and the horse with the widdler next to it as I wrote the abstract for this chapter. I mis-located those imagined drawings in Freud's case study. Falsehood! Catastrophe! The whole chapter is junk! POW! Sometimes find a grid box for myself, to try to localize elusive experience, although the grid is meant to be a notation template for a session; I hope Bion doesn't mind. There was a creative catastrophe involved in writing this chapter.

Eigen (2014) said:

> Beta elements can become frozen or be envisioned as agglutinated bizarre masses that cement caesuras. They can form part of the psi-barrier in column two of the grid, partly made up of lies that act as a contact barrier between unconscious and conscious processes.
>
> (p. 34)

A linking force in me grabbed onto objects indiscriminately, ignoring reality. These bizarre masses formed the contact barrier between my creative unconscious and my annoying, nitpicking conscious processes. "My kingdom for a widdler!" began its birth process. The creative process ground to a halt, and I needed to fact check to continue the birth of meaningful language to public-ate potentially useful bits of imagination. The C2 Box seemed an Alice in Wonderland portal between the positive and negative grid, but was becoming a coffin. I opened the coffin lid and re-membered a dream (Teitelbaum, 2014) which included a big baby giraffe with a feminine triangle of thick black mesh covering its feminine widdler and wiwi-macher, which, unlike those of Hans's and all men (including Eigen), do not co-exist one within the other. In women, they are separated by a "dark continent" (Freud, 1926e/2001, p. 212). Perhaps the falsehood was a parapraxis pressured by my unconscious to reveal its union–distinction work differentiating my Eigen thinking and my own. More fact-checking. Lo and behold! There is a cartoon by Hans's father of a giraffe with a long skinny black widdler in the case study (Freud, 1909b/2001, p. 14). Linking boy and the big baby girl giraffes happened after I crawled out of the C2 rabbit hole.

Eigen (2014) said:

> I see beta and alpha as interweaving. Often, they are presented as opposed. I feel they are interwoven not just in the sense of beta feeding alpha impacts for storage and digestion, but more thoroughly interwoven, so that you do not have one without the other.
>
> (p. 36)

Rabbinic commentators puzzle that the first word of the book of Genesis – B'reisheet – begins with a bet rather than an alef. The first row (A) of Bion's grid is the row of beta elements. The alef is open and closed, in some places framing the light, in other letting the light flow in an infinity of direction. Bet is closed, with open spaces for the light to come through, but definitively pointing to the next character. Robert Alter's (2004) translation of the first phrase of Genesis is "When God began to create heaven and earth ..." (p. 17). This language opens space to contemplate God living. Eigen's (2018, pp. 1–10) "alternate infinities" before getting busy creating the world we know. There is also no solid line in Bion's Grid before Row A. Eigen (2005, p. 156) talks about an inner vagina opening within him. Post bet, in the second creation story, human is both male and female. Pre-bet, there is perhaps a Lilith Eigen. Reading Eigen has been both alef and bet for me, and every bit a beginning in my human development. Enlightened ideas very clearly framed in their roots of psychoanalytic thinkers, and unframed wild thoughts. The framed Eigen work and the framed bet, the Hebrew alphabet letter, lead me to Bion's (1990/2018, Vol XI, p. 199) idea of the Pythagorean function of a Henry Moore sculpture. The materials of the sculpture are there to frame the place where there is no material. The shards of the broken vessels of sephirot nodes form graphics through which wild thoughts (Bion, 1977b/2018, Vol X, pp. 175–86) shine through.

Eigen (2014, p. 38) ponders that the grid and Sephirot are upside-down images of each other; sense impressions at the top of the grid and the Bottom of the Sephirot (Malchut, Kingdom). Keter the Crown at the Top of the Sephirot, empty space beyond calculus at the Bottom of the Grid. The realms of "infinities of infinities."

Beta elements can have various functions in psychic life, feeding, stimulating, blocking or even destroying processing. There may be benefit of
thinking of positive and negative beta elements depending on how they
function in a given context, similar to positive–negative grid, sephirot
and z functions.

(Eigen, 2014, pp. 35–6)

The z work refers to Winnicott (1967). The dimension in which the baby
can no longer maintain the affective reality of the Mother's existence.
The healthy baby survives z experience and grows a sense of faith and
confidence in a capacity to survive. I suspect Margot's z experience was
a ghastly experience of empty eternity. She needs to cling to the real
therapy space as her z space becomes the court of the hollow crown in
Shakespeare's *Richard II* (Shakespeare, 1597/1936). Eigen (2014, pp. 31–2)
likens the POW BANGS of beta impacts experienced by the analytic
couple with so-called "borderlines" to the experience of reading a
Shakespeare play.

within the hollow crown
That rounds the mortal temples of a king
Keeps Death his court
      (*Richard II*, Act III, Scene II, p. 369)

An empty and death-saturated space at the same time. Catastrophe. The
upside-down negative crown.

Harold Bloom (1998), in his text *Shakespeare: The Invention of the Human*,
points out that Richard III shocks audiences. In his favourite stage performance by Ian McKellan, Bloom (1998) sees a Richard with no inward capacity, and that Shakespeare's attempt to imbue him with a sense of inwardness
is a dramatic disaster (pp. 64–71). In sessions with borderline phenomena,
analysts experience the hide and seek of inward capacity and see that bad
drama as a fine dramatization of the disaster in a personality that cannot
sustain the pain of an inner world. The subtopic (super topic to me) theme
of the 2019 International Psychohistory Association is "The contributions of
Michael Eigen to human understanding." The music in the phrases Birth of
Experience and Invention of the Human harmonize in a distinction–union
tonality. Poly-tonal, perhaps, like Stravinsky's (1913) *Rite of Spring*. Disney
Studios intuited the pow-bang impact of that music and brought animated
cartoon expression of the music into its birth of the world segment of *Fantasia*. The boulders shooting out of the lava have some similarity to the concrete
projectiles disabling the treads of a tank on the battle terrain in Director
Richard Locraine's (Bayly Pare, 1995) 20th century film setting of Richard
III. I suspect Margot could have some more of the life she wants if she could
tolerate polytonality in human relationships. She sometimes seeks the perfect

psychotic attunement that Bion (1990/2018, Vol XI, p. 304) expressed in a metaphor of "perfect pitch." I imagine her toleration of the union of human music contact in the parallel organum of Gregorian chant. Sounds like an orgasm.

Richard's fight with the polytonality of interior and exterior surrenders yield to a single tone of villainy. Gives up on the struggle of "trying to dream what cannot be dreamt" (Eigen, 2014, p. 42). This and the following quotes are from the Opening Soliloquy from *Richard III* (Act I Scene I, p. 113).

> And therefore, since I cannot prove a lover
> To entertain these fair well-spoken days,
> I am determined to prove a villain
> And hate the idle pleasures of these days.

BANG!!

In the BBC's 2014 *Hollow Crown*, we first see the young Richard III in a doorway, his twisted body darkening the sun behind him, spying like Richard spies on "my shadow in the sun." The doorway frames Richard's body and the light. I felt myself inside Plato's cave looking out, Richard blocking escape. Benedict Cumberbatch dazzled with an innocent, attractive, adolescent-like face. The distinction—union of beauty and deformity. POW!!! As the Cumberbatch Richard ages, traces of interiority which dramatize such dissonance are gone. He is a saturated villain itself and can be nothing else. Unlike the "Immoral Conscience" of which Eigen (1996b/1991, pp. 91–9) writes, Margot has a deeply moral conscience. Her goodness bars her from the relief of saturated villainy into which Richard descended. She remains an observing self, hating the deforming mutilation that a life-saving ileostomy perpetrated on her body. Her morality morphed into a destructive attack Eigen (1996a, pp. 49–54) called "Moral Violence." She grimaced and smiled sadly as she read from my pages.

> Deformed, unfinished, sent before my time
> Into this breathing world, scarce half made up,
> And that so lamely and unfashionable
> That dogs bark at me as I halt by them.
> > (*Richard III*, Act I, Scene I)

OUCH!!

Eigen (2014) said, "Perhaps pressure from unknown beta elements becomes painful (beta, alpha) and the pain among other things translates into dream" (p. 42). I have found no information confirming historical Richard's deformity. Bloom (1998) said, "We will never know how Shakespeare truly regarded the historical Richard III, the Tudor cartoon was wonderful *materia poetica* for playful purposes, and that was more than enough" (p. 64). In his critique of a pre-human Richard, Bloom says "think of Falstaff as the author of Richard III, and you can't go too far wrong." Eigen (2014) tells us that Bion found Falstaff more real than many people he knew. I feel the same way about Richard III. Shakespeare's Richard gave me a tableau of deformed beta experience. This Richard might be Shakespeare's own "animated demonic being outside him on which I descant on mine deformity" (Shakespeare, 1598/1936, p. 113). In a personal communication, Mike spoke of Shakespeare's gift of dramatizing deformed psyche. Richard III could be Shakespeare's rendition of Eigen's (2014) "Being trying to dream what cannot be dreamt" (p. 42).

Loncraine's (Bayly/Pare, 1995) Richard III, played by Ian McKellen, shows Richard trapped in an inanimate tank, its treads unable to grip and move over the broken concrete shards I saw in *Fantasia*, his head emerging from a metallic birth canal crying out for the flesh and the flesh and blood mobility of an animate horse. I can easily imagine that eviscerated tank widdling fuel. The noise of battle and the motor of the tank is deafening. Such an image links easily to the photo of a disabled tank such as Bion the solider would have seen (1997a/2014, Vol III, pp. 42–3). I hear Bion's un-screamed scream at the sight of the tank with its back sinking into the mud like a turtle, the useless caterpillar tread legs kicking in the air. Eigen's (2014) words evoke similar agonizing noises of psychical jeopardy:

> Beta elements can make themselves known as physical pains. I have heard psychotic individuals' express fright over whirring sensations in their brains … crackling, whirring tensions as signs that his brain was in psychical jeopardy. One might regard these sensations as beta elements signaling catastrophe in progress, lacking capacity to locate the latter.
>
> (p. 35)

Cumberbatch's Richard III's deformities were extreme enough to cripple him. Thrown from his horse, stuck in the mud on his back in his inanimate metal armour like a wounded Teenage Mutant Ninja Turtle (Eastman and Laird, 1984) and/or an upside-down tank, he can neither stand nor curl into a fetal position as he cries out for a horse. The image of Richard The Turtle leads me to Ferenczi's (1938, pp. 44–51) Thalassa; phylogenetic regression to the turtle in a human's evolutionary past. Although Eigen speaks highly of Thalassa, that work is not central to his written body of work. Hearing this cry for a horse sparks my fantasy of amphibian Richard longing for an evolutionary rebirth to a pre-human but mammalian Richard in the form of a horse. Chausseuget-Smirgel (1987) called Bion a Wise Baby Grandson of Ferenczi, linking the familial tie of Ferenczi's traumatic atomization of experience, and Bion's infinite splitting in psychosis. I call Mike Eigen, Ferenczi's Wise Baby Great Grandson, sharing a common genetic marker in the "alternate infinities" (Eigen, 2018, 1–10) of prehistoric moments of birth and rebirth.

A table or a tank with a widdler would be bizarre objects, but such bizarre elements in my fantasy linked Mike, Doctor Eigen, Doctor Freud, Captain Bion, Doctor Bion, Hans, Richards II and III, Elmer Fudd, a Teenage Mutant Ninja Turtle, Igor Stravinsky, Rodgers and Hammerstein, Margot, and me. Perhaps the Seder table on which Elijah's cup rests has a widdler. I now smile reading that paragraph, hearing Bion's discourse in his baby voice. I try to experience the horizontal and vertical movement of Hans's epistemophilic instinct from the sensory impact of the sight of the widdling engine, to his distinction–union of table and horse relentlessly seeking the truth about babies.

A birth of a beta concept is still in process in me. I think it unlikely that the fruits of this labour will ever be ripe enough to harvest. Mike (Eigen, 1993/2018, pp. 275–6) ponders the on-going growth of the analyst, and the analyst's being able to be a good match for the growth state of the patient. Margot and I share some shame when grown-up professionals make us feel like babies. When I dress up (the first typo was stress up) in a grown-up analyst persona, I can pontificate about things like Freud's instincts in and of themselves residing on the frontier between soma and psyche and beta elements as primitive representations of the instincts in and of themselves. Maybe not so far off and useful, but out of tune in orchestrating this Eigen music. I did have to look up agglutinated as Mike used it in an earlier quote. Very grown-up. Perhaps, when Elijah drinks his cup of wine from Bion's Seder table and decodes the mysteries of the TEIKU (the acronym for unanswerable halachic questions), he will also explain the beta element more fully. It is through 20 years of encountering Dr Mike Eigen in person and in books that I learned I can tolerate waiting for Elijah and/or Mike's next book for more clarity. Whichever comes first. Or I can shed my grown-up disguise and be satisfied by a childhood joke to communicate my thoughts about beta experience. How can you tell if an elephant has been in the refrigerator? By the footprints in the peanut butter.

YUM!!!

References

Algar, J et al. (1940). *Fantasia*. Walt Disney Productions.
Alter, R. (2004). *The five books of Moses*. W.W. Norton.
Bayly/Pare (1995). *Richard III*. Bayly/Pare Productions, R Loncraine, Director. R Loncraine, I McKellan, writers, based on William Shakespeare's Richard III.
Bion, WR. (1997a/2018). War memoirs 1917–1919: WR Bion (C Mawson and F Bion, Ed.), *The complete works of W.R. Bion* (Vol. III). Routledge (original work published 1997a), pp. 42–3.

Bion, W.R. (1963/2018). Elements of psycho-analysis (WR Bion, C Mawson Ed., and F Bion, Ed.), *The complete works of W.R. Bion* (Vol. V). Routledge (original work published 1963), pp. 12, 61.

Bion, W.R. (1971/2018) Two papers: The grid and caesura (C Mawson and F Bion, Ed.), *The complete works of W.R. Bion* (Vol. X). Routledge (original work published 1971), pp. 7–32.

Bion, W.R. (1977b/2018). Taming wild thoughts II: Untitled (C Mawson and F Bion, Ed.), *The complete works of W.R. Bion* (Vol. X) (original work published 1977b), pp. 175–86.

Bion, W.R. (1990/2018). Cogitations (C Mawson and F Bion, Ed.), *The complete works of W.R. Bion* (Vol. XI). Routledge (original work published 1990), pp. 199, 304.

Bloom, H. (1998). *Shakespeare: The creation of the human*. Riverhead Books/Penguin, Putnam, Inc. (pp. 64–71).

Chasseguet-Smirgel, J. (1987). An encounter between the "wise baby" and one of his grandsons: (Ferenczi and Bion). *Free Associations*, 10, 57–62.

Eastman, K and Laird, P. (1984) *Teenage Mutant Ninja Turtles* (Mirage Studios) ViacomCBS (via Nickelodeon).

Eigen, M. (1986). *The psychotic core*. Jason Aronson.

Eigen, M. (1996a). Moral violence, In M Eigen, *Psychic deadness*. Jason Aronson, pp. 49, 55.

Eigen, M. (1996b/1991). The immoral conscience. In M Eigen, *Psychic deadness* Jason Aronson (original work published 1991), pp. 91–3.

Eigen, M. (2005). *Emotional storm*. Wesleyan University Press, p. 156.

Eigen, M. (2014). *The birth of experience*. Karnac.

Eigen, M. (1993/2018). The recoil of having another person. In M Eigen and A Phillips, *The electrified tightrope* (original work published 1973), pp 21–4.

Eigen, M. (2018) *The challenge of being human*. Routledge, pp. 1–10.

Ferenczi, S. (1938). *Thalassa: A theory of genitality* (HA Bunker, Trans.). Routledge, 2018 (originally published in *Psychoanalytic Quarterly*), pp. 44–51.

Freud, S. (1900a/2001). *The interpretation of dreams: The complete and definitive text* (J Strachey, Ed. and Trans. Vol. IV). Vintage, The Hogarth Press, and the Institute for Psychoanalysis (original work published 1900a).

Freud, S. (1909b/2001). Analysis of a phobia in a five-year-old boy (J Strachey, Ed. and Trans.), *The complete and definitive text* (Vol. X). Vintage, The Hogarth Press and the Institute for Psychoanalysis (original work published 1909b), pp. 1–150.

Freud, S. (1915/2001). Instincts and their vicissitudes (J Strachey, Ed. and Trans.), *The complete and definitive text* (Vol. XIV). Vintage, The Hogarth Press, and the Institute for Psychoanalysis, pp. 109–40.

Freud, S. (1926e/2001). *The question of lay analysis: The complete and definitive text* (J Strachey, Ed. and Trans. Vol. XX). Vintage, The Hogarth Press, and the Institute for Psychoanalysis (original work published 1926e), p. 212.

Goold et al. (2012–16) *The Hollow Crown*. Mendes, S. Executive Producer

Rodgers, R (Composer) and Hammerstein II, O (Lyricist). (1959). The sound of music. Williamson Music, Inc., owner of the publication and allied rights throughout the world. International copyright secured.

Shakespeare, W. (1597/1936). *The tragedy of King Richard II*. In WA Wright (Ed.), *The Complete Works of William Shakespeare*, Cambridge Edition. Doubleday & Co., 1936, pp. 351–86.

Shakespeare, W. (1598/1936). *The tragedy of King Richard III*. In WA Wright (Ed.), *The Complete Works of William Shakespeare*, Cambridge Edition. Doubleday & Co., 1936, pp. 111–56.

Stravinsky, I. (1913). *The rite of spring*. Public domain in the USA.

Teitelbaum, S. (2008). Allergic to people: Building bridges in a ripped psychic-soma. *American Journal of Psychoanalysis*, 68 (2), 177–88.

Teitelbaum, S. (2014). No-baby: Mourning an unthought baby. *Other/Wise*. Retrieved from www.wordpress.com/2014/05/03/no-baby/.

Winnicott, DW. (1967). The location of cultural experience. *International Journal of Psycho-Analysis*, 48, 368–72.

Part V

Expanding the psychoanalytic frame

Chapter 17

A tribute to Michael Eigen's brave opposition to a legacy of dogma, torture, and manufactured truth

Burton Norman Seitler

History is tortuous. It neither proceeds in isolation nor in a vacuum. It is shaped by events, which are themselves influenced and determined by the actions of the participants in the epic human saga. The metaphorical road upon which history travels is replete with the maelstrom of human misadventures marked by cavities, chasms, cliffs, gaps, punctures, rifts, apertures, and abysses. There are many twists and turns on that road and more than an occasional point in which an actor in this great play of life must make a choice as to what direction will be taken. Some choices are based on conviction, some on convenience, and some on the anticipation of condemnation and ensuing cruel treatment by the powers that be.

Many of the sharp rocks and crevasses along the way illustrate a heartbreaking history of inhumanity punctuated by some of the vilest atrocities. Torture is but one example of this. Although torture only appears to affect certain individuals, its ramifications are far greater because it alters reality, distorts the truth, and produces intergenerational trauma.

This chapter will extract from Michael Eigen's formal works and numerous conversations with him, a smattering of his thinking about how the mind has been subject to external influences as well as intrapsychic ones, some of which were not necessarily conducive to the growth of the individual or to society. Furthermore, in order to properly guide us along the path towards Eigen's thinking, we must be prepared to encounter various modern traditions that have diverted us away from seeing a fuller portrayal of humanity, one which took us down the primrose path of expediency born of simplistic reductionistic outlooks. These include Cartesian dualism notions, behaviourism, and the mania for reductionistic diagnoses of emotional problems.

Learning from the chequered past of the history of torture – when psychopaths attained positions of power – Michael Eigen commented about the current connection with America.

> It almost seems as if this country has two sets of enemies. Its economic and political leaders, its own power elite and those who come from the outside to wound it. I would not want to minimize the external threat,

but at this moment of history, I fear the greatest threat to the good of the land comes from those who profess to guide us.

(2006)

He presciently made that observation in 2006, with prophetic insight and clarity. Eigen's observations have since been born out. To wit:

> our sense of truth is one of the greatest casualties. Facts or presumed facts and situations are repeatedly misrepresented for the sake of getting one's way, whether to win, to gain power, money, establish position, or set of strategies of world domination ... We are in the midst of an Age of Psychopathy, with the present years being one of its high points.
>
> (p. 128)

His words are eerily reminiscent of earlier times of great darkness and anguish descending on the human spirit. About this, he wrote:

> Sometimes we wake up screaming. A scream that begins in our dreams wakes us up. Sometimes the dream vanishes and we can not find it. We sense a paralysis. For we know other dreams in which we try to scream but can not. We are paralyzed in face of danger, in face of a dread that tortures us.
>
> (p. 129)

Past is prelude

Recognizing that past is prelude, Freud emphasized the salience and prepotency of primacy over recency regarding human experiences. Thus, traumas that occur early in life will be more powerful and will have greater destabilizing effects than equivalent forms of trauma that take place later in an individual's life when s/he has more resources with which to contend, adjust to, or defend against.

The legacy of trauma gets passed down intergenerationally. In that manner, history speaks to us, often dictating the future by virtue of precedents that were established in the past – that themselves were probably influenced by traumatic events. Centuries ago, one's physical safety was imperilled. Now, a person's reputation or livelihood are endangered. Often, these suffice to silence most voices.

Part of our going astray towards the beginning of the modern Western epoch can be seen in Descartes and his devotees, who bore witness to, or experienced, vicarious trauma – and modified their stated views (either consciously or subliminally) to avoid any possibility of calling undue attention to themselves for fear of offending the Grand Inquisitors. Descartes hints at his awareness of danger in his writings:

But like a man who walks alone and in the shadows, I resolved to go slowly and to use such *circumspection* in all things, that if I did advance but very little, I would at least *guard* against falling.

(1637, p. 33, italics mine)

Descartes published this work in Holland, *anonymously* at first, and in French, rather than the customary Latin, suggesting his understandable wariness and need for *circumspection*.

Descartes' loyal supporters were undoubtedly influenced by the atrocities committed in the name of religious piety. It makes sense that their transcriptions of Descartes' work would contain further distortions of reality. This unwittingly influenced countless generations that followed. It was only recently that Descartes' work has been deeply questioned, mainly for his mind–body dualism. Until now, few noticed that his views were "modified" because of extrinsic exigencies.

That many were drawn to Descartes' "rational" approach is not in dispute. What is a subject for disagreement is the contention that his followers held; one that I maintain was largely shaped by the shadows of death that surrounded them. Unfortunately, their manufactured truth insinuated itself into some of the most fundamental assumptions upon which science, itself, is based. Because these assumptions lasted this long, they were assumed as fact. Rarely have they made their way into consciousness and even less frequently have they been debated. For example, *minds* and *bodies* are separate. Having different words like, "mind" or "body," creates the artificial impression they are distinct from one another. They are no different than thumbs and pinkies; different specialities, but integral members of the hand. Mind/body are distinct in function, yet part of a unitary whole – the human being. Much of the dualism that detracts from our full humanity has roots in Descartes' doctrines.

Regrettably, we did not take *the road less travelled by* those who took issue with and dissented from reductionism. We chose, instead, the "rational" route adopted by Descartes' followers, and, in that manner, we witnessed the triumph of mechanism and reductionism over humanism, thus constructing a major obstacle on the path to our own agency and divergent thinking. The legacy of reductionistic inquiry has been an ever-present ghost haunting and foreclosing the door to humanistic lodgings, understandings, and approaches to personal problems.

Mind–brain identity explanation

A descendant of the Cartesian tradition of reductionism involves identifying the mind with the brain. Even if it were true that reductionism could account for the disposition of every atom in the brain, we would still be unable to precisely spell out and elucidate reasons for humans to develop spiritual beliefs, for example. The mind–brain identity theory that some have proffered as a possible end-run around Descartes' dualism dilemma is logically appealing, but is itself somewhat reductionistic. It falls short because it too incorrectly assumes that mind and brain are identical and that if we know the properties of one, we can automatically apply that to the other. McLaren (2010) disagreed, "mind is not and can never be identical with brain, simply because there are attributes of mind that are not also attributes of brain and vice versa" (p. 13). Correspondingly, stating that we are *pre-wired* to invent a Supreme Creator merely excludes deeper examinations of spirituality, and offers no cogent explanation for the near universality of religious beliefs or transcendent experiences that many have independently attested to having undergone.

Eigen views mind and body as part of a unitary whole. He considers the mind–body duality as heralding in the notion of spirituality, and by transcending mind he is able to unify these constructs. He regards these terms as representations of shifts in our attention by which we can get in and out of our bodies. He contends that when we are ultimately able to attain such heightened levels of experience, we may be able to get in touch with the Great Spirit:

> We can get into and out of our bodies with a shift of attitude. We can relish surface sensations or dip into deep, interoceptive, quasi-sensory streams. Sitting still, or moving in various ways, alters our sense of aliveness.
>
> (2018, p. 130)

Learning is complex, multi-layered, and over-determined

Another influential reductionist tradition in psychology is behaviourism. For Eigen, behaviour is associated with desire or lust, which he argues in *Ecstasy* (2001) and *Rage* (2002) is basic to humans. For him, emotion precedes behaviour, while for many behaviourists there is a singular emphasis on learning. Paraphrasing Osgood (1964), the idea that learning is simply a direct, unsophisticated, uncomplicated process – occurring purely because conditioning that produces a neural reflex arc – is overly simplistic and utterly naïve. Reductionism has been hard-pressed to satisfactorily explain learning even in less complex organisms, like rats (Spence, 1956; Tolman, 1932). Nowhere does reductionism explain the impacts, intricacies, and differential contributions of socialization, culture, reinforcement, individual, and/or intergenerational trauma in shaping the mind, personality, and behaviour.

The mind has evolved over countless millennia. How can we justify viewing all that flows from it as one-dimensional? Gestalt psychology has long held that the whole is greater than the sum of its parts. Each individual human being needs to be respectfully viewed and treated in this holistic context.

In contrast, Kandel, Nobel Laureate, testified on behalf of the beneficial role played by reductionism.

I spelled out my belief – almost a manifesto – that to understand behavior one had to apply to it the same type of radical reductionist approach that had proved so effective in other areas of biology.

(2006, p. 236).

McLaren strongly takes issue with this:

The goal of a reductionistic "new science of the mind," for psychiatry, based wholly on the biology of the brain, rests on a fundamental error: the conflation of information and its physical substrate. Because of this error, the project will fail because it looks the wrong way along the arrow of causation.

(2010, p. 14)

Thus, if depression, schizophrenia, bipolar conditions, and ADHD are now reflections of our present existential reality, it is so because we are shocked to find ourselves living in a realm of mystification, bewilderment, and confusion. In a culture of smoke and mirrors, where progress becomes paradoxical and absurd, and reality becomes incomprehensible, we desperately seek refuge in a technology that offers us nothing more than the illusion of an escape, and which leads only into the void of *virtual reality*. Despite the fact that our civilization has advanced to such a spectacular degree – due to our technology – that we have accumulated an amazing amount of information and know an enormous amount of *stuff*, the paradox of it all is that we understand very little about what is truly important – love, compassion, genuine empathy, understanding, and acceptance of – and curiosity about – that which seems strange, odd, or different from us.

While we celebrate the apotheosis of reason, in the midst of such ostentatious revelry, we suddenly become aware that something is amiss and something is fundamentally missing. We have failed to distinguish understanding from knowledge – presumptively treating them as equivalent. Understanding, as Max-Neef pointed out, is the result of integration, while knowledge, particularly how we define science, is the result of detachment. Understanding is holistic; knowledge is fragmentary. Our passionate pursuit, but misguided and necessarily incomplete rendering of knowledge, has postponed and severely limited our attainment of understanding, says Max-Neef (2010). Gandhi (1925) presciently admonished us that: "The things that will destroy us are knowledge that is without character and science that is without humanity" (p. 135).

One would think that because of all our advances there ought to be nothing that could impede the undertaking of such ventures now, until we recognize the role that an economics which, as practised under the spell of the biopsychiatric, big pHARMa, discourse, has increasingly distorted reality, and has contributed to our confusion and to the falsification of knowledge itself (Young, Ioannidis, and Al-Baydli, 2008; Ioannidis, 2005).

Truth is not easily pinned down. Paraphrasing Alfred North Whitehead (1933), truth was the confirmation of appearance to reality. Reductionism's approximation of truth cannot replace the ultimate "Truth" itself. Reductionistic, mechanistic approaches are too limited to apply the final word about Truth.

Even using quantum physics to obtain some semblance of eternal Truth produces idiosyncratic results. This is particularly so in view of the startling revelations amassed by research in physics regarding the nature of light. Until Einstein in 1905, light was thought to consist of waves. Einstein showed that light had two distinct and seemingly opposing features: Waves and particles. Bohr's 1926 notion of complementarity proposed that light was both a wave and a particle. What made the problem difficult was that one could observe only one of these phenomena at a time. Whenever researchers set up investigations to measure waves, devices used to measure waves would not detect anything but waves. Similarly, measuring instruments set up to measure particles only found particles. In each case, results were due to measuring instruments' artefacts. Thus, even "hard" sciences, like physics, have unavoidable limitations.

Heisenberg (in Davies, 1983) boldly announced: "The common division of the world into subject and object, inner world and outer world, body and soul, is no longer adequate …" (p. 112); adding, "Natural science does not simply describe and explain nature; it is part of the interplay between nature and ourselves" (1958, p. 102). Hence, the very act of observing something changes it. Leonard Shlain (2001) describes this in his discursive, visionary discussion of art, physics, space, time, and light. He writes:

> According to the new physics, observer and observed are somehow connected, and the inner domain of subjective thought turns out to be intimately conjoined to the external sphere of objective facts.
>
> (p. 23)

Hence, we must now fashion new dialectics about human circumstances based on humanism, empathy, understanding, and respect, not labelling as practised by the old guard's discourse of and obsession with power, profit, fear of difference, or anxiety about and countertransferential reaction against the primitive impulses and images that live within all of us, and to which we defensively attach diagnostic labels.

Labels and stigma

Kierkegaard observed – once you label me, you negate me. Paradoxically, with all of our incredible technology, fMRIs, PET scans, or CAT scans, we have become too much like the physicians of old – that is before germ theory – who were baffled by childbed fevers that they themselves spread with their own un-washed hands. We do the same iatrogenically, with most of our high-minded diagnostic labels and pseudoscientific terms. Anu Garg (2009) insightfully notes, "if you torture words long enough, they will confess to anything."

And it was Moliere (1673) who reminded us,

> Once you have the cap and gown of the doctor, all you need to do is open your mouth. Whatever nonsense you talk becomes wisdom and all the rubbish, good sense.
>
> (p. 273)

To which, Thomas Szasz (1997) added:

> Much of modern psychiatry consists of a compounding of these prevarications – the lies steadily concealed by a ceaseless relabeling of the patient's deceptions as new diseases, and the psychiatrist's as new treatments.
>
> (pp. 189–90)

Researchers demonstrated that using diagnostic terminology on people experiencing profound personal inner turmoil, unwittingly stigmatizes them. Mehta and Farina (1997) found that people who fell under the medical model's "biochemical" or "brain disease" explanation of emotional problems were treated more harshly than those whose problems were considered to be the result of psychosocial reversals or traumatic events. They stated: "We say we are being kind, but our actions suggest otherwise" (p. 407).

This is because the biomedical narrative about so-called "illnesses" like "schizophrenia," subtly promulgate assumptions that genetic, biological, or biochemical abnormalities break the brain – thoroughly and permanently. Blaming the brain, or our neurology, is fairly common. Although "brain" explanations sound scientific, they are unproven suppositions, not established givens. Mehta adds, "Viewing those with mental disorders as diseased sets them apart and may lead to our perceiving them as physically distinct. Biochemical aberrations make them almost a different species." Explanations claiming problems result from one's neurology or biochemical imbalances not only fail to eliminate stigmas attached to having personal problems, but actually increase stigmatization.

The moment human beings in the throes of emotional upset receive diagnoses, they begin to identify themselves with that label. The diagnosis becomes reified: "I am bipolar," or "I am schizophrenic" become the clarion cries of the recipients of these labels. This often produces the following misunderstanding: "Therefore, my actions are caused by my bipolar disorder, or my schizophrenia, or my ADHD." Our wholeness as a human becomes reduced to our diagnosis.

Merely naming something is not the same as knowing something

Actually, diagnostic pronouncements bear little or no resemblance to the complex inner workings of an individual's mind. Merely naming something is not sufficient to claims of knowing something. Naming a person's "condition" merely situates that person in a particular psychiatric or psychological domain. Worse yet, labels are often perceived as pejorative and felt by the receiver of such labels as akin to being called "crazy." Because they sound scientific, they are considerably more potent and more dangerous.

Sounding "scientific" accrues extra gravitas

No matter how far off the mark diagnoses may be, they convey an aura of truth. Diagnostic terminology implies the existence of an explanation for behaviour. Yet no satisfactory explanation can possibly be provided that fully clarifies human woes in a few words.

What human beings go through and how they process their individual experiences is complex, multi-layered, and nuanced. An individual's phenomenological subjectivity is a tapestry of all of one's life experiences, desires, fears, wishes, perceptions (or misperceptions), attitudes, spiritual beliefs, and the state of one's physiology.

Diagnosis and subjectivity

Furthermore, most diagnoses are grossly imprecise. Their accuracy largely depends upon the person doing the assessment and his/her sensitivity, intuitivity, and experience. Normally, assessment is not predicated on the use of established, time-tested, standardized psychodiagnostic instruments. Instead, diagnoses rely heavily on the vagaries and inexactness of the subjectivities of clinical judgement. Witness the pronounced differences in diagnoses seen in different countries, wherein one nation tends to classify certain individuals as *schizophrenic*, another perceives such individuals as *bipolar*.

Clinical judgement and/or statistical measurement

Meehl and others' (Grove et al., 2000; Grove and Meehl, 1996) meta-analytic comparisons of clinical judgement and actuarial predictions consistently indicated that not more than 5 per cent resulted in the clinician's informal predictive procedure being more accurate than a statistical one (p. iii). Instruments like the MMPI came out on top. Projective tests like the Rorschach, using scoring systems demonstrating statistical validity and reliability (e.g. Exner,

1993, or others), were shown to be more accurate than clinical interviews alone. Meehl recommends integrating both methods.

Rosenhan's studies (1975, 1973), although dated, still lend dramatic credence to warrant viewing diagnoses for emotional problems with suspicion. Rosenhan felt that labels become self-confirming. In a well-documented account, Rosenhan (1973) and cronies hoodwinked a host of psychiatrists and other trained personnel at various hospitals across the country into believing Rosenhan and company were seriously "disturbed," ultimately convincing the "experts" to admit them to mental hospitals for treatment. Although this gambit fooled all of the professionals, most patients were not taken in. In fact, the *patients* differentiated themselves and their problems from Rosenhan's. They told him they felt he was clearly not "disturbed" and wondered why he had *ever* been admitted? Rosenhan (1973) responded, "One thing is certain: Any diagnostic process that lends itself so readily to massive errors of this sort cannot be a very reliable one" (p. 252).

Modifications, as well as replications of this study, have consistently shown that professionals using "clinical judgement" alone are generally not able to reliably differentiate individuals who are experiencing severe emotional disturbances from those who are not.

Folly, fiasco, and failure of psychodiagnostic formularies

Ronald Abramson (2013, personal communication) pointed out that Robert Spitzer, one of the chief authors of the *DSM-III*, took Rosenhan's study to mean the *DSM-II* (the version that was current at that time) was not *detailed* enough, and created yet another version, the *DSM-III*. This produced an incredible upsurge of children being diagnosed with ADHD, and subsequently as "having" a similarly invented condition, paediatric bipolar disorder, for which enormous amounts of prescriptions were filled for powerful pharmacological agents to be administered – horrifyingly enough – to toddlers and infants! Decades later, Spitzer said that perhaps there was an over-reaction to the *DSM*s of the time, but that it was unanticipated, as well as unintended. In a BBC2 interview in 2007, Spitzer stated:

> What happened is that we made estimates of the prevalence of mental disorders totally descriptively, without considering that many of these conditions might be normal reactions which are not really disorders. That's the problem, because we were not looking at the context in which these conditions developed.

Fellow former *DSM* editor, Allen Frances, recently criticized the *DSM-IV* (his own creation) and also came out against the latest edition, the *DSM-V,* predicting that:

The *DSM-5* promises to be a disaster – even after the changes introduced this week, it will introduce many new and unproven diagnoses that will medicalize normality and result in a glut of unnecessary and harmful drug prescriptions.

Frances went further, declaring:

The [American Psychiatric] Association has been largely deaf to the widespread criticism of the *DSM-5* stubbornly refusing to subject the proposals to independent review.

(2012, p. A19)

Even so, the horse was out of the barn, and it seems a bit hard for them to explain in hindsight and verbally lament so many years later their not having attempted to close the door sooner to these repugnant practices. Moreover, as strong as their arguments now sound, they are not sufficiently potent or come soon enough to avert the harm they predict will ensue, or to undo the harm that has already occurred under their respective watches after the introduction of attention deficit disorder, paediatric bipolar disorder, and other diagnoses. Now *grief* and *shyness* are going to be medicalized and pathologized, along with other so-called disorders, which Enrico Gnaulati (2013) has described as responses to the rigours of ordinary everyday living.

Circular reasoning

The following illustrates the fundamental problems of circular reasoning inherent in psychodynamic formulations. I invited several psychotherapist colleagues of mine to my house for a Super Bowl party. Enclosed with the requisite directions for travelling to my home was the following "psychodiagnostic" admonition: "Coming early means you are *manic*; coming late means you are *passive-aggressive*; and coming precisely on time means you are *obsessive compulsive*. Pick your poison."

On a serious note, this shows that anything, and anyone, at any time, can be labelled. The ultimately chosen label depends on who is the judge, what is his/her background, training, life experiences, state of mind, and biases.

Who does the judging and why?

Judging contains a power dynamic. Paraphrasing Joseph Lyons' musings:

If the *patient* categorizes the therapist in accordance with other similar people s/he has known – we call it *transference* [italics mine]. When the *therapist* categorizes a patient in accordance with other people s/he has known, we call it *diagnosis*.

(1963, pp. 203–4)

Diagnoses as countertransferences against therapists' uncertainty

The *DSM* series is clearly an influential set of constructions. Nevertheless, they too are simply other forms of reductionism. In truth, labels are momentary "snapshots," not ongoing motion pictures. They do not constitute an adequate sampling of a person's life or "durable essence." Thus, we cannot say with certainty that a *DSM* diagnosed individual actually matches a specific description of that person's behaviour most of the time. *DSMs* are incapable of accurately clarifying the content and/or structure of an individual's "*typical inner life*." Even individuals experiencing psychosis have many lucid moments.

Diagnoses simply serve countertransferential wishes for certainty in order to assuage therapists' anxiety regarding not knowing, trepidation dealing with ambiguity, or trouble experiencing our own terror inherent in the conflicts our patients induce in us.

The sacrosanct unassailability of diagnostic pseudo-sounding sense

Although they do not start out dominating our theological engravings, once arbitrarily derived diagnostic criteria are inscribed in the Holy Bibles of psychiatry, the *DSMs/ICDs*, they eventually acquire the status of sacred lore. In a pointed reaction to the circularity of diagnoses, RD Laing (1972) once quipped:

> There must be something the matter with him because he would not be acting as he does unless there was. Therefore, he is acting as he is because there is something the matter with him.
>
> (p. 5)

Laing presciently anticipated the establishment of yet another diagnostic category, one that fits well with his notion of a closed system, the advent of the diagnosis of "anosognosia," in which not believing that one has a problem is itself indicative that there is a problem. Here is Laing's perfectly on-target provocative dart:

> He does not think there is anything the matter with him because one of the things that is the matter with him is that he does not think that there is anything the matter with him.
>
> (p. 5)

Definitional issues combined with difficulties involving the odd use (or misuse) of logic and language have their own sets of serious problems. As Frank Summers remarked (2010, personal communication), "he who controls the *terms* of the discourse, wins the discussion." Kipling once said, "Words are the most powerful drug used by mankind" (Kipling, 2012, p. 51). Voltaire further commented on the use of words to deceive. He declared, "Those who can make you believe absurdities can make you commit atrocities" (Voltaire, 1765–1961, pp. 277–8).

Finally, how can we seriously and meaningfully define and discuss psychopathology when we have no universal consensual agreement about what constitutes "normality." Damasio (1994), noticing the rather conspicuous omission of studies of school curricula concerned with investigating "normal" writes:

> Few medical schools, to this day, offer their students any formal instruction on the normal mind, instruction that can only come from a curriculum strong in general psychology, neuropsychology, and neuroscience. Medical schools do offer studies of the sick mind encountered in mental diseases, but it is indeed astonishing to realize that students learn about psychopathology without ever being taught normal psychology.
>
> (p. 255)

Do we need diagnoses?

The reasons for having diagnoses rests on an anachronistic medical model, which proclaims that if we have a name for a malady, we automatically know how to treat it. This is patently false. Although the medical model may work for medical diseases, diagnoses are not as helpful for people who are in the midst of emotional distress, which are not due to diseases, lesions, so-called biochemical "imbalances," or twisted neurons. Let us say we have ten patients exhibiting symptoms of anxiety, each one would be different from the others in significant ways, save for the fact that they all are scared (mostly for different reasons).

Arguing that diagnostic terms are shorthand communications for researchers runs into problems plaguing the *DSM*s and *ICD*s since their inception – of agreeing on a standard set of definitions. If they had it right the first time, why the continuous need for all these emendations?

For rigorous research to take place, there would have to be *a priori* agreed-upon standards against which all variables could be assessed in a uniform, consistent, inviolate, reliable manner. For this reason, the United States Bureau of Standards exists, to ensure that the influence of extraneous variables on physical instruments involved in basic measurements, such as the "ruler," are minimized against Brownian movement, for example.

Embracing human wholeness

Given the prevalence of reductionism, how then do psychoanalysts, other therapists, and assorted Homo Sapiens, seeking to embrace our human wholeness proceed? Let us turn again to Michael Eigen (2011), who coura-geously departed from the crowd of advocates who held fast to venerating diagnoses, by noting that it was perfectly fine not to know, in fact, it was preferable:

> Not knowing doesn't mean you have to say it. Just keep it to yourself. As long as you know that you don't know, that's the most important thing. Flexibility is important … If you have a "know it all" attitude, your pa-tient will leave you or get worse. He won't get better.
>
> (2012, Listserve personal communication)

Michael's Eigen's capacity for creative thinking and his fearless stance against being bound by the rigid structures of society's demand for uniformity in all things is clearly seen in his writings, as well as his overall approach to life. He privileges paying attention to emotions, to the primary process, and to words and the meanings they convey. He is as playful and creative with words as he is in the way he interacts with and relates to people. His is not a mien that conveys superficiality. While he has a light bearing, he does not take things lightly. On the contrary, he examines things quite deeply. In particu-lar, words are regarded with great reverence, even when he is in the midst of playing with them. He is unafraid of going where many dare not go – into the inner depths of despair and into the pits and throes of psychotic expe-riences. He joins their mad minds, without losing his. It is no wonder that he writes books about faith, about waiting, about the flames of the uncon-scious. Even the titles of his works are telling: *The Psychotic Core*; *Flames from the Unconscious*; *Contact with the Depths*; *The Electrified Tightrope*. An original thinker, he has wondered, studied, and written about spirituality in an effort to go beyond doctrinaire psychotherapy aversions that have been summarily dismissed and passed down through the generations. But, in all of his writ-ings, whether works that were influenced by Bion, Winnicott, or Lacan, he stresses the common denominator of humanness. Labels take a back seat in his thinking. Understanding what an individual is struggling with is central, along with trying to appreciate how to empathically bear a patient's anguish so that they both can experience and suffer through the pain together. He sees and responds to psychic reality as spanning a multitude of dimensions (2020). His mission: Interlocutor.

> The dialectics of psychodynamics is rich and colorful and plenteous. You feel the alive psyche when you read someone like Winnicott, who says he is trying to find expressive language to give voice to living feelings. Bion, too, speaks of helping areas of psychic life come alive, e.g. blowing on seemingly dead ashes to birth living sparks. One thing I felt from them: If they can be them, I can be me, or try to; to find one's own living language to begin to do justice to therapy experience. Keep on working – finding

words that touch live nerves for you. What's real for you and gives expression to living reality?

An acceptable label: Human being

I accept one universal label, human being. I work with human beings, not labels; try to engage each individual humanly; approach each person with humanity, and interact humanely. I respect each one's individual differences, and try to learn about each individual's personal story, which I hold in my mind. Holding the patient in my mind as a person with unique needs, fears, sadness, anxiety, and an assortment of different dynamics, is much more significant than attempting to pin a label on an individual and then treating that label.

I believe we help people feel better when we relate one human being to another, rather than inventing a diagnosis and having the label get stuck to the patient for life (even after substantial progress has taken place). In the latter regard, it is quite commonplace for doctors to refer to individuals who once were, but are no longer, in the throes of a "schizophrenic break," as having "schizophrenia in remission." In their minds, the schizophrenia is still present, but merely dormant. This is an odd view, one that denies the existence of resiliency and ignores substantial research showing patients can get well and remain well (Karon and VandenBos, 1981; Bola and Mosher, 2002; Harrow et al., 2005; Harrow and Jobe, 2007). This attitude keeps alive the faulty premise that those who have endured the agony of emotional problems are diseased and that their malady is forever. Nothing is further from the truth.

As children we were told that "sticks and stones may break my bones, but names can never harm me." This well-meaning aphorism did not reflect reality then, nor does it now. Words can, and do hurt – often causing lasting harm. Diagnoses for emotional problems contribute to this more than most professionals realize. Fortunately, words can also help. This is what human relationships are all about, and this is what good therapeutic practice ought to be all about.

Ultimately, as HS Sullivan reminds us, we are all more simply human than not. Names can all too easily be applied, and be damaging to each one of us. Accordingly, *let s/he who be without label cast the first stigma*.

References

Abramson, R. (2013). Personal communication.
Bola, J and Mosher, L. (2002). At issue: Predicting drug-free treatment response in acute psychosis from the Soteria Project. *Schizophrenia Bulletin*, 28, 559–75.
Damasio, A. (1994). *Descartes' error: Emotion, reason, and the human brain*. Penguin Books.
Davies, P. (1994). (1983). *God and the new physics*. Simon & Schuster.

Descartes, R. (1637). Discourse on the method of rightly conducting the reason, and seeking truth in the sciences. Retrieved from http://www.gutenberg.org/ebooks/59.

Eigen, M. (2001). *Ecstasy.* Karnac.

Eigen, M. (2002). *Rage.* Wesleyan University Press.

Eigen, M. (2006). *Age of psychopathy.* Retrieved from http://psychoanalysis-and-therapy.com/hukman.../...pref.html.

Eigen, M. (2007). Guilt in an age of psychopathy. *Psychoanalytic Review,* 94 (5) 727–49.

Eigen, M. (2011). *Eigen in Seoul, Volume 2: Faith and transformation.* Karnac.

Eigen, M. (2018). *Reshaping the self.* Routledge (originally published by Karnac, 1995).

Eigen, M and Daws, L. (2020). *Dialogues with Michael Eigen.* Routledge.

Exner, JE. (1993). *The Rorschach: A comprehensive system* (Vol. 1, Basic Foundations: 3rd Edition). Wiley Books.

Frances, A. (2012). "Diagnosing the *DSM.*" *New York Times,* May 11, 2012, A19.

Gandhi, M. (1925). Young India. In *Collected works of Mahatma Gandhi* (Vol. 33). GandhiServe Foundation, p. 135.

Gnaulati, E. (2013). *Back to normal: Why ordinary childhood behavior is mistaken for ADHD, bipolar disorder, and autism spectrum disorder.* Beacon Books.

Greenberg, J. (1981). An interview with David Rosenhan. *American Psychological Association Monitor,* 4–5.

Grove, WM and Meehl, PE. (1996). Comparative efficiency of informed (subjective, impressionistic) and formal (mechanical, algorithmic) prediction procedures: The clinical, statistical controversy. *Psychology, Public Policy, and Law,* 2, 293–323.

Harrow, M and Job, TH. (2007). Factors involved in outcome and recovery in schizophrenic patients not on medications: A 15-year multifollow-up study. *J. Nervous and Mental Disease,* 195 (5), 406–14.

Harrow, M, Grossman, L, Jobe, TH and Herbener, E. (2005). Do patients with schizophrenia ever show periods of recovery? A 15-year multifollow-up study. *Schizophrenia Bulletin,* 31, 723–34.

Heisenberg, W. (1958). *Physics and philosophy.* Harper Publishers.

Ioannidis, JPA. (2005). Why most published research findings are false. *PLoS Med* 2(8), ei124. doi: 10.1371/journal.pmed.0020124.

Kandel, ER. (2006). *In search of memory: The emergence of a new science of mind.* Norton & Company Publishers.

Karon, B and VandenBos, G. (1981). *Psychotherapy of schizophrenia: The treatment of choice.* Jason Aronson.

Kierkegaard, S. Retrieved June 25, 2013, from BrainyQuote.com: http://www.brainyquote.com/quotes/quotes/s/sorenkierk152222.html.

Kipling, R. (2012). In JR McElfresh. Spiritquest 2: *Interface with creation: Creative words, their power and their use.* Abbott Books

Laing, RD. (1972). *Knots.* Vintage.

Lyons, J. (1963). *Psychology and the measure of man: A phenomenological approach.* Glencoe Free Press.

Max-Neef, M. (2010). Chilean Economist Manfred Max-Neef: U.S. is becoming an "underdeveloping nation" Interview by Amy Goodman, In, *Democracy now! A daily independent global news hour.* September 22.

McLaren, N. (2010). *Humanizing psychiatry.* Future Psychiatry Press.

Mehta, S and Farina, A. (1997). Is being "sick" really better? Effects of mental disorder on stigma. *Journal of Social and Clinical Psychology,* 16 (4), 405–19.

Moliere, JB. (1673). "The imaginary invalid." In, *The Misanthrope and other plays* (D Coward Trans., 2000). Penguin Books.

Osgood, CE. (1964). *Method and theory in experimental psychology.* Oxford University Press.

Rosenhan, DL. (1975). The contextual nature of psychiatric diagnosis. *Journal of Abnormal Psychology,* 84, 442–52.

Shlain, L. (2001). *Art and physics: Parallel visions in space, time, and light.* William Morrow Press.

Spitzer, R. (2007). *British Broadcasting Company.* Interview with Robert Spitzer.

Summers, F. (2010). Personal communication.

Thomas, A and Wood, P. (2009). The philomath speaks: An interview with Anu Garg. *National Association of Scholars,* December 15.

Voltaire [Francois-Marie Arouet] (1765–1961). *Questions sur les miracles.* Trans. Norman Lewis Torrey: *Les Philosophes.* Capricorn, 277–8.

Whitehead, AN. (1933). *Adventures of ideas.* Collier Macmillan.

Young, NS, Ioannidis, JPA and Al-Ubaydli, O. (2008). Why current publication practices may distort science. *PLoS Med* 5(10). doi: 1371/journal.pmed.0050201.

Chapter 18

Missed opportunities in the history of psychoanalysis

Howard Covitz

Good-Enough Analysts vs Analysts Acting Badly

Questions: What makes a psychoanalyst or what constitutes the psychoanalyst we aspire to be? It cannot be institute certifications, alone. It's not the ability to pass *the pin test* on the *Standard Edition of Sigmund Freud*, either (to know what words lie at the hole a pin makes as it pierces the pages of a given volume). But what is it then? What constitutes a Good-Enough Psychoanalyst?

Ella Freeman Sharpe (1930) suggested testing in theory, literature, and mythology which could include questions about why the farmer's wife cut off their tails and why the Three Blind Mice were blind to begin with? Freud recommended broad studies when he wrote while defending Theodore Reik against charges of quackery for not being the right kind of analyst!

Adler asked (Nunberg and Federn, 1962/1907) at a meeting of the Vienna Psychoanalytic Association if psychoanalysis could be taught? He was asking a related question to "what is a psychoanalyst?" If it couldn't be taught, was it some inborn capacity to promote healing? Freud responded unhelpfully, saying that when we can get rid of argumentative folk, psychoanalysis would be teachable. Freud, thereby, refused to answer the question. Not answering questions in early psychoanalysis was all the rage. Not answering questions, though, may not be a necessary constituent part of the Good-Enough Analyst.

Oscar Sternbach and I sat together as part of a committee trying to formulate a licensing exam 30 plus years ago. The exam would determine who could call themselves psychoanalysts in New York. We were against including any multiple-choice questions, and cheekily offered the following sample question to our committee:

The Oedipus Complex is: (a) a strip mall 6 km outside of Athens? (b) …

I could blame that one on Oscar, as he is no longer about to defend himself, but I'd like to take some credit for it. I guess I'm thinking that one of the constituent parts of the Good-Enough Psychoanalyst is a capacity for symbolic humour. The Aspired-to-Analyst should quip about such matters as whether life is a tragic comedy or a comic tragedy and smile and laugh like the Buddha!

Posit: *The Good-Enough Psychoanalyst displays characteristics precisely antithetical to those we find in severely personality disordered individuals, those who combine borderline, narcissistic, and sociopathic tendencies.*

I offer six interrelated stigmata of severely character disordered folk:

1. They appear incapable of responding in an emotionally empathic way to another's feelings. They do not see others as *subjects in their own right.*
2. They feel/reason – when wounded but otherwise with some frequency, too – in black-and-white. They split the World into those who are *with'em* and those who are *agin'em.* They have weak group allegiances.
3. They are generally unable to reflect on their impulses before acting; they are quick thinkers.
4. They have little-to-no respect for established organizational, governmental or legal sensibilities and are allergic to alliances between others. They live by *apres moi le deluge.*
5. They think without nuance; they demonstrate no ability to see more than one *not-unreasonable* view. Their views can flip. What makes new attitudes acceptable to them arises from a *my-will-be-done* syndrome: "It is important because I said/did/felt it."
6. Finally, they display little interest in distinguishing between the *real* and the *wished-for/imagined.* They willingly distort the truth to further their own interests.

In contrast, we have the Good-Enough Analyst.

1. S/he sees others as *people in their own right.* Others have ideas, relationships, schedules, pains, and joys all of their own and s/he cherishes those. This ability is more than cognitive used-car-salesman empathy. S/he emotionally resonates with her patient and not only as the patient relates to the analyst. The Jewish mystics that Eigen cites pondered how a Creator that was everywhere could create something else? Where would it fit? They suggest a process they labelled *Tzimtzum* – a means by which God redacted Him/Herself. The Good-Enough Analyst makes space for others.
2. The Good-Enough Psychoanalyst doesn't see "A or B" but embraces the complexity of *das Unbewusste,* the unconscious. Indeed, "A is like B" lives alongside "A is not like B." "A acts on B" is right there with "B acts on A" and "A acts on others," too. When the patient hates the analyst, s/he suspects love and, importantly, vice versa. Inside dances with outside and much dancing is good!
3. The Good-Enough Psychoanalyst reflects and reflects, again. S/he accepts Waelder's notion that everything is multiply determined and s/he is forever ready for a Reikian surprise. No heels dug in, here. The power

of ongoing associating to affects and images rules. Without memory or desire, s/he works in the space between successive images.

4. In many legal codes, we have *stare decisis*, a conservative principle that embraces previous thinking and precedent! The Good-Enough Analyst considers earlier studies and cases and uses intuition with novel solutions. S/he considers what the new would say in the language of the old, as that informs, as well.

5. Thought is nuanced for the Good-Enough Analyst. S/he recognizes that just because two notions are mutually exclusive, doesn't mean that one of them must be wrong. She doesn't elaborate, perhaps, beyond imagining the rental of one elephant and ten blind wise men. She knows that science never captures truth but assiduously attempts to approximate towards truths. The Good-Enough Analyst sees differing well-thought-out models perched on different branches of the same tree. All seek the sun. Which one is higher? Who knows? As a mortal, s/he accepts that in the end s/he'll choose without the benefit of Godly omniscience.

6. Eschewing absolute truth and ever-sceptical of her own, s/he seeks to find solutions that comport with multiple conflicting truths that take up residence in clinical offices and s/he admits inevitable mistakes.

I've met a surfeit of analysts in whom these goals are obviously met and who well-fill the shoes I've cobbled for the Good-Enough Analyst, *and I have met many who do not.*

I met Michael Eigen on a listserv when internet handshakes still sounded like dysarthric cats trying to speak Hebrew with each other. It was nominally a discussion group about Bion's contributions. It was much more. It followed on a 1997 conference in South America. I do not remember most of the participants on the listserv, but I do remember, indeed, Marilyn Charles, Corbett Williams, Paolo Azzone, and Mike Eigen, and I'm not certain about Paolo. Maybe the Milan-based analyst was on another listserv. In any case, those four people were/are, in my estimation at that time and now, Good-Enough Psychoanalysts, even if Corbett was an Engineer and not a clinician and even if I only met Mike Eigen once outside a paperback with his name on the front. Oh, yes, they knew a lot, too, and except for Corbett had the right letter salad after their names. But largely, it was a matter of how they behaved! They/we granted each other the right to be *subjects and thinkers in our own right* and never played the "You call yourself an analyst?" game. I can't recall any of us claiming a monopoly on a singular truth or the right metapsychology. And there was, too, a sense of caring, of cherishing each other.

Alas, I keep running into analysts who are incapable of granting others the right to differ and who lack the scepticism that Ferenczi suggested 100 years ago was missing among analysts. I decided that the best way I could think about Mike Eigen's work was to talk about this problem of *Analysts Acting Badly* and hints of why there weren't more *Good-Enough Analysts.*

These *are* trying times

Much of the World's landmass is under the control of would-be or actual despots and controlled by rising nationalistic administrations that rule with the suggested stigmata of severe personality disordered folk: Lack of empathy; splitting; no nuance and no truth. The turn-of-the-21st-century was and is a difficult era with some three-dozen hot-or-cold wars raging and war-technology sufficiently portable to add to a rise of terroristic acts. Maybe the smaller actors felt less threatened when the Superpowers were at each other and, now that the Cold War ended, imagine they must tame the set-loose giants who are no longer busy fighting each other? Who's to say?

On *our front*, though, the wars in American psychoanalysis were a bit quieter after the Great Settlement in 1988 that interrupted the medical monopoly of American psychoanalysis and after the infusion of humility from the paucity of psychoanalytic patients and candidates. The 1970s and 1980s furore against self psychology, modern psychoanalysis, object relations theories, and developmental psychology quieted *a bit*. Still, there were clear indications that *Pax Psychoanalytica* was a yet-to-be fulfilled dream.

Let me speak personally of what it was like for me, someone who trained as a lay analyst 45 years ago. In 1998, when I published my model for an emendation of the Oedipus Complex, some friends *de-friended* me. Two cited my training in the lay community that they said made me vulnerable to theoretical perfidy and put me in bed with Jung. And the relational people didn't want to talk because I came out of a different church/training.

Lest I appear anti-medicine, let me recount another story from years around the events of 9/11. Johanna Tabin, one of the founders of the American Psychoanalytic Psychologists, invited me to apply for Distinguished Senior Diplomate status in ABPP some 20 years ago. I had my reservations about the invitation as the anonymous case they wanted me to discuss was not only ill-handled but both superficial and thoroughly unanalytic. I did send in, as requested, my credentials and writings and showed up for a planned meeting on the Upper East Side. The grand inquisitor came out and explained that if it were up to him this meeting would not occur, and that I had "trained wrong." He would still invite me in after the others arrived, and he had the chance to have his objections heard. He explained that he had gotten a PhD, then gone to the Army, and then trained psychoanalytically ... "that's the way it's done, Son." I was, admittedly, less than 60 years old.

When I was at last beckoned into the meeting, a second Inquisitor explained that, while I was more than likely among the most qualified ever to apply for this status, they were uncomfortable about my training; I told them that I was not. I was analyzed by Feldman, Feldman by Harbour, Harbour by Sachs and Sachs arguably by Freud. My training, I went on, was mainstream classical cum Hartmann, Kris and Loewenstein, and the analysts at the Psychoanalytic Studies Institute were all dyed-in-the-wool psychoanalysts, most of whom hadn't yet accepted radicals like Mahler! In a calm voice, I opined: "Why the fuck did you invite me, here?"

"No, no," the third explained, "we have every intention of inviting you to join, are very impressed with your writings, but wanted to say what we said." It turned out that the grand inquisitor had not bothered to read my published pieces.

Staying with the personal with a nod to kindness, it was about this time that Arnie Richards invited me to join a faculty of the online *Journal of the American Psychoanalytic Association*. I was moved to tears as I heard his words resounding in my head. I was being invited to talk alongside mainstream psychoanalysts! How different this was from dealings I had with a medical analyst in 1978 who kicked me out of his office. I had been looking for consultative-supervision on a difficult perversion case. He told me I should toddle-off and "do some university tutoring and keep (my) nose clean."

Equally disturbing, though, is the "you call yourself an analyst" game. It's a specific form of the orthodoxy game. Like the ancient split after the gnostic heresy and the centuries-later splitting of Islam into a multiplicity of orthodoxies, like the dozens of Jewish practices each believing itself to have gotten it from God and like recent Holy Wars in other religious and political groups, analysts who have not learned the joys of entertaining others' ideas in a *primus inter pares* way – without either agreement or disagreement – are prone to play this game. "You're wrong because you disagree with me. And, by the way, don't convert; just get out of here!"

Analysts Acting Badly, indeed!

Missed opportunities and the community

Cooper (2008) wrote about schisms in psychoanalysis and the need for research to settle disputes. I (2007) wrote about internecine conflict within Philadelphia psychoanalysis. Eisold (1998) wrote about the destructive nature of psychoanalytic authority and how it played out in the era of the European refugees. Richards (1998) edited a collection on "Politics and paradigms." Frosch (1991) wrote his history of "the New York psychoanalytic civil war(s)." And Roustang (1976) compared the psychoanalytic community around Freud to a primal horde suffering from guilt about cannibalizing the psychoanalytic Father.

Indeed, many of our scholars have taken a bite out of this paradox wherein the most analyzed group of people don't metabolize differences sufficiently to avoid splitting of their groups and/or are incapable of living in peace with each other after groups have fragmented. People who prosecute these wars don't fit my impressionistic view of the Good-Enough Psychoanalyst. Freudian, Jungian, Modern, and the dispersed offspring of the interpersonalists? We/they all seem to split.

Ellen English (unpublished film by Alex Burland) described the friendship-turned-icy-chill between her husband, Spurgeon, and Gerald Pearson, his co-author on many projects. Her fond memories of nights with each other's family while "the boys" were working on their books and papers are followed by her memories of the cold disregard they showed each other at meetings after the split that caused a rift in Philadelphia Medical psychoanalysis for generations. She ended her comments on this matter with the haunting: "And they were analyzed and should have known better." We've all been analyzed and all should know better.

The mentioned scholars typically addressed the sociology of such schismatization: The old Europeans with lefty politics in the world but righty politics inside of psychoanalysis, the new wave of immigrants vs. those from earlier immigrations! Indeed, the ground of psychoanalytic comity has been bloodied by wars under diverse conditions and contexts. Recently (2019), I heard Rolnick paradoxically argue that growth in the Israeli Psychoanalytic Society only arose due to a relatively stable, hopeful, and peaceful surround that was necessary for creative and productive growth of intellectual curiosity. This promoted, he thought, the rapid growth of introspective psychical thinking and research in the early 1900s in Vienna and in the 1920s to 1940s in Israel. Peaceful Europe and Israel? I cannot accept that either our progress or our wars are understandable as internalized from a larger context nor that the two mentioned arenas fit the bill.

Undetonated landmines still threaten to maim anyone whose footfalls veer far from the paths set down by their institutes. In fear of these dangers and others, perhaps, there have been many moments in psychoanalytic history when costly choices were made to go-in or not-to-go-in particular directions.

Cooper (2008) gives multiple examples of the cost of missed opportunities; I won't repeat them, here. The reasons for these disputes, alienations, and excommunications were typically rationalized in the name of maintaining a cohering science or explained by the sociology of the group or by fealty to *Papa Freud*. Still, candidates do well to this day to recognize that each choice of training or control analyst may come with a price. Fail to fear friendly fire, at your peril!

I offer an 11th Commandment: Thou shalt not take the name of a cohering science in vain. It was in 1912 that Freud purportedly wrote to Jung on the importance of not abandoning the absolute bulwark of the *Movement*, the *sexual theories*, in order not to hurt the Movement. Too bad Jung couldn't stay and Freud couldn't bring himself to permit Strange Fires in the Temple, and couldn't allow room for the Other!

We know that, as theories complexify without major renovation, the cone of possible new discoveries narrows, even in hard sciences, thus delaying and/or preventing novel thought that may fit the data but not the model. This bodes poorly for the construction of unification models and may add to theoretical claustrophobias that precipitate break-outs. Let me give a simple example: Harold Blum (*ex officio* president of psychoanalytic organizations, editor of major journals with 700 listings on Pep_Web: No slouch!) gave the following account of the rift between Bowlby and mainstream psychoanalysis at a recent Mahler symposium in Philadelphia (2019):

> The film (Bowlby, Robertson, and Roseblitt, 1972) was interpreted by Bowlby and Robertson as a reaction to separation from her mother. Many British analysts, however, attributed the girl's distress to her guilt over destructive fantasies about her pregnant mother and in utero sibling.

Blum continued:

> Bowlby was aware that his interest in attachment was stimulated by his own traumatic separations.

Blum attributed the difference between Bowlby and the Sages to the exigencies of Bowlby's childhood and youth. I would have been satisfied had he then explained that these two different views were not incompatible. We learn in Physics how to determine the trajectory of a single object projected at a certain angle with a given force within the domain of a specified gravity. As analysts, though, we try to map the paths taken by an ever-changing, progressively subjective (self-directed-and-propelled) psyche that is travelling with dozens of other psyches interacting with it, impacting its path. Blum's comments came some 50 years after Anna Freud offered us a great theoretical advance. She suggested that we consider a multiplicity of *developmental lines* – many of them, even if she only offered handfuls. Why not for Blum on Bowlby? And remember: When Kohut suggested a novel developmental continuum for narcissism that was separate from the psychosexual line, he was harshly castigated. And Kohut, in turn, didn't make it easy for Gedo and the beat goes on!

Too often either the model or the preferred guru in psychoanalytic thinking trumps the question of representation of the data. Indeed, the *skinny* was/ is that data could only come from the analytic situation, and it was/is the data from the most powerful analysts that held/holds the key to acceptance. As if: The word of God is only available from those who have been anointed to receive it. We may but speculate about when the growth of object relations theories, pre-Oedipal developmental observational studies, the place of the Father or the relational turn might have occurred if Sigmund had given but a little flex to Carl?

Orthodoxies

I want to pay respect to orthodoxy. Among my proffered characteristics of a Good-Enough Analyst was that s/he studies and evaluates precedent. Cooper, though, described a characteristic of the psychoanalytic endeavour that is, indeed, much like the generation function among religious sects. In both cases, we have a world of competing orthodoxies that each began in a heterodoxical move away from some orthodoxy by becoming a separate orthodoxy.

There have been, though, brave authors who have broadened the cone of *the possible* in our enterprise, sometimes without fracturing the groups in which they were hatched. Eigen is one such person; as far as I know, he has never sought an Eigenian label. It is such people who are my psychoanalytic heroes. They fight a difficult war, one in which to disagree may lead to being disfellowshipped. Such clinical/theoreticians accept that it is fair to say about those who differ with them that:

- They know of which they speak clinically;
- They speak it well;
- They care deeply for their patients;
- They, with a presumption of good intentions (something the severely personality disordered lack, as well), disagree with "us" not to be contrarian or because they're members of some *great unwashed illiterati* or because they're neurotic, and not because they haven't resolved their oedipal dilemmas but rather because they have thought about their data deeply and carefully and arrived at different conclusions.

My internet friends were such people – Corbett, Marilyn, Mike, and Paolo – who could accept that others thought deep and hard, just as they did.

Orthodoxy occurs when members of a controlling subgroup aver that there is but one path that is consistent with membership in that group. The maintaining of orthodoxy is the way tribalism works to keep the tribe intact, whatever the leaders' explicitly stated motives might be. LeBon (1895) postulated a terror of dissolution of the group that moves groups to transgress ethical precepts and individual's value systems. Each member in an orthodoxy trembles in fear of being thrown out of *the gates of the city*. Thus, we see fealty by an implied *threat of excommunication* threatening ego disintegration, disintegration anxieties, soul murder, or the sequelae of a *dead/absent mother syndrome*. Alas. This is the way we members of Clan Anthropos roll before and, for some of us even after analysis!

Orthodoxy aims to maintain clonal transmission of whatever it is that marks the group – sometimes, little more than a name. If we accept LeBon's thinking, what holds tribes together is the fear that the glue will come loose in the absence of fealty to the leader and the leader's words; leaders stoke this view.

Before I'm accused of partisan polemicizing, let me also look at my own group of origin. I was born into Orthodox Judaism and studied in their Yeshivas. Were I from a devout Moslem family, my Yeshiva would have been called a Madrassa. I was to live life according to *Halacha*. i.e. The Way. Tao,

Shariya, Mahabarata, and the writing of the Curae in Rome – whatever you call it. It was The Way. The Only Way!

Cooper certainly could have written his piece on competing orthodoxies for my group; a simple example is illustrative. Many of my relatives are members of the Black Hat anti-Chassidic movement in Lakewood, NJ. A Rabbi with a handful of students founded a *Kollel*, a Study Collective on the shores of New Jersey 90 years ago. That handful has become a community with 9,000 adult males, each studying there maybe 60 hours each week. They follow the guidelines for living that they believe were set out by their forebears. Not so long ago, one of my cousin's grandsons decided to marry a woman from the Skver community of Chassidim. They don't wear Lakewood black hats; they wear tall black cylindrical fur *shtrommels*. Are the rules in Lakewood and Skver the same? Pretty much and assuredly to outsiders but not exactly to insiders. Are there different details in customs? Yes, but slight! Their question was: "What to do? Do we attend the wedding?"

The Old Testament put it simply, and it has applied to the world of psychoanalysis, too often:

> Guard carefully in accordance with that which God, your God has commanded you; you must not deviate to the right or to the left.
>
> (Deuteronomy, 5, 29; also, 17, 10–11)

And elsewhere:

> Be careful to observe only that which I enjoin upon you: neither add to it nor take anything away from it.
>
> (Deuteronomy, 13, 1)

Indeed, psychoanalytic orthodoxy is a term many might consider oxymoronic. Psychoanalysis offered a radical programme and not because it talked about sex. Indeed, we don't spend a lot of time talking about sex-proper but rather about obsessions and compulsions and prohibitions that distort *vita sexualis*. We welcome the analysand to say it all, believing, as we do that *the non-thought is father to the deed*. Those who come to us and learn to freely associate to their feelings and images discover *Sophrosyne* (σωφροσύνη), the moderating sanity of which the Ancient Greeks spoke. That, alone, makes psychoanalysis a radical enterprise, radically different than the equation of thought and deed in Christian theology and behavioural psychologies.

Arguably, the part of the frame in psychoanalysis that is most essential is not the couch, nor the fee and not the metapsychology but a novel psychoanalytic contribution to human nature that precipitates from free association (not to ideas but) to affects and images. Beginning with the pressure technique (an earlier name for Shapiro's EMDR) in 1893–5, it was this chaining of associations that brought about something new, not health, per se, but something novel.

Orthodoxy is a system of clonal regeneration – from generation to generation and from whole to parts – that seeks to bind members' thinking and behaviour using the rules, regulations and admonitions of a power class: *Stare decisis on steroids!*

Orthodoxies seek to maintain a cherished homeostasis, a state – borrowing from Eigen – that represents a *bug-free universe*, one delineated by its leader or leaders. It represents a return to a culture of presumed edenic bliss where the messy decisions of life have all been made *au nom du pere et la mere*, where all forks in the road are marked and where its laws and its Caesars, at any given moment, are presumed to be righteous.

Until – and maybe even after – Glover's paper on "inexact and incomplete interpretations" (1931), some psychoanalysts believed that if one but were to welcome someone to lay on a couch with some frequency for many years and prompt them to free-associate under the witnessing eyes of a well-trained psychoanalyst, it mattered little who the analyst was. The result would be the same unfolding of transferences in the treatment. The patient would work through their conflicts, and Analyst A would do it just like Analyst B would. We still speak in generalities: "I was analyzed" … as if that were akin to saying "cooked to perfection."

I object! While some of us are analytic siblings or cousins, and the preponderance of us are likely third cousins or closer, analytically speaking, we have reason to believe that our experiences and results vary broadly. I was analyzed in the classical psychoanalytic technique of the middle of the last century. Glover's iconic paper might have me, therefore, considering whether I was well analyzed – after all, ideas presumably improved and I had an old analyst, even then!

Losses to orthodoxy

I earlier mentioned a cold Vienna night in the Fall of 1907 when Adler asked those assembled in Freud's Berggasse flat if psychoanalysis could be taught. It is, if nothing else, an interesting question as to whether there is what we could call a therapeutic personality that is necessary, if not sufficient, to carry out good and healing treatments.

Freud, however, chose not to reply maternally with the *pause-cum-common-courtesy*: "I'm so glad you asked that question." Instead, Freud responded that (essentially) when arbitrarily obstreperous swine – presumably, such as Adler – could be constrained by proven rules, well, then, *yes it could be taught*. We know that Adler was already thinking of social constructs and community matters to be included in a psychoanalytic notion of health, just as Jung was reasoning in those years that, covarying with the sexual tensions that Freud was investigating, there must lie non-sexual matters, as well. We know that Malinowski's work on the varieties of oedipal experiences would be largely trashed, Kosawa and Okinogi's work on a Japanese variant on the oedipal would be buried, as would Bowlby's work on attachment and Franz Alexander's new thinking about the reconstructive emotional experience. We know that analysts like Fromm (who sold more books that almost all the analysts of the past 100 years, put together) and Kohut and Minuchin and the likes of Speck and Beck were driven out from under the psychoanalytic umbrella, at an arguably great expense to both our community and to progress in our field. Talk of a death instinct! There is no reason, to my way of thinking, that all of these different ways of conceptualizing treatment couldn't live under the same psychoanalytic umbrella except, of course, for therapists' way of disagreeing disharmoniously and agreeing disagreeably.

Much emphasis in the literature on internecine conflict in our field focuses on certain dominant clefts: Adler, Jung, the Anna–Melanie rift, Lacan–Paris split, the departures from the New York Psychoanalytic Society and the *Chicago renegades*. But, truth be told, the rifts and expulsions are in most every Society and within the preponderance of rival schools. Kohut and Gedo didn't get on real well. And when Charlie Brenner began saying that the Structural Model was too clinically distant to be useful, he took flack. Two classically trained folk were driven out of the institute I later directed because they were in Kohut's. Occasionally some Jungians in Europe would try to join with some object relational theorists, two American Societies joined 40 years after splitting, and a Fred Pine would come along trying to synchronize four different Freudian postures. In general, though I think it fair to say, that efforts such as Pine's were unsuccessful. (You can likely buy his cogent book online for $1.98 + Shipping.)

Curiously, too, many contributions that were made by these auslanders, those who were treated as others, were later co-opted by leading classical or mainstream psychoanalytic subgroups.

Let me be clear: Orthodoxy is as necessary as gravity is on our planet. But, add to gravity a couple of feet per second/per second of gravitational acceleration, and you can kiss basketball and swimming goodbye. We need magicians who can find a good-enough balance between respect for the past and openness to innovation.

Closing this call for ecumenism, then, I would note that when Martin Bergmann (who was only permitted entry into the American Psychoanalytic Association very late in life and as an honorary member, at that) invited analysts to a roundtable discussing "Dissidence and controversy in psychoanalytic thinking" (2004), participants were all members of the American Psychoanalytic Association, with the single *outsider* being André Green. That is to say, in order to be invited to Martin's party, one had to be a member of the American Psychoanalytic Association or André Green! It would be, I once suggested to him, something akin to having a discussion about the Holocaust and inviting no Jews or akin to discussing Jim Crow psychology at a sheets-optional whites-only roundtable!

Otto Kernberg reported during the Bergmann roundtable that when he arrived in New York, ranking members of NY Psychoanalytic Society warned him that he would never rise in the New York Institutes if he tried to hawk his South American Kleinian perfidies. We know that Adler, Jung, not-quite-Ferenczi, Bowlby, Klein, Sullivan, Horney, Thompson, Fromm and Kohut, Beck and Speck, and Minuchin were all given *ye ole-heave-ho* and forced to find lodging elsewhere. We know, too, that much of these innovators' works were later co-opted or, shall we say, *purloined*. Freud, in 1914, spoke of the narcissistic way of connecting. He compared it to the Amoeboid and how, with its pseudopodia, it absorbs its nutrients; the captured becomes part of the protoplasm. This is, perhaps, the most extreme form of narcissistic attachment.

If the fear of group fragmentation fuels the mob and, perhaps, contributes to understanding the maintenance of transgenerational group identity, we may ask: What form does it take in the psychoanalytic world and, importantly, how is it transmitted?

Posit: *Psychoanalysis has had a multi-step method for responding to novel/deviant contributions*:

(a) The Community, initially, Ignores, Denies, or Minimizes the value of the novel contribution;
(b) It then waits for about eight years;
(c) Thereafter, it introduces the novel notion as a possibility, citing deficiencies in earlier incarnations of this concept by people outside the mainstream; and finally
(d) It accepts the idea into the mainstream, while footnoting the original authors.

Pesky little matter (Eigen's bug-free universe?) that new innovators keep rising. When and where I was in training in the 1970s, Melanie Klein could only be read *under the covers* and reading the Sullivan, Horney, Rosenfeld, and Fromm Gang required a wrapping of their books in a marble composition-book cover; still, it was done.

The case of Spielrein's death drive is worth mentioning briefly before closing. In 1912, she offered up a notion of a self-destructive programme inside each element of God's good creation to go alongside a program for survival. However, one feels about the *Todestriebe*, Freud would eight years later proffer something similar while footnoting her work:

A considerable portion of these speculations have been anticipated by Sabina Spielrein (1912) in an instructive and interesting paper which, however, is unfortunately not entirely clear to me. She there describes the sadistic components of the sexual instinct as "destructive."

(Freud, 1920, p. 55)

Almost enough said. I would just add that Jung similarly co-opted her work on the collective unconscious and nary a child analyst mentions her early work with children done long before Melanie and Anna squared off in their decades-long rift; Spielrein sometimes gets a footnote.

This is not typical of other sciences. Einstein had the decency to hold a meeting apologizing to Stekel's student, Velikovsky, whom he had accused of pseudoscience when that pseudoscientific screed turned out to be consistent with science. And the great British Mathematician, George Hardy, travelled to visit a young Indian clerk who had written to him claiming that certain of his theorems were false when it turned out they were. Indeed, it didn't matter to George that Ramanujan claimed to learn precisely which theorems were wrong from hypnogogic and hypnopompic visitations by a beautiful fairy princess. The theorems were wrong and needed to be changed. So, I ask, how does this not happen under our psychoanalytic umbrella?

Transmission lines

I've gone on long enough polemicizing (not against psychoanalysis, the attempt to understand the soul by seeing how it interacts with another soul under controlled conditions that Eigen describes so well without getting hooked into orthodoxy but) against the politics of psychoanalysis.

I'm left, then, wondering about the structural dynamics of this transmission. Psychoanalytic training is tri-partite. I close with a sentence-each about its three elements. I should note that there are training facilities that have chosen different and more inclusive methods, but, in general, it is as follows:

Didactic coursework … The teaching of metapsychology and material are chosen from the writings of the prince or princess and his or her closest attendants in each psychoanalytic community.
Training Analysis … analysts are hand-chosen by the Dynasty with an eye for picking only those who do the heavy lifting for that Royal Family and no other.
Control Analyses … supervision? You guessed it! Supervision is performed by those chosen by the Monarchy and in its name.

Parting words

When someone comes thinking to train with me, I recommend that they – within limits afforded to them by circumstance – seek out a variety of the available orthodoxies. I tell them: "Choose an analyst of a type different than the type of analysis you intend to practice and do similarly with choosing a heterogeneous collection of control analysts." I tell them that *psychoanalyse* was *a common noun* and lost much of its meaning when it became the *proper noun Psychoanalysis* and that I prefer *the common noun version*. I think I know some of the arguments against this advice and I reject them. I, then, tell them to read the works of Michael Eigen. "Oh, taste and see."

References

Bergmann, M. (2004). *Understanding dissidence and controversy in the history of psychoanalysis*. Other Press.

Cooper, A. (2008). American psychoanalysis today: A plurality of orthodoxies. *Journal American Academy of Psychoanalysis*, 36 (2), 235–53.

Covitz, H. (2007). The possibility of multiple models for oedipal development. *American Journal of Psychoanalysis*, 67 (2), 162–80.

Eisold, K. (1998). The splitting of the New York Psychoanalytic Society and the construction of psychoanalytic authority. *International Journal of Psychoanalysis*, 79, 871–85.

Freud, S. (1920). Beyond the pleasure principle. *The Standard Edition of the complete psychological works of Sigmund Freud*, Volume XVIII (J. Strachey, Ed.). Hogarth Press, pp. 1–64.

Frosch, J. (1991). The New York psychoanalytic civil war. *Journal of the American Psychoanalytic Association*, 39, 1037–64.

Glover, E. (1931). The therapeutic effect of inexact interpretation: A contribution to the theory of suggestion. *International Journal of Psycho-Analysis*, 12, 397–411.

LeBon, G. (1895). *Psychologie des Foules*. Hach livre-BNF.

Nunberg, H and Federn, E. (1962). *Minutes of the Vienna Psychoanalytic Society, Volume 1*. International Universities Press.

Richards, AD. (1998). Politics and paradigms. *Journal of the American Psychoanalytic Association*, 46 (2), 357–60.

Roustang, F. (1976). *Dire mastery: Discipleship from Freud to Lacan*. Johns Hopkins University.

Sharpe, EF. (1930). The analyst. *International Journal of Psychoanalysis*, XI, 255.

Chapter 19

Elemental contact

From madness to mysticism in celebrating the work of Michael Eigen

Willow Pearson

Elemental

The title of this chapter is "Elemental contact." I'd like to begin with three definitions of the word *elemental* (Merriam-Webster, 2020) and then focus on the first two.

As an adjective, *elemental* is defined as "forming an integral part," and "of, relating to, or being the basic or essential constituent of something." And also, "of, relating to, or resembling a great force of nature." For instance, a thunderstorm is the natural outcome of atmospheric elements battling one another.

And then there's also *elemental* as a noun – a curious turn. *Elemental* is defined as a noun in this way: "A supernatural being."

Applying these definitions, this chapter is *elemental* in the sense of me being a beginner in studying Dr Eigen's work, making elemental or *foundational* contact with his texts, with a community of scholar-practitioners engaged in his work through an international online Listserve since 2014 and with him on occasion, directly, through his generous email correspondence. In the second sense of the definition, I mean to describe the myriad ways that Dr Eigen makes contact with us, his readership, through the portal of his psychoanalytic opus of 26 books and more. By that I particularly mean Eigen's making contact with us, his readership, through fire, water, air, earth, and space. So I'd like to describe both these contexts of elemental contact with Dr Eigen's work and his work with us as I experience it. To return to the first sense, the sense of elemental contact as my beginning contact, my elementary contact with Dr Eigen's work, allows me to expand the story of how it is that I came to the 42nd International Psychohistorical Association Conference, where I presented this paper on Dr Eigen's work.

Connecting

The way I came to this work was very personal. Let me begin by telling you how I *imagine* that I got here. When I returned to graduate school in 2010,

I happened to discover (or perhaps they discovered me) two seminal books from Eigen's catalogue. The first book was *The Psychoanalytic Mystic* (1998), and the second book was *The Psychotic Core* (1986). Having *The Psychoanalytic Mystic* and *The Psychotic Core* quietly take up residence on my bookshelf, as I studied at the Wright Institute in Berkeley, California, provided a background support of which I was scarcely conscious. These volumes unsuspectingly extended the reach of my capacity to engage depth of spirit, on the one hand, and depth of psychopathology, on the other hand.

As these two books quietly rested there on my bookshelf – unread – in my tiny library, they expanded my thinking. How is that you might ask? Well, they allowed me to begin to move in two directions at once. They allowed me to move in the direction of more space for the true depths of psychopathology – of suffering, of challenge, of limitations that we face. And at once, in the very same breath, they allowed me to make more space for the depths of mystery. So as Eigen quietly expanded my library, and so expanded my mind to the depths of pathology and mystery, spirit and difficulty, challenge and capability, I gradually found my way to making contact with two other important people who helped me open those books and open into Eigen's work: Dr James Grotstein, whom I had the privilege of consulting with by phone during the four years prior to his death; and Dr Robin Bagai, whom I had the great pleasure of meeting through the International Association of Relational Psychoanalysis and Psychotherapy (IARPP). It's through my encounters with Dr Grotstein and Dr Bagai that my capacity for engaging with the work of Bion and of Eigen took root, which I'm really still beginning. This happened somewhere in the neighbourhood of 2011 or so. Then lo and behold, something really beautiful happened at the Wright Institute: One of my most influential professors, Dr Alan Kubler (who for many years was the editor of *Fort Da, The Journal of the Northern California Society for Psychoanalytic Psychology*) brought in an article by Dr Eigen on primary aloneness (2008). Read in Dr Kubler's comparative psychoanalysis course, this article on primary aloneness included Eigen's commentary on and extension of Winnicott's notions of background support and the incommunicado core.

Another world opened at that very moment – the person whose work lived on my bookshelves was now brought into the seminar and given a place in discourse and conversation, which I could then elaborate on in dialogue with Drs Grotstein and Bagai. Eigen's words came alive in the community and off the page. That was very exciting for me. I remember Dr Kubler saying something like, "Well, yeah. There is no one like Eigen, but he's in New York" (personal communication). So yes, given that I was in the San Francisco Bay Area, it took a bit of a journey to open up into Eigen's work. That's the beginning of the story of how I got here – from two texts sitting unread on my bookshelf, yet emanating their wisdom, to conversation in a seminar, to conversation with Drs Grotstein and Bagai, to the conversation at the 42nd International Psychohistorical Association Conference.

Be a light

"Be a light, unto the world." This phrase was sent to me by Dr Eigen (personal communication, December 4, 2018) on the third night of Chanukah this past year, when he generously responded to my initial email message. I had sent him a review that I had written on his most recent book, *The Challenge of Being Human* (2018a), which was published in *Fort Da* (see Pearson, 2019). Dr Eigen shared with me that, in reflecting on my review, the phrase "Be a light, unto the world" came to him. Reading this, the prayer, "Be a light, unto the world" captivated my attention and was a beacon for it. Only as I began to sing the prayer, to find a melody for it, to emerge as an embodied vessel, did I begin to unfold the prayer's living wisdom. Inside of that prayer, the whole of my contact with Dr Eigen's teaching opened up for me, now heart to heart. By bringing a melody into being to accompany Dr Eigen's refrain, the soul became flesh, and that was my first direct instance of meeting Dr Eigen, soul to soul.

My first language is dreaming. My second language is music. I have been a singer and a songwriter my whole life and a nationally board-certified music therapist for 20 years. For me, music comes before words. Yet this business of what comes first and what comes next is so vexing – and wonderfully so. What comes first in song, the words or the music? Happily, it is a question with endless answers and with no answer at all. Regardless, singing is a great passion of mine. It won't surprise you, then, to learn how deeply I am inspired by the fact that Dr Eigen is a jazz pianist and, moreover, that he opened by playing piano when he was teaching in Korea several years ago. His twin loves of music and psychotherapy, which he has written and talked about in tandem throughout his career, mirror my own. Moreover, his own twin identities of psychologist/psychotherapist, on the one hand, and musician, on the other – in a culture that would try to separate that natural twinship – moves me and gives me the courage to stand by my own integration of the sung and the spoken, the wordless and the word.

Perhaps that context of kinship with Dr Eigen for psyche and song helps to explain why through that email exchange "Be a light, unto the world" became a refrain, why that little song became a chant, and why that chant became a prayer. And in just this way, the prayer that Dr Eigen shared with me in 2018 has crept inside of my psyche and taken residence there in beautiful ways – from the light of Dr Eigen's words to the light of our words together through music. So if you'll indulge me, I'd love to seed the way with a moment of music, just a little songlet, a tiny invocation, a little bit of a prayer. I'd like to sing, and for you to sing from wherever you are sitting as you read this chapter, if you'd be so kind as to lend your voice to this simple prayer to "Be a light, unto the world." I welcome your voice to open into our shared space here together and to create a melody that is pleasing to you. I invite you to be brave. Don't worry about what it might sound like. Just enjoy the opening into the river of sound.

I'll give you the four refrains and then invite you to join me for a few more. Here it is: "Be a light, unto the world. Be a light, unto the world. Be a light, unto the wo-or-orld. Be a light, unto the world." Join me: "Be a light, unto the world. Be a light, unto the world. Be a light, unto the wo-or-orld. Be a light, unto the world." Beautiful. Thank you very much.

Convergence/*dis*integration

Michael Eigen's extraordinary body of work explores the convergence of psychoanalytic, psychotherapeutic, and spiritual streams through the confluence of themes from madness to mysticism. That in Dr Eigen's teaching the human condition is bound by a negotiation of these two apparent poles of experience, these poles being madness on the one hand and the mystical on the other, is a window to his generosity of spirit and genius of soul.

Dr Eigen's work allows his reader to imagine and envision the psychoanalytic mystic who has a psychotic core and to see those two truths of madness and mysticism harboured within as genuinely confluent, and even generative, rather than as necessarily discordant or only as destructive. Dr Eigen allows the reader to imagine herself as such a being – endowed with this human inheritance of psyche's majesty and psyche's catastrophe within her alike – and indeed allows the reader to regard psyche's inheritance within all beings – as potential for contact with the depths in all their majesty and catastrophe. In this way, Dr Eigen's work allows the reader to become more fully human, more completely herself.

I know I am not alone when I underscore that Dr Eigen's work has been as transformative for me personally, emotionally, and clinically, as it has been catalytic for me intellectually and theoretically. I came to Dr Eigen's work at a time in my own life when I had a lot of integration work to do, and these paradoxical aspects of clinical work that he describes so brilliantly in his scholarship were as personally illuminating as they were professionally fascinating, for which I am very grateful. Through his work, I was able to allow the *dis*integration to simply be, which was the beginning of integration in its own time. This simple truth was as compelling for me personally, and it was captivating intellectually.

Contact

Let's further consider contact with the elements: Fire, water, earth, air, and space. We are repelled and compelled at once to make contact with the natural elements, just as we are with the elements of psychic life.

In terms of contact, we both seek to be protected and sheltered from the elements in their extremities and also to delight in their temperate expressions in more measured doses. We are delighted by a gentle spring shower, but a torrential flood can sweep our home away. We are warmed by a tame winter fire, but an out-of-control blaze can burn a city block to the ground. Dr Eigen helps us to approach these psychic elements in their nakedness, allowing us to make sense of the drive to extremes, paradoxically offering a kind of shelter in this manner of looking closely and seeing directly. His contact with the elements and vivid descriptions and interpretations of what he discovers there affords us this view.

In his 2011 publication of *Contact with the Depths*, Dr Eigen writes: "We oscillate between grandiose and abject states and find these profoundly linked. Scratch one, get the other, a kind of psychic law: Live one side, the other comes" (6–30). An example of this is in the psychic life of his patient Abe, who is struggling with alcoholism. Dr Eigen describes his work with Abe as an admixture of trauma and support, and Abe's experience of the radiance of all beings was something that both Dr Eigen and Abe were birth attendants to through the therapy, in the midst of grappling with the madness and trauma of addiction and its tendrils. What strikes me in Dr Eigen's work with Abe is his presence to the catastrophic dimension of Abe's life even as Dr Eigen also attends to Abe's birth of radiance. Dr Eigen never collapses one side of this doubleness. Even as radiance is born, catastrophe is in view.

The catastrophic

In his chapter entitled "Wordlessness," also in *Contact with the Depths* (2011a), Eigen writes that

> Bion's work, however, functions as a marker, a notation, calling attention to a catastrophic sense that is pervasive, that is one of the elements that knits personality together. To overlook the claims of our sense of catastrophe is itself catastrophic.
>
> (pp. 65–6)

Dr Eigen emphasizes and extends Bion's adage of learning from experience to exhort us to learn from both catastrophe and ecstasy alike. His attention to the catastrophic with Abe seems to contribute to the veracity of radiance and its birth in Abe's life through the therapy.

The elements

The elements are both radiant and potentially catastrophic. Living water, living fire, living earth: Psyche's taste, touch; living air: Psyche's scent, sound, sight; spirit indwelling – these are not for the faint of heart. The whole of Eigen's work can be read as a voyage into the radiance and catastrophe of psychic elements.

To draw from his library, allow me to name just a few volumes. *The Psychotic Core* (1986), *Flames from the Unconscious: Trauma, Madness and Faith* (2009), *Madness and Murder* (2010), *Rage* (2002), *Lust* (2006), and *Ecstasy* (2001b) read to me as testaments to fire.

Feeling Matters (2007) and *The Sensitive Self* (2004b) read to me as a river, inviting the waters of the self to lend expression. *Damaged Bonds* (2001a) and *Toxic Nourishment* (2018b) read as having to reckon with muddy waters throughout our development.

The Electrified Tightrope (2004a) and *Coming through the Whirlwind* (1992) read to me as efforts to gentle our earthwalk by virtue of the expanded space that navigating the tumults of fire, air, and water afford.

The Psychoanalytic Mystic (1998), *Faith* (2014b), *Faith and Transformation* (2011b), *The Birth of Experience* (2014a), *Image, Sense, Infinities, and Everyday Life* (2016), and most recently *The Challenge of Being Human* (2018a) read to me as treatises on the incarnation of and the expansion of space, together with what can happen when that space collapses.

Each of these texts read as the inspiration of psychic oxygen, air for the psyche to breathe, which in turn allows for more space for the materiality of this earthwalk, this task and trial, trauma and blessing of living.

Blessing

Dr Eigen's work is, for me, a profound blessing. In the Buddhist lineage, blessings are tied as knots on crimson thread. Perhaps this is both a concrete and a symbolic tie to recognition that karma is forever threaded by doubleness – samsara and nirvana inseparable. Paradoxically we seek the blessing from another, and then we can envy that person for their generosity of spirit and their capacity for genuine service. Yet, perhaps therein lies the benefit of blessing. We are tied, caught, linked. Perhaps we could see the tie itself as a contract to recognize the inseparability of wisdom and confusion in the very bodhisattva who ties the knot – akin to Eigen's "necessary phases of dependence with all its wounds and pleasures" (2018a, p. 18) – and see that it is we too who tie our own blessing cord merely by choosing to extend our wrist to the one who blesses. Our wrist is the bridge between our arm, which rests close in to our body, and our hand, which links us to the world.

This blessing is a profound form of contact that is ushered in on the wings of the elemental. Allow me to quote from "Opening to the Challenge," my recent book review in *Fort Da* (2019):[1]

> I am struck by how Dr Eigen holds up what resonates for me as a mirror to my mind (with regard for the unknowable) that is simultaneously unflinching and compassionate with its open, honest questions for an invitation to self reflection. I am compelled and helped to go further because he suggests to do just a bit at a time, to keep beginning, to not have to have all the answers, to open to what I am really, actually feeling and experiencing.
> (Pearson, 2019)

This is a profound blessing.

Distinction–union: The paradoxical doubleness of psychosis and mysticism

Again, I quote from my review in *Fort Da*:

> From Dr Eigen's new book *The Challenge of Being Human* (2018a), chapters titled "O, Orgasm, and Beyond," "Just Beginning: Ethics of the Unknown," and "Life Kills, Aliveness Kills" bring the reader into direct contact with what he has called "this double capacity two-in-one, one-in-two, a distinction-union structure that is made up of both dimensions, a paradoxical monism, a kind of psychic DNA/RNA."
>
> (2018a, p. 61).

> Eigen goes on to discern, "They can be more dissociated or fused and take myriad forms in spectrums of experience. Sometimes we feel the forms they take are inexhaustible and sometimes we feel trapped in rigid organizations."
>
> (p. 61; Pearson, 2019)

One way of reading Dr Eigen's work is that psychosis and mysticism necessitate such a distinction–union structure. In the face of such a challenge, how are we to cope, how are we to proceed? What liabilities and what gifts are discovered between psychosis and mysticism in both their distinction and also in their union?

> Eigen wonders with us, encouraging us to merely begin to look into this doubleness – this distinction-union structure of psychic life – and plants seeds of being able to go further. At the same time, Eigen suggests that we have barely begun to enter into our capacity to work with others and ourselves in this inherent dilemma and to take responsibility for our condition. He shows us how – at every turn in psychic life, in every instant – we are connected to others and how we are also separate beings. We exist inside of one another, endlessly, and, at the same time, the one who exists is just uniquely herself. We cannot escape this paradox of distinction–union. It is a riddle of our nature, to be lived.
>
> As Eigen brings us into contact with this immense and seemingly overwhelming challenge of being human, he does so from an equal challenge issuing from the ground and goal of an ethics of care and the power of love. He invites us to embrace our profound sensitivities in the service of opening to the infinite, impossible profession [of psychotherapy]. In so doing, possibilities open up; we might surprise ourselves. With Eigen as fellow traveller, we receive immense support along the way.

Through this blessing, Eigen helps us to open to the challenge of being human just a little bit more.

(Pearson, 2019)

The depths of darkness, light, and space

So now, through Dr Eigen's blessing, as I sing "Be a light, unto the world," I realize for the first time that to illuminate the darkness has a double meaning that is literally brought to life through the aperture of Eigen's work. One meaning I think I've always well understood is literally bring-ing light to the darkness, illuminating the darkness, making the darkness a little bit lighter, making the darkness a little bit softer, a little bit less harsh, a little bit less blinding, to be able to *enlighten*. At the same time and on another level, I begin to realize in uttering this chant – this song, this prayer that comes from my elemental, elementary, beginning contact with Dr Eigen – what it is to illuminate the darkness, to as William Sty-ron (1990) put it, render the *darkness visible*, to allow us to begin to see the darkness as it is, on its own terms as it were and, in *that* illumination, to be grateful. In tying together illuminating, as in *lightening the darkness*, and illuminating, as in *rendering visible the darkness*, I'd like to close by singing this prayer one more time and then inviting you to join me in singing; even as you read this book, set it down and sing: "Be a light, unto the world."

But first, an ode to darkness itself:

> What is the sound of darkness illumined?
> Is it a plaintive cry?
> What is the sight of darkness illumined?
> Is it an inward eye?
> What is a beam of intense darkness?[2]
> Is it this man, this woman, who radiates obsidian clear light for all to see?
> What is clear, light, black?
> Is it O, Ein Sof, Yum Chenmo, Prajnaparamita, The Noble Lady, the Tree of Life, the Refuge Tree all regarded as the many one infinite Beloved?

So let's raise our voices and hold in view this expression from Dr Eigen to the Bion Collective on December 9, 2018, when he wrote:

> See you the day after Chanukah
>   With Lights Brighter Than Ever In Love With the Translucent Oil Darkness

I'll repeat that one more time. Eigen wrote to the Bion Collective on December 9, 2018:

> See you the day after Chanukah
>   With Lights Brighter Than Ever In Love With the Translucent Oil Darkness

I think this prayer that Eigen offered to me is a way to be in love with the "translucent oil darkness." So I invite you to sing with me for a second time, holding these two modes of illumination in view.

See where the song takes you, through the tantra of song, the dream of song, this closing prayer to "be a light, unto the world" So, again, you can start singing anytime. Feel free to get up and move around and let the song move you.

> Be a light, unto the world
> Be a light, unto the world
> Be a light, unto the wo-or-orld
> Be a light, unto the world
>
> Be a light, unto the world
> Be a light, unto the world
> Be a light, unto the wo-or-orld
> Be a light, unto the world

Thank you!

Notes

1   This chapter extensively references portions of "Opening to the challenge," Willow Pearson's book review of Michael Eigen's *The challenge of being human*, which was originally published in *Fort Da*, Spring 2019, XXV(1), 68–71.
2   This psychoanalytic phrase is also the title of Dr James Grotstein's 2007 book, *A beam of intense darkness: Wilfred Bion's legacy to psychoanalysis*. Karnac.

References

Eigen, M. (1986). *The psychotic core*. Jason Aronson.
Eigen, M. (1992). *Coming through the whirlwind*. Chiron.
Eigen, M. (1998). *The psychoanalytic mystic*. Free Association Books.
Eigen, M. (2001a). *Damaged bonds*. Karnac.
Eigen, M. (2001b). *Ecstasy*. Wesleyan University Press.
Eigen, M. (2002). *Rage*. Wesleyan University Press.
Eigen, M. (2004a). *The electrified tightrope* (A Phillips (Ed.). Karnac.

Eigen, M. (2004b). *The sensitive self.* Wesleyan University Press.

Eigen, M. (2006). *Lust.* Wesleyan University Press.

Eigen, M. (2007). *Feeling matters.* Karnac.

Eigen, M. (2008). Primary aloneness. *Psychoanalytic Perspectives,* 5(2), 63–8.

Eigen, M. (2009). *Flames from the unconscious: Trauma, madness and faith.* Karnac.

Eigen, M. (2010). *Eigen in Seoul: Vol. 1. Madness and murder.* Karnac.

Eigen, M. (2011a). *Contact with the depths.* Karnac.

Eigen, M. (2011b). *Eigen in Seoul: Vol. 2. Faith and transformation.* Karnac.

Eigen, M. (2014a). *The birth of experience.* Karnac.

Eigen, M. (2014b). *Faith.* Karnac.

Eigen, M. (2016). *Image, sense, infinities, and everyday life.* Karnac.

Eigen, M. (2018a). *The challenge of being human.* Routledge.

Eigen, M. (2018b). *Toxic nourishment.* Routledge.

Eigen, M. (2018, December 9). Re: Bion. [Online forum comment]. Retrieved from https://groups.yahoo.com/neo/groups/BIONCOLLECTIVE/info

Merriam-Webster. (2020, January 19). Elemental. Retrieved from https://www.merriam-webster.com/dictionary/elemental

Pearson, W. (Spring, 2019). Opening to the challenge. *Fort Da: The Journal of the Northern California Society for Psychoanalytic Psychology,* 25 (1), 68–71.

Styron, W. (1990). *Darkness visible: A memoir of madness.* Random House.

Chapter 20

Permission and gratitude

Michael Eigen's gateway to possibility and freedom

Merle Molofsky

Ode for Michael Eigen
Mystic, psychoanalyst, visionary, story weaver
Imagining for us an invitation to play.
Creating a path with shattering faith in word,
Hope for self-discovery, another act of faith that you
portray,
An ardent access to a flowing river:
Ecstasy. We raise our voice in song that must be
heard,
L'Chaim! Live life and learn to lust
Energetically. Each sensitive soul returns
Inwardly, outwardly, with eternal mirth.
Gratitude. Your humanity inspires trust.
Every flame from the unconscious burns
Naming what we always need, survival and rebirth.

Love and Blessings, Merle

I am so grateful to Michael Eigen for the myriad contributions he has made to psychoanalysis. And, in so doing, he is making myriad contributions to the world. His depth and insight will continue to shape many lives, and thus will continue to shape the history in which we are embedded.

I am grateful for this opportunity to once again participate in homage to Mike's achievements. I contributed a chapter to *Living Moments: On the Work of Michael Eigen* (2015, pp. 289–305), edited by Stephen Bloch and Loray Daws. The book is a *Festschrift*. The word means "celebration writing," referring to a book that celebrates someone. Also, the International Psychohistorical Association 2019 Conference tribute certainly was in large part a gathering celebrating Michael Eigen.

Mike's 27 books to date have expanded psychoanalytic theory and technique. He has taught in quite a number of psychoanalytic institutes, and has taught seminars and workshops in various parts of the world. In my encounters with Michael Eigen, through his books and his seminars, I discovered permission to be my true self, my true psychoanalytic self. Reading *The Psychoanalytic Mystic* (1998) was electrifying. My psychoanalytic training taught me that an interest in spirituality was regressive, that oceanic feeling was an infantile undifferentiated state. *The Psychoanalytic Mystic*, and Eigen's seminars on Psychoanalysis and Kabbalah, allowed me to value my vision of the world, which resonated with the way that Eigen integrated contributions by Bion and Winnicott, the sense of play, the value of creativity and originality, so that infinity and a sense of the divine is woven into quotidian experience. I am eternally grateful to Michael Eigen for the permission I discovered to be true to myself, creative, resonant, fully engaged, to engage the other, as Bion suggested, without memory, desire, or knowledge. Eigen's descriptive phrase, "barbed wire surrounds the soul and cuts into it" helps us avoid the barbed wire, and enter the gateway of possibility (Eigen, 2010).

And, if indeed barbed wire cuts into the soul, we have two mystic poets, one from the 13th century CE, and one from the 20th and 21st centuries CE, to teach us how to accept the barbed wire, as Michael Eigen also does.

> The wound is the place where Light enters you.
> (Rumi, n.d., p. 94)

> Ring the bells that still can ring.
> Forget your perfect offering.
> There is a crack, a crack, in everything.
> That's how the light gets in.
> ("Anthem," Cohen, 2011, p. 188)

Mike offers us the possibility of having wounds, acknowledging wounds, using wounds. How? By using the possibility of being human, acknowledging being human, using our human nature. He identifies the essence of being human, exemplified in the titles of his books, beginning with *The Psychotic Core*. And onward: *Lust*; *Rage*; *Ecstasy*; *Psychic Deadness*; *Faith*; *The Sensitive Self*. And, a most perceptive of possible titles, *Feeling Matters*.

Seven years ago, Regina Monti conducted a video interview with Mike on Dharma Café (dharmacafe.com), which is hosted by William Stranger. The interview began with Monti calling attention to Mike's integration of spirituality in his approach to psychoanalysis, and Mike added that he also values social reality. Therefore, he integrates every sort of "reality" into exploring the human psyche, the conscious and unconscious mind, the inner and outer world, sensory experience, spiritual experience, environmental experience.

An example of Mike's resonance with social reality, outward reality, the reality that becomes psychohistory, is his valuing of Wilfred Bion's major

contributions to psychoanalysis, emphasizing Bion's life experiences as forming his insights. Bion was a soldier in armed conflict during the First World
War, and suffered extreme trauma. He manifested the expected symptoms of
PTSD. Mike has offered a seminar on Bion for many years, and has sponsored
showings of a film about Bion's life, *A Memoir of the Future*, based on Bion's
autobiographical writings with that title, and directed by Kumar Shahani,
written by Kumar Shahani and Meg Harris Williams. The film itself shows
an admixture of fantasy and realism, exemplifying the essence of the way the
human psyche processes experience, thought, and feeling. Mike resonates
with Bion because, like Bion, he wanders between fantasy and reality in an
unbounded way, abolishing the borders.

If Mike freely bypasses boundaries and borders in conceptualization, of
course, he respects the boundaries of others. Somehow, like Rumi and Leonard Cohen, he manages to find that essential "crack in everything," to find
a way to help the people he works with, supervises, teaches, the people who
read his books, to "see the light." "That's how the light gets in," and that's
how the inner light shines through.

In Monti's interview, Monti postulates, with reference to Bion and PTSD,
that there is ambivalent connectedness. Mike responds that everything is connected, and talks about implicit order and explicit order, inside and outside,
that we are perceptually discrete. I was moved by, indeed, stunned, by his
saying, "What is space? There is no end to the kind of space you can imagine.
We need both." He questions the "separate individual" by saying, "What are
you separate from?" He points out that we are connected and distinct at the
same time, permeable and resistant at the same time, that we have plasticity
and strength (Monti, 2006).

The chapter I contributed to *Living Moments*, the Karnac tribute to Michael
Eigen, is titled "On fragmentation, expansion, pieces of more." That title
reflects my experience of encountering Mike's way of being, his willingness
to encounter and use fragmentation, and somehow discover the "more." How
do we approach the "threat" of fragmentation, as fragmentation implies annihilation? Mike has said that the shattered self, the annihilated self, poses an
evolutionary challenge.

By identifying that "evolutionary challenge," Mike provides a pathway,
or possibly a vista, by which we can contemplate what it means to be a human animal, mortal, aware of our mortality, capable of envisioning a future,
capable of fantasy. Our capabilities lead us to consciously and unconsciously
shape the world.

Dissociation, depersonalization, derealization, are defences against fragmentation in the face of overwhelming trauma. When we cannot bear reality, when we cannot bear what is happening to us, we find we can use a
pervasive denial of anything being real. We experience our wounds as being
totally deadly, and we escape death by escaping experiencing what is happening to us. We dissociate.

Mike approaches the wounded, those who feel as if they are psychically mortally wounded, he approaches the wounds because he is willing to experience with the wounded person. This is beyond empathy, beyond identifying with the wounded person. This is inner knowledge of something beyond the personal boundaries of the analyst. There is no border. There is pain. There are wounds. We fragment to survive, and then we have to survive fragmentation.

Mike reminds us that we all have a psychotic core, and that boundaries are permeable, shared, and yet, respected in the analytic situation.

I gleaned some refreshingly startling statements Mike made in the interview conducted, in order to illustrate what I think is Mike's essential approach.

He referenced Winnicott, and then said that as personality begins to form, trauma begins. We are shattered, wounded. He elaborated that this is real for every human being, that you are vulnerable, and trauma will hit. That is our nature, our very sensitive nature. We don't have resources to handle what goes wrong. We shatter, and return. Shatter, return.

These ideas are fundamental to how he thinks, works, feels, directly reflected in the titles of two of his books, *The Psychotic Core* and *The Sensitive Self*. Mike is willing to follow the shattering, the fragmentation, and to believe in the light, the inner light, the outer light, the light that escapes through the wound, the light that enters the wound, the possibility of return, through encounter between a self and another, the psychoanalytic dyad.

We live in a world of unspeakable horror, and a world of something very different, what has been called the ineffable, divine experience. Ineffable, of course, means something unspeakable, something so grand, so beyond us, that there are no words.

Unspeakable horror is unspeakable trauma. Planet Earth is riddled with violence, with wars, with pestilence, with famine, with horrendous suffering. Some people die of the inflicted trauma. Others survive. Mike works with those who hover between psychic death and psychic life. Perhaps what we can learn from him, from a psychohistorical perspective, is to address the reality of horrendous trauma, social and environmental trauma, to acknowledge the severity and extent of the wounds, and to strive for life. For genuine life.

Chai in Hebrew translates to the English word life. *Chaya* in Hebrew translates to the English word animal. The English word "animal" is derived from the Latin word *animalis*, which itself is based on the word *anima*, which means "breath," and means a sentient breathing being. In what way does Michael Eigen evoke life?

Mike's openness to spiritual experience is life-affirming. He said that Thomas Merton said, "The secret of our identity is that divine mercy is possible." Several of Mike's book titles, *The Psychoanalytic Mystic*, and *Ecstasy*, and *Faith*, and his seminars on Kabbalah and psychoanalysis that were brought together in his book, *Kabbalah and Psychoanalysis*, speak to this openness, this immersion in spiritual experience. In the Introduction, he cites Bion as having told him that "I use Kabbalah as the framework for psychoanalysis" (Eigen, 2012).

When Monti asked Mike how Mike endures traumatic fragmentation in the people with whom he works, Mike answered, "In meditation." He said that in meditation, he is surprised by peace. Mike also recommends meditation to his analysands. He said that a phrase came to him, "unknown intimacies," that we become intimate with ourselves in unknown ways.

Mike has said that psychoanalysis is a form of prayer. Using Bion, and using his own innate self, Mike boldly links catastrophe and faith. He links faith with the psychoanalytic attitude. Faith becomes the light that touches the wound.

I return to the interview because Mike said something I found breathtaking. He spoke of ecstasy. He described the "glow," saying, "aliveness glows." He went on to say that we respond to sunsets, and with sunsets, you can't miss the glow. The glow is real. The whole system sees the glow during the day and goes right past it. But where has it gone?

By anchoring the spiritual in the quotidian, Mike reminds us that spirituality is a living, breathing element of being human. Encountering another human in all the animal, psychological, spiritual reality of that person, within the psychoanalytic situation, with full attention on anything and everything, is a spiritual undertaking.

Mike is what Patrick Kavanaugh, in his 2003 article, "The Dead Poets Society ventures into a radioactive analytic space", called a Mind Poet (p. 342). Kavanaugh describes the "poet's sacred obligation to be The One Who Remembers" (p. 341), and attributes that function now to psychoanalysis. Mike boldly uses metaphor and poetic imagery to convey the otherwise unvoiced psychic reality that emerges in that "radioactive analytic space," because Mike is not only an exceptionally gifted psychoanalyst, but as well an exceptionally gifted writer. The two functions meet in a poetic sensibility. Just as feeling matters, to use Mike's wonderful title, language matters. Mike speaks of essential psychotic communication as covered up, yet a genuine distress signal, an SOS. A desperate soul tells the analyst, "whatever I say, what I'm really communicating is a catastrophe in the process." Mike sees this as "a person going under." With this imagery, Mike communicates to us the sensation of drowning. His Mind Poet sensitivity to language creates in us something akin to the physical sensation of drowning. He has felt what the desperate psychotic person is feeling, he knows it in his body and soul, and, if we pay attention, we also know it.

Gratitude is prayer. I am grateful for the opportunity I have been given to become a psychoanalyst, and I am grateful that Michael Eigen confronts wounds and shines light, and that the light illuminates the pathways and the vistas that are always there.

References

Bloch, S and Daws, L. (Eds.) (2015). *Living moments: On the work of Michael Eigen.* Karnac.

Cohen, L. (2011). *Leonard Cohen: Poems and songs* (R Faggen, Ed.). Everyman's Library, pp. 188–90 (originally recorded 1992).

Eigen, M. (1998). *The psychoanalytic mystic.* Free Association Books.

Eigen, M. (2010). *Eigen in Seoul, Volume 1: Madness and murder.* Karnac.

Eigen, M. (2012). *Kabbalah and psychoanalysis.* Karnac.

Eigen, M. (n.d.). Recorded on video by William Stranger, DharmaCafe.

Kavanaugh, PB. (2003). "The Dead Poets Society ventures into a radioactive analytic space," *The Psychoanalytic Review*, 90 (3), 341–60.

Monti, R. (2006). "Faith and disillusionment: An interview with Dr. Michael Eigen," video, Dharma Café. Retrieved from http://www.dharmacafe.com/ lifecycles/faith-and-disillusionment-an-interview-with-dr-michael-eigen.

Rumi (n.d.) in Corzo, M (Ed.) (1999). *Mortality immortality? The legacy of twentieth century art.* Getty Conservation Institute.

Index

For Product Safety Concerns and Information please contact our EU
representative GPSR@taylorandfrancis.com
Taylor & Francis Verlag GmbH, Kaufingerstraße 24, 80331 München, Germany